The Acoustic Guitar

University of Oklahoma Press
Norman and London

The Acoustic Guitar

Adjustment, Care, Maintenance, and Repair

Don E. Teeter

Library of Congress Cataloging-in-Publication Data

Teeter, Don E
    The acoustic guitar.
    Bibliography: p. 195
    1. Guitar—Construction.   I. Title.
ML1016.G8T44   787'.61'2   74-5962

787.61
2
Teet
B

ISBN: 0-8061-2814-3

6 7 8 9 10 11 12 13 14 15

For all my innumerable friends and customers,
who have shown their faith in me,
and without whose support I could never
have written this book.

I am writing this manual with the hope of filling a need that becomes more apparent as time goes by. Many people are dropping by my shop wanting to learn how to repair guitars. I just don't have the time to answer all the questions and also get my repair work done. With one exception, there seems to be a lack of information in general on major repair of the guitar, and this is what I am trying to remedy. There are several manuals on minor repair work in existence, but only one of these, Irving Sloane's *Guitar Repair*, covers major work in any detail. Sloane covers quite a bit of major repair, but I have decided to go into greater depth and detail on quite a few more topics that I think should be included in a book of this type. Most of the other books say to take the instrument to a qualified repairman for any major repairs. This is fine if there is a qualified repairman in your area. The main problem is the great shortage of qualified repairmen. There are many large cities without any kind of repair facilities, or even part-time repairmen. I started out repairing part time and making a guitar once in a while. Things started happening after the word got around, and in four years I had to go into the repair business full time and had little time to make anything except a dulcimer once in a while and an occasional guitar. During one four-year period I managed to make only one guitar, owing to the load of repair work.

I have approached this vocation from a machinist's viewpoint, working at it as a hobby and being forced to go into it full time. Being a machinist, I have designed and made quite a few of my own tools. Some of the ideas I have picked up from other shops and people and either used "as is" or redesigned to fit the job at hand. I will give them credit on these ideas as we get further along in the book.

Some of my techniques may be a little on the controversial side for some people, but they work very well for me. I am still in the learning process, even after spending ten years working on all kinds of fretted instruments. It is my own opinion that when you stop learning

or close your mind to new or controversial methods without giving them a chance, it is time to try a new vocation. There are just too many things involved in guitar repair and construction for any one person to learn it all.

This manual will be concerned primarily with the so called "Spanish" or round-hole, flat-top guitar. Most of the techniques, however, such as fret work, crack repair, string action settings, bridging and intonation, straightening of warped necks, adjusting tension rods, refinishing, etc., may be applied, with slight variations, to almost any of the fretted instruments, such as banjos, mandolins, F-hole acoustic and electric guitars, solid-body electric guitars, dulcimers, etc.

Quite a few of the techniques listed in this manual, such as adjusting tension rods, adjusting string heights (action), repairing minor cracks, setting movable bridges for proper intonation (noting accuracy), dressing and polishing frets, gluing loose bridges, changing machine heads, and, of course, the proper care and maintenance of the instruments, are within the capabilities of the average amateur with limited tools.

All instruments, even those of identical make and model, are different. Each has a personality of its own, just like a human being. There are variations in wood grain, hardness, density, grain direction, dryness, and in how well all the connected factors work together. Even the chemical composition of the soil where the tree was grown is a factor in the tonal quality of the wood. If you have an instrument that has all of the wood working together, you can have an exceptional instrument. Without this co-operation, an identical instrument can be below average. It is really hard to predict what a given instrument will sound like before you string it. Some of the larger companies are now experimenting with electronic analysis, trying to improve the sound and tonal qualities of their instruments, with varying degrees of success. Some of the results are very interesting.

A word of warning to beginners acquiring this manual. This book is not guaranteed to make you an instant expert guitar repairman. I can tell you how to do things

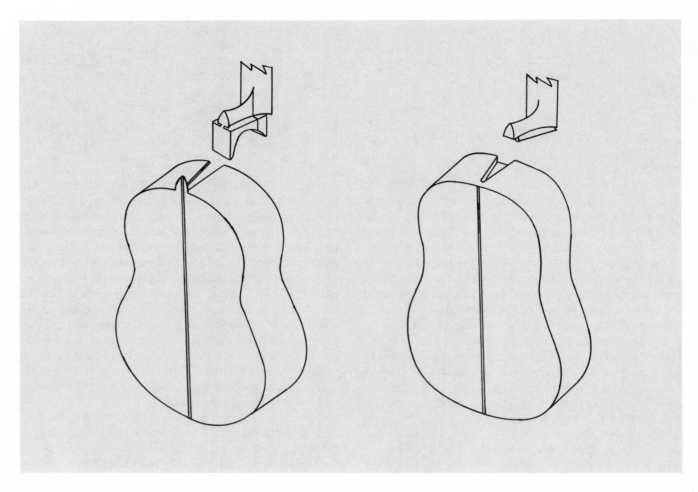

Fig. 1—Left: Spanish-Mexican-type construction with integral neck and neck block and laminated on heel. Right: European-American-type construction with neck dovetailed into body and neck block after body assembly.

all day long, but until you actually do the jobs yourself, not once, but time after time, until you have the technique down pat, you cannot call yourself a repairman. I am assuming, in writing this book, that the person actually using the book does know something about woodworking and power tools as well as various hand tools. It is very hard to describe some of the techniques, such as handling a spray gun with ease, and the best way to learn this is to practice on junk or have somebody experienced show how to do it. If you are just getting into the repair field, I would recommend starting as I did. Make a guitar from scratch using one of the many available books on constructing a classic guitar. In fact, the purchase of all the different books available on guitar construction and anything you can find on guitar repairs will give you a valuable library of reference books. They will show the differences between the Spanish-type construction and European construction and the various

ways that different ideas are used to achieve the same results. Most of these books are on the classic or nylon-strung guitars, but the basic construction techniques are the same, with changes in the strength of various components of the guitar and changes in the type of bracing, particularly in the sounding board or top of the instrument. The bracing or strutting must be much heavier for steel strings, and the layout of the struts is usually completely different from the bracing of the classic guitar. As an example of the types of construction used in different countries, the Spanish style has the neck and neck block inside the guitar as a single unit. The sides of the guitar are set into notches cut in the sides of the neck and block assembly. The European, the most popular construction for steel-string guitars, has the neck set into a dovetail cut into the block through the sides where they meet at the upper bout of the guitar. The Spanish guitar is constructed around the neck and top as a unit, and the European is constructed completely without the neck, which is fitted after the body is removed from the mold.

For the person just starting in repairs, I would also recommend finding a few old junk instruments and trying to put them back into playable condition. Try to figure out exactly what is wrong with them and how to correct the problem. Also, try to figure out why the particular problem occurred. If it was some basic weakness in the design of the guitar, try to figure out how it could be corrected, if possible, and then do it. Tear it up and put it back together again. Repair it, refret it, and then try your hand at refinishing it. Get your techniques to working and get the feel of them. This all helps to get your confidence built up, and after all, if you don't have confidence in yourself, nobody else will either.

Another thing required for becoming a qualified repairman is a large measure of patience. Outside of your knowledge, techniques, and tools, I would say that patience (or the lack of it) would be the determining factor in whether or not you make it as a repairman.

Another thing you will have to learn is whether or not a particular instrument is worth repairing. Some of the real cheapies would cost more to repair than the original purchase price. Unless there is some sentimental value attached to one of these, it would be better to replace it. I have done repair jobs on some of these that cost three or four times as much as the instrument was worth, but, because of the sentimental value attached, the customer wanted it done. Also, some of the old beat-up guitars such as the old Martins are worth quite a bit as collector's items, and the expense of the repairs would be justified in many cases. It just takes time and experience to know when to repair and when not to.

For you experienced repairmen, I hope some of the information in this book will be of some use to you. I am not claiming that my techniques are the only way to go, or that they are better than yours. Perhaps they are not as good as yours for your particular style of working. What will work well for one person will sometimes cause problems for others. All I am saying is that the techniques set down in this book have worked well for me. I have tried them all and know that they will work if applied properly. I am just trying to set up some sort of basic guideline to help others with ideas and to assist them in developing their own ideas and techniques. If I succeed in this purpose, then I will have achieved my goal in writing this book.

Don E. Teeter

Oklahoma City, Oklahoma

Contents

The Acoustic Guitar

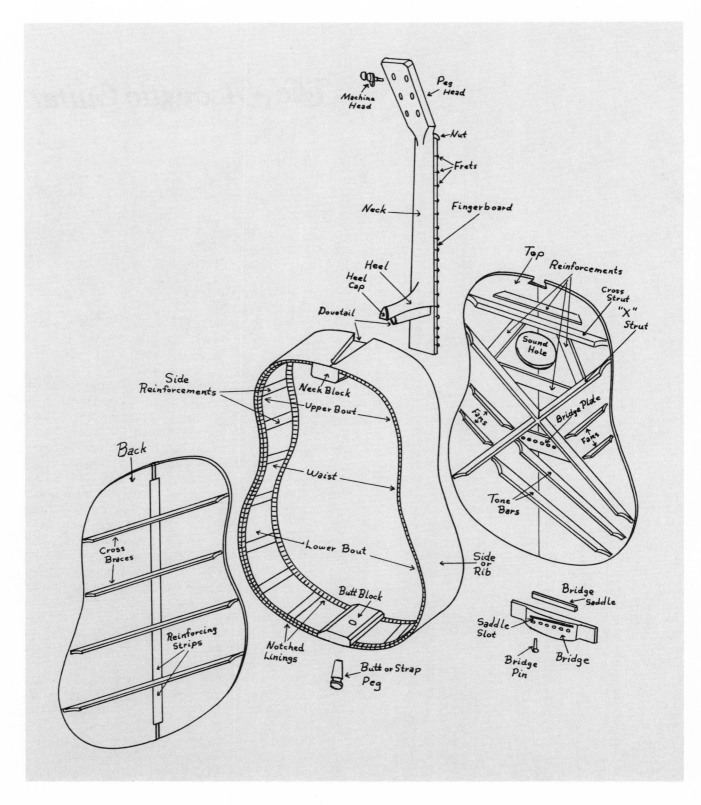

Fig. 2—Exploded drawing of a steel-string guitar.

The Acoustic Guitar

The acoustic guitars we have today are said to have their roots clear back to pre-biblical times in the form of the lyre. This was a many-stringed instrument with a sounding box at the base of the instrument. It was developed in various countries into different shaped instruments, some plucked with the fingers and others played with a bow. These developed farther along into the various types of lutes and violins and on into the two basic types of acoustic guitars we have today, the F-hole and the Spanish guitar.

The F-hole guitar still used the arched top and back with the long "f"-shaped sound holes and the neck canted away from the body at a steep angle to allow a rather high and usually adjustable bridge. The bridge is movable, not being glued to the top, and a tailpiece is used to fasten the strings to the butt end of the instrument very much like the violin. Unlike the violin family, which uses one strut under the bass side of the arched top and a sound post between the front and back on the treble side, the F-hole guitar uses two struts running the length of the arch (see illustration). This tends to give more resonance and sound sustaining ability to the guitar. This is unnecessary with the violin because the sound is sustained with the bow and both the top and back are allowed to vibrate. The F-hole guitar is usually played with the back of the instrument held against the body, and if it were equipped with a sound post to connect the front with the back, a loss of resonance would result.

Most of the F-hole guitars the modern repairman will face will be those with the tops laminated (plywood) under pressure to form the arch and will usually be very shallow in depth and equipped with electric pickups.

There are a few of the old jobs around that were painstakingly carved by hand and are not electrified. A few of the modern companies make a couple of models of carved-top instruments, but they are very expensive. These non-electric F-hole guitars were and are primarily used for orchestral work as a rhythm instrument or by jazz guitarists as a lead instrument. I believe its popularity as a jazz guitar is probably because a note does not sustain as long as on the flat-top guitar. Jazz music, being very complicated, requires many notes to be played in a short space of time, and musicians can grab a note and it's gone, allowing them to proceed to the next note cleanly and smoothly.

Except for the angled neck, the arched top, and back, these guitars were assembled like most any of the other European-type instruments, with the neck being dovetailed into the body after assembly.

These guitars are almost invariably equipped with metal strings because nylon or gut strings simply do not have the strength and weight to move the arched top.

Any disassembly of these guitars is practically the same as other types of guitars, but with one difference. Where interior repairs can be done on the round-hole guitar through the sound hole, the F-hole guitar, in most cases, will have to have either the top or back removed.

The Spanish guitar was more or less developed from the lute. The lute, having a pear-shaped body, many strings, many different versions, and about as many different tunings as strings, was awkward to transport and was very fragile and difficult to keep in tune and to handle while playing. The Spanish guitar evolved through various stages of development, such as flattening the lute back, changing the shape, shortening the body, lengthening the neck, relocating the bridge more towards the center of the top so the neck could be lengthened even more to give more playable frets, lessening the number of strings to four courses, increasing this to five courses, and then to six courses, as we have today on the modern guitar.

Probably the biggest development in the classic guitar was made in the 1850s by Antonio Torres. He enlarged the body of the guitar and developed a fan bracing that has been widely copied. Variations of this strutting pattern are used in most of the commercially produced classic guitars today. The classic guitar is usually made with rosewood backs and sides on the more expensive models and Honduras mahogany on the less expensive

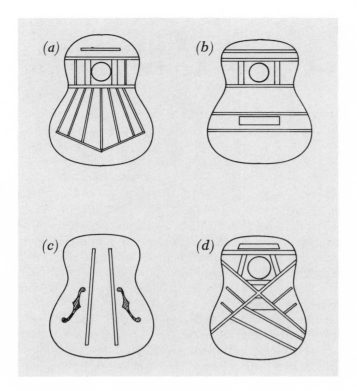

Fig. 3—Most common types of top strutting used with variations in modern instruments. Top left (a): Torres classic. Top right (b): Inexpensive steel-string. Bottom left (c): F-hole. Bottom right (d): Martin steel-string.

models. The top is almost always spruce, although some of the luthiers are using Spanish cedar or quarter-sawn redwood.

The classic guitars of Spain, Mexico, and quite a few individual craftsmen have the neck and neck-block assembly as one piece, while most of those made elsewhere have the neck dovetailed into the body. Otherwise the construction is quite similar, with the wide flat fingerboard, usually from two inches to two and one-eighth inches wide at the nut, the flat top with round sound hole, slightly arched back, tie-type bridge located in the center of the belly, rounded upper and lower bouts with fairly narrow waist, and the neck joining the body at the twelfth or octave fret.

The flamenco guitar of the Spanish gypsies is similar to the Spanish classic, except that it is made almost feather-light so that the back resonates along with the front. The strings are deliberately set low so that they rattle to a certain extent.

The back and sides are usually made of Spanish cypress wood, and the spruce front of the guitar is strutted very light, quite often with only five fan braces instead of the

Fig. 4—Front view of pre-World War II Gibson F model L-7.

seven or more usually found on the classic guitar. This results in a harsh metallic sound instead of the rich mellow sound usually associated with the classic guitar.

The guitar is held and played in such a position that the back of the guitar is held away from the body to allow it to vibrate.

Fig. 5—Back view of same F-hole Gibson guitar.

As for the difference in sound between the classic and flamenco guitars, I don't claim to be an acoustic engineer, but I have read up on acoustics to a certain extent, and from what I understand, the following theory seems to hold water. The guitar is basically an air pump. The sound we hear is from the air waves created by the guitar striking the ear drum and the sound is created in our brain. The strings, in vibrating against the bridge of the guitar, causes the guitar top or sounding board to move up and down moving the air in two directions. The air moving inside the guitar is bounced from the inside back of the guitar out through the sound hole. When the air moves out of the sound hole in phase or at the same time as the air is moving outward from the top moving forward, we get a rich mellow sound. This is what appears to happen with the rigid reflective back of the classic guitar. The flamenco guitar with its resonant back, vibrates with the air column hitting it instead of completely reflecting it, throwing the air moving out of the sound hole a few micro-seconds out of phase with the air moving off the outside of the top, causing a harsher sound. Make sense? Study the acoustics of the bass reflex or ducted port speaker enclosures. The speaker cone moves air in much the same way as the guitar top, and if the porting of the enclosure is off, the sound generated is of a different quality than a properly ported one. I believe the principle is parallel with that of the guitar.

There are a couple other differences I think should be mentioned between the flamenco and classic guitars. The flamenco traditionally uses wooden friction tuning pegs such as those found in the violin family, but this is not always so. Some of the luthiers now use geared machine heads.

Also, while there are a few fine solo artists, the flamenco guitar is most commonly used when working with flamenco dancers, the harsh driving sound of the flamenco guitar blending perfectly with the click of the castanets and the pounding heels of the flamenco dancers.

Here in the United States in the early 1900s, the steel-string guitar gained in popularity as people began demanding more volume from their guitars. The plectrum or pick style of playing gained in popularity also, and to make the guitar easier to play, guitar makers narrowed the necks and fingerboards. The strings were set closer together to facilitate the plectrum style of playing. This resulted in the rather narrow fingerboards found on today's steel-string guitars, with some models being only about one and three-quarters of an inch wide at the nut. Also, it was found that by ovaling the surface of the fingerboard slightly, although not as much as on the violin, it was easier to select the individual string with the pick. As a result, most of the fingerboards used on the steel-string guitars have this ovaled surface.

Guitars were also being made larger in various shapes as the demand for volume, particularly in the bass ranges, became stronger. This resulted in the large, almost straight-waisted guitar called the "Dreadnought," designed in 1917 by the C. F. Martin organization. This guitar was originally produced with the neck joining the

Fig. 6—Front view of classic guitar made six or seven years ago by the author.

Fig. 7—Back view of the same classic guitar.

6

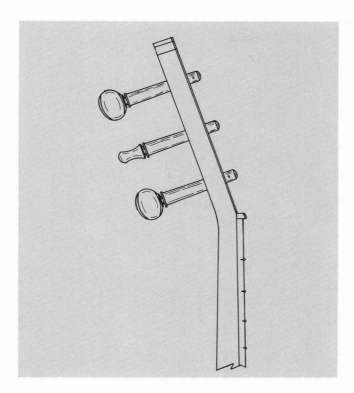

Fig. 8—*Wooden friction pegs found on traditional flamenco guitars. Martin guitars were available before 1920 with ivory friction pegs on special order. These were regular models and not flamenco models.*

raise or lower the string height in relation to the body of the guitar. The neck retaining screws should be checked periodically for tightness as the vibrations have a tendency to loosen the screws, causing the strings to be too high and promoting a loss of tonal qualities owing to the lack of rigidity between the neck and body.

This should give you some idea of the types of guitars you will be running into nowadays. If you wish to delve thoroughly into the history of the guitar, the bibliography in the back of this book will really fill you in and provide some interesting reading. If you cannot find them in your library, Vitali Import Company does stock most of them.

body at the twelfth fret. Later Martin squared off the upper bout of the guitar and relocated the bridge slightly to allow a full fourteen frets free of the body. This fourteen-fret neck, Dreadnought body, and Martin's own X-strutted top became a standard for the guitar-making industry. Almost all of the better steel-string instruments of all sizes use the "X" strutting or variations thereof.

Some of the more inexpensive types of steel string guitars use the old lute-type or "ladder" strutting, as I call it, because the struts are laid across the top like the steps of a ladder.

Some of the modern guitars you will run into will have the neck screwed to the body. The screws will be usually four in number, being inserted through the back of the instrument through a rather massive neck block. These models may be spotted rather easily because of the absence of the curved heel on the bottom of the neck and a decorative metal plate on the back of the guitar to conceal the screw holes. This neck is a feature on many models of electric guitars also.

One of the advantages of this design is that tapered shims may be used between the neck and its socket to

Tools Useful in Guitar Repair

Tool requirements for doing repairs on musical instruments vary with the person doing the repairs and the techniques used. I will outline some of the tools I use, their various accessories, and the jobs they perform. Many of the tools are custom made or adapted for a particular job, and I will show in drawings how to modify, adapt, and in some cases, how to make them from scratch. Some of you will not, of course, have the machinist's know-how or equipment to make some of the tools. They can usually be made by just about any machine shop, and although the initial cost may be rather high, the time saved and improvement in quality of a given job is worth the original cash outlay. You will usually pay for a tool in a couple of jobs. I have found out the hard way that to try to scrimp on tools is a bad mistake. Buying the proper tools of *top quality* will save you money in the long run. You can, with the proper tools, do as much work as it would normally take two or three people to do in the same amount of time by hand.

At times, when you are having to do the same job over and over, such as refret work, it pays to set up special tools and jigs to speed up the job without losing quality. In regular repairs also, it is a good idea to make jigs universal so they may be used on just about any make of guitar. If you set it up for only one make, chances are that it will not work properly on another make, so the thing to do is to design it for adaptability. On some jobs, you may have to make several different jigs because there may not be any way to make them universal. You have to learn to improvise in this kind of work. That is one of the biggest secrets in repair. If one system will not work on a particular application, improvise. Figure another system, and if that won't work either, figure out yet another. I guess I probably spend more time trying to figure the best way to do a particular job than I actually spend in doing the job at times.

Selecting Hand Tools and Measuring Instruments

There are many hand tools I consider necessary for a complete shop, and every once in a while I still add things as I find a use for them. I guess you never get everything you need. It is rather hard to know where to start, but I will start with selecting wrenches you will probably be using to adjust necks and other parts of the different instruments you will be working on in this business.

You will need a good set of ¼"-drive deep-well sockets with a breakover and rachet handle, two-inch and four-inch extensions for same, open-end and box-end wrenches in both American and metric sizes from ¼" to ⅝" and 5mm. to 11mm., the metrics being for foreign instruments, a set of Allen wrenches in both American and metric sizes, and a good set of screwdrivers of different sizes in both standard and Phillips blades. A good set of nutdrivers is also handy. Between the wrenches and screwdrivers, you should have enough tools to adjust most of the different sizes of tension rod setups you will come up against. We will get into that a little later when we discuss the adjusting of necks and what you will be running into.

You should have several types of pliers also. A good pair of standard pliers, needle-nose pliers, diagonals, or "dikes" as they are usually called, end-nippers (their use will be explained later), and a pair or two of Vise-Grips. The dikes or sidecutters should be of the special kind designed to cut piano wire, if you can find them. Otherwise, expect to buy a new pair every few months, because cutting guitar strings will chew up the jaws pretty fast. Check the index of suppliers for the address of Brookstone's Hard To Find Tools. They stock all kinds of special pliers, cutters, files, and all sorts of top quality goods, including measuring tools and saws for special purposes, all of which are fairly hard to find in the average hardware or industrial supply house.

A *good* set of wood chisels is a must. Spend some money here. You can get cheap ones for a dollar or two apiece, but it is better to spend four or five dollars for one that will hold an edge. (Better yet, maybe you will get lucky, as I did, and inherit a set of good old ones. My grand-

Fig. 9—Front view of a custom-made steel-string guitar constructed by the author.

Fig. 10—Back view of the same custom steel-string guitar.

father left me all his old woodworking tools, and the chisels are beauties. They will take and hold an edge you can shave with.) The secret of working with cutting tools is keeping them sharp. You will have far more accidents with dull tools because you know they are dull and will be careless with them. With sharp tools, you have a natural tendency to be more careful because one slip can carve up a finger or ruin a guitar. A carved up hand can be healed, but to fix a messed up guitar can be trouble. Keep your cutting tools sharp and be careful with them. Now, as to chisel sizes, the ones I find myself using are as follows: ¼₆", ⅛", ¼", and ¾" widths. Get a good rock to sharpen them, such as the Norton India stone. This is fairly fine, and when used in combination with a piece of #600 Wetordry sandpaper and a little oil, will put an edge on the chisels or knives that will shave the hair off your arms.

As for knives, a good sized set of X-acto knives and replaceable blades will do the trick. The blades can be sharpened also. One of the tricks I have learned with the X-acto blade is to use a cloth buffing wheel and jeweler's rouge on a grinder to put a razor edge on them. I hone them maybe once a week and buff them every day or so. They get to where they look like surgical scalpels after a few polishings. Also, a good heavy stainless steel electric knife blade should be acquired, along with a thin pancake spatula. On the spatula, it would be better if it is of high carbon steel, about .020" thick, as stainless steel this thin has a tendency to curl when sharpened to a very thin edge. Sharpen it two thirds of the way around the end and about an inch or two down one side. It should be sharpened so that the edge is very thin. The purpose of this spatula is to remove pickguards, bridges, and what-have-you. It is especially useful to remove instrument backs and tops, as will be described later. An artist's palate knife, sharpened the same way, may be used instead of the spatula. This is one of my pet tools, and I have already worn out one spatula.

There are several kinds of files that should be acquired. For rough work in wood, the Stanley Shurform files, in various shapes, really do the trick. For smoother cutting files, I use the common double-cut bastard file. They are available in half-round types and can be purchased in several lengths. I keep a good 6" and 10" size on hand. A pair of mill bastards in the same sizes should be purchased for use in finishing out fret work and other uses. A good set of X-acto or other brand of needle files are a must for making and reworking nuts and setting string actions. These are available at most hobby shops.

I use several types of small saws in my work. One of the handiest is the jeweler's saw. This looks like a small coping saw, but it takes saw blades that will cut stainless steel. I use this saw to cut fret wire and mother-of-pearl

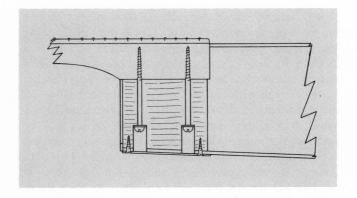

Fig. 11—Cutaway side view drawing of screwed-on neck. Note the decorative plate over neck retaining screws. On some models, such as the Fender, the neck holding screws come all the way through the metal plate and are used to retain the plate as well as the neck.

for inlay work. Another saw that comes in handy is the X-acto razor saw. This is available with replaceable blades of several sizes and can be used also to cut fret wire and other metals. There is a slightly larger saw available, called a guitar maker's saw, that has two blades, one for wood and the other for metal use. These are available from Vitali Import Company and several other sources. The blades from the guitar maker's saw and razor saw, when dull, may be used for other jobs. I break them up into different sizes and shapes to use for cleaning out cracks, etc. The razor saw blade, with the teeth and back removed, makes an excellent glue spatula. It does a superb job of forcing glue into tight cracks.

A couple of block planes should be acquired also. I have one, a Stanley #220, that I wouldn't take anything for. It is a very small plane, and the blade takes a razor edge and holds it. It is very useful in planing fingerboards of small sizes and the spot planing of larger fingerboards. I also have a large 14" jack plane, that I use for the same purposes.

Now let's get into measuring instruments. *The one most important measuring tool in my whole shop, to me, is the vernier caliper.* If I had to do without my calipers, I think I would get out of the business. When read properly, they are accurate up to .001 of an inch. You may not be able to work to that close a tolerance when working in wood, but it helps to know that when you take a measurement or set a saw guide or depth, you are going to be as close as humanly possible. I can really appreciate measurements. Being an ex-machinist, I have worked to less than .001 tolerances. Besides, when you work with precision tolerances, you make fewer mistakes.

You should also purchase a good stainless steel straight

edge at least 30" to 36" long. Spend some money on this and get a precision ground one. This is used in checking fingerboards when truing, checking string actions and checking for bow in necks. It can also be used for checking alignment when resetting a neck or checking whether a neck is true with the top of an instrument when re-cutting dovetails, should you have to reneck an instrument. A good one such as the Starrett, which may be purchased at most industrial supply houses, can set you back as much as thirty dollars. Be very careful with both the calipers and straight edge and do not drop them at any time. If you do, they will either have to be replaced or repaired, because their accuracy will be impaired. Be touchy with them and don't let other people handle them unless they know what they are doing. Have a safe place to keep them. When you are through using them, replace them in that safe place.

Another good investment is a small set of draftsman's tools. This should include a couple of small compasses, scribes, pens, a steel $\frac{1}{32}$-graduated rule, and, depending on the expense of the set, many other things. A small set of French curves is handy, should you have to design a different pickguard or do other layout work.

Another *very important measuring tool* would be a machinist's master square. This is not a common square, but one that is ground to within .001" accuracy on all surfaces. This is another tool that should not be dropped, or you can count on replacing it. This tool is invaluable in setting or checking the accuracy of band saws, table saws, other squares, or anything that should be square to a high degree of accuracy. A protractor square is another good investment, as it is marked in degrees. This will allow you to check various angles and to duplicate them. Another tool along this line would be the "Copy Cat Contour Gauge." With this handy tool, you can check a contour, such as the back of a neck, and duplicate the contour perfectly on paper or actually check and duplicate dimensions while carving a new neck from scratch. This is particularly handy when you are trying to duplicate the fit of a banjo neck to the pot. I know, for I've had to do this more than once while duplicating a neck or making a five-string neck to take the place of a tenor or plectrum neck.

A good selection of clamps of several types should be purchased. A half-dozen of the number one and two Hargrave spring clamps come in handy for many things, such as regluing loose struts after removing a guitar back for repairs, holding patches in place, etc. In case you cannot find that particular brand and wonder what the clamps look like, they resemble somewhat large metal clothespins. A half-dozen 4" and a pair of 5" or 6" steel "C" clamps are a must. These are used for many things, but I use them primarily for fret work. Also, pur-

chase or make three or four wooden bridge or "cam" clamps of at least three depths' reach. I probably use the 6" and 8" ones most in repair work, but when you need the 10" clamps, it's a little late to stop and make or order them. I would suggest going ahead and buying a couple of the 10" or making them, if you like. I also have a handful of 2" model-maker clamps, which are useful when working in tight places or on small parts. Purchase a few dozen wooden spring-type clothespins to be used in case you have to make and install new notched linings around the sides of a guitar during repairs. Sometimes this is necessary if the guitar doesn't co-operate during disassembly and you have to get nasty with it. Another invaluable clamp, used for pulling loose bindings and sometimes even a loose section of back or top into place, is the common filament tape used for taping cartons where strength is needed. It is semi-transparent tape with fiberglass reinforcing filament throughout the length of the tape. *Do not try to tear this tape with the bare hands.* This is a very good way to receive a nasty cut. Use a sharp knife or scissors to cut it. I use this tape almost entirely to rebind instruments during assembly after repairs. Some shops like to wrap the body with stout cord or twine while binding, but the tape method seems to work well for me, so I stick with it.

Another very important tool for the shop is masking tape. The best place to purchase masking tape is a place where they sell a lot of paint and body rebuilding supplies for automobiles. They use a good grade of tape, and it is almost always fresh. Paint and body men won't buy tape unless it is of good quality, and it must be fresh. I know, because in my younger days I worked at an auto supply store that specialized in paints and supplies. Buy only as much as you plan on using within a month's time, because tape will deteriorate with age, especially if it gets hot. I keep three sizes on hand: $\frac{1}{4}$", $\frac{1}{2}$", and $\frac{3}{4}$". Masking tape can save you a lot of work and time when used properly. If I run out of tape and have to do a glue job, I will shut down and go buy a new supply, rather than have to clean a mess of glue off the finish. Sure, you can use water to remove excess water soluble glues, but if the finish is cracked a little, the first thing you know, you have the finish peeling. Why not just use a little more time and a little masking tape, and not run the risk? You can work most of the glue out on the tape, or even clean it off the tape while it is still wet, and then when the glue dries, just pull the tape off and clean up what little remains with a chisel. I seem to get a neater looking job by doing it this way, and neatness helps sell your repair work.

A good woodworker's bench vise is a necessity. I also consider a steel mechanic's or machinist's vise necessary. When you are working with a piece of metal and use the wooden faced woodworker's vise, you will surely ruin the jaws. I also use a small hobbiest's vise for use in cutting fret wire and a good used drill-press vise that is adjustable to various angles for use in the drill press when you have to drill on an angle, such as in bridge work, etc. Another tool classified as a vise would be the pin vise. This is nothing but a small hand-held drill chuck used to hold miniature drill bits too small to be used with standard chucks on hand or electric drills. These usually come with several size chucks from o to 1⁄8" capabilities. They come in handy for use with jeweler's screwdriver bits also.

A few other tools that could be possibly classified as hand tools would be a common electric iron of the household type (used in removing fingerboards, etc.), a good small soldering iron with a spool of *resin* core solder, a couple of squirt cans (pump type) for naptha and lube oil, and a handful of artist's paint brushes of various sizes.

You should set up a couple of workbenches of a comfortable height for you. I find that a bench set at belt-buckle height is most comfortable for me. You don't have to bend over so much, and if you work at this type of work very long in a bent-over position, you will know what I mean. You should have a piece of carpet covering the bench where you will be doing most of the work. It should not be tacked down, as you will need to remove it for cleaning once in a while. The carpet is used to prevent scratches when working with finished instruments. Do not get the very long shag-type carpet, because you will spend a lot of time looking for lost small parts, which seem to disappear into the pile. You should have several other small benches or shelves to set instruments on while glue is drying, etc. These benches or shelves can be hinged to the walls and folded up out of the way when they are not in use. I have one in my paint room that is extremely handy. I can use it when I am stripping finish and have the exhaust fan right there to remove the stripper fumes. Then when I am ready to spray finishes, I just fold the bench up against the wall out of the way and shoot. I also use it when touching up finishes, since I have a piece of carpet on it also.

It is a good idea to go to your local lumber yard and purchase a few square feet of peg board and a good supply of various types of hangers for it. This can be fastened to the wall behind your bench, and most of your tools can be hung right where they are handy. I have found that I save a lot of time by knowing exactly where my tools are, and can select a tool from the board almost blindfolded. The tools should be replaced as soon as you are through with them, as this keeps them from getting lost or misplaced. This also will help keep the

sharp tools, such as chisels and knives, from getting knocked around and having their edges dulled. It seems that if one of these gets knocked off, it automatically falls on the cutting edge, and if a foot is in the way, you have instant trouble.

There are a few more hand tools that I use, but I will bring them up later on. They are mostly specialty tools, some handmade or adapted from other tools.

SELECTING POWER TOOLS AND ACCESSORIES

Most minor repairs on musical instruments can be done with hand tools, but if you are trying to make a living at repair work and/or if you are having to handle a large volume of repairs, some power tools are a must. The selection of the tools should be done with care. Good used tools can be purchased if you are careful in checking them out. Sometimes you can buy good used name-brand power tools at the same price as new off-brand ones and have a much better tool. Replacement parts are readily available for most name-brand tools, even the older ones. I have a mixture of new and used tools in my shop. With a small amount of reconditioning, the older tools are good as new at about half the price of the new ones.

An air compressor is a must if you are doing any finishing work. It is very useful for repair work also. Some of the instruments coming into my shop are filthy inside, and to do any glue work in there, you need to blow the dust out. I have a two-cylinder, one-horsepower compressor that puts out around six cubic feet of air at 50 psi. I have a quick coupling system so I can snap on a blow nozzle or change to a spray gun in a matter of seconds. The refinishing chapter gives a more complete picture of the filtration system, spray guns, and air brushes I use in finish work.

You should have a well-ventilated area in which to do the spray work. I have a small room nine feet square with an exhaust fan to do my spray work in. The exhaust fan is a necessity, especially if you are working with lacquers. Fans can be very expensive because their motors should be sealed to prevent explosions. The average motor can spark at the points when started and stopped and should not be used unless it is belted out of the way with a long "V" belt. I found an excellent small fan in the seventy-dollar range that will almost suck me out of my paint room. This is about a third of what most of the exhaust fans sell for. It is made by Dayton Electric Company of Chicago. It is the Dayton 12" Explosion-Proof Fan, model number 4C020. The fan is mounted in a well-constructed, burglar-proof frame that will screw or bolt into a 13½" hole in the wall. An inexpensive louvre system can be purchased along with it to weatherproof the opening. This fan is large enough for a room up to around ten or twelve feet square.

A band saw is a necessity in my opinion. It will do a lot of things that you cannot do with a table saw, and if you are limited in funds and must choose between a band saw and table saw, I would choose the band saw. I have a Delta Rockwell #28–290 with the height attachment. This attachment will allow you to cut up to 12" in thickness, and that can be useful in cutting woods for replacement backs, sides, or tops. A miter gauge and rip fence are necessary accessories for both the band and table saws. A word on band saw blades: I have found through experience that the best blades to buy are the skip-tooth design. Just looking at them, you would think they would cut very rough, but they will cut smoother than any blade I have found and do not gum up as fast when cutting resinous woods such as the rosewoods. They can also be used in cutting non-ferrous metals such as brass, magnesium, aluminum, etc. This metal-cutting capability can help in the making of some of the specialty tools and jigs. You can saw the parts out of one of these metals, and using a belt and disk sander, smooth them up.

Speaking of the belt and disk sander, this is another tool I would not do without. You can purchase these in just about any price range and get a pretty decent sander. For light duty, the American Machine and Tool Company of Royersford, Pa., sells a sander kit for a very reasonable price. I used one of these for four years. It is a combination 4" belt with a 6" disk. Abrasives are available from Sears. You will find advertisements for the AMT Corporation in the back of almost all the science magazines such as *Popular Science*, etc. I now have a Sears Model 13–22541 Craftsman sander combination that is a dilly. It has a 6"-wide belt with a 9" disk. I use a 60-grit belt with a fine-rated sanding disk. The aluminum oxide abrasives are probably the best to use for longevity and cutting ability. I use mine every day for shaping things such as ivory nuts and bridge saddles and parts of all kinds. Without the sander, repairs are much more difficult.

Should you decide to buy a table saw, get a good name-brand one. Most of the top brands, such as the 9" Delta Rockwell Model 34–600 saw, are very well constructed. You are, in guitar repair, working with hardwoods such as rosewood, ebony, the maples, and others. These are very hard on saw blades. It would be to your advantage to buy a tungsten carbide-tipped saw blade. When I first bought my saw, I was using the hollow-ground planer blades. These cut nice and smooth but need sharpening quite often. In fact, I was having mine sharpened every two weeks. With the hollow-ground blade, you can sharpen them around six or eight times

and then throw them away. This can get expensive after several years. I paid a little over $110.00 for a 60-tooth, $\frac{3}{32}$"-kerf (thickness) carbide-tipped blade. I have been using it for almost two years now and have had it sharpened once. In the long run, it's much cheaper to buy the carbide blade. You get another plus with the carbide blade, too. They cut so smooth you almost have to scuff up the wood to glue it. If you think it sounds like I'm sold on the carbide blade, you're right.

Another tool I consider necessary is an electric drill motor. I used a hand drill for years until I finally bought one of the new $\frac{3}{8}$" variable-speed drills. You can control the speed even closer with the variable speed than you could with the hand drill, and you have both hands free to control the drill. You should purchase a set of drill bits in $\frac{1}{32}$" increments from $\frac{1}{16}$" to $\frac{3}{8}$". Some of the sizes you may never use, but if you need them you will have them. Also, purchase #3, 6, and 7 taper pin reamers. These can be used with a hand reamer holder or with the drill motor. Since I have the variable speed drill motor, I don't use the hand holder much any more. The #3 taper pin reamer is just the right size to ream bridge-pin holes for most tapered bridge pins. The #6 and #7 reamers are used to ream butt-peg holes and enlarge machine-head holes for Grover Rotomatic and Schaller machine heads. The reamers work better than trying to drill an existing hole out larger with a regular drill because the taper reamer is, more or less, self-centering. The taper pin reamers, being made to ream steel or cast iron for repair pinning of cracks, are made of high-speed steel and should last for years if cared for. They may be purchased at almost any industrial supply and are a lot cheaper than some of the reamers I have seen listed by some of the guitar supply houses.

A small drill press is an asset also. Check around the want ads in your local newspapers and see if you can find a used one. Sometimes you can get a large used press for the price of a new small one. I used a conversion stand that takes a drill motor for several years as a drill press. They are pretty handy but aren't particularly accurate. I bought an almost new Compactool drill press for less than half of the new price, and with a $\frac{1}{2}$" chuck, it does most of the work the average guitar shop will need. This is one tool you can get by without, though, if necessary.

Now we come to one of the most important power tools in my whole shop. It is the Model 280 ball-bearing Dremel Moto-Tool. With the accessories available for it, it is almost a work shop in itself. I use mine in bridge work, grafting patches into holes, inlay work, cutting binding and purfling grooves, engraving, marking tools, reworking tools, and the handiest thing of all, my system of fretting and refretting. Taking this tool away from me would be like cutting off one of my hands. In fact,

I recently purchased a second one so I could have two different setups ready at all times. I use the #229 router attachment for about half of the work I do. I have reworked the base specially and have redesigned the edge guide so that it can be used normally and with a special guide to use the #115 or #196 high-speed steel cutters to rout out the edges of guitars for purflings and bindings. The special guide allows you to go around just about any type of curve or radius and maintain the same depth of cut. (See drawings of special adapters for the Moto Tool to see how to make this and also the smaller base.) The smaller base is to make the tool easier to handle when using it for fret work. Check in with your dentist and talk him out of a bunch of his used dental burrs. A cousin of mine, a dentist before he retired, gave me a couple of pounds of used dental burrs of all sizes. He said that they could use them on only one tooth before throwing them away. They are still plenty sharp and will work in wood for a long time. I use the small straight-shank ones to clean out fret slots in fingerboards and the larger ones for shaping string slots in bridges and all kinds of grafting and inlay work. If you can't talk your dentist out of any burrs, you can buy engraving cutters from your Dremel dealer. They have several types of cutters, burrs, grinding wheels, polishing wheels, routing cutters, and even some carbide cutters for working in steel and other very hard substances. I will describe the use of the Moto-Tool more thoroughly as we get into the repair chapters.

A small router, such as the ¾-horsepower Black and Decker, can be of some use, too, if you plan to try your hand at installing tension rods. With the proper cutters, it can be used to cut binding and purfling grooves. I will show how to build a jig to slot necks for tension rods and other jobs in another chapter.

For rough sharpening of tools and other work, you should have a small bench grinder with two heads. I keep a fairly fine stone on one end of my grinder and a cloth polishing wheel on the other. When used with a bar of red jeweler's rouge, the cloth wheel can be used to polish parts of all kinds, and I particularly like the way it puts a fine edge on a knife. It, of course, should be honed to a fine edge first, then polished on the wheel for a scalpel-type edge. When used to finish the edge on the taper-point X-acto blades, the pin-sharp point is rounded slightly. After several sharpenings this rounding becomes more pronounced. This blade is then perfect for trimming masking tape without marring the finish underneath the tape. Using very light pressure, you can tell by the feel when you have gone through the tape.

If you are doing a lot of refinishing, a power buffer can be a real time saver. I have a Black and Decker Model 676, type AA, with a 7" #61824 backup pad. Should you order one of these, make sure you specify the 1,000 rpm gearing. If you use more speed than this, you are asking for trouble. A higher speed would be fine if we were working with metal, but wood just doesn't dissipate the heat well enough to keep from overheating the instrument. This can either melt the finish in an extreme case or make the finish cure prematurely in spots, causing checking of the finish.

The next tool mentioned does not fall under the category of power tool, but is rather an electronic tool. It is the Conn "Strobotuner," used by many bands, school orchestras, music teachers, voice teachers, and some piano tuners. I use it primarily to adjust the adjustable bridges on electric guitars and for quickie tuning the strings while installing new ones. It is great for twelve string guitars when tuning from scratch. Mine paid for itself in three months' time just from adjusting the electric guitar bridges. It is invaluable for checking the bridging of any instrument, and I will explain its use later in the chapter on bridging.

There are quite a few other power tools that are real handy but not necessary. I do find a 6" metal lathe useful in making wooden plugs of exacting sizes for repairing holes of different kinds, e.g., filling machine head holes in preparation for drilling to a different patterned head. I use the lathe also in rebuilding some of the antique and obsolete machine heads, while trying to maintain authenticity of an antique instrument. It is handy to make some of the parts for special purpose tools, such as the strut jack shown in one of the drawings of custom tools, and for quite a bit of other metal work.

A couple of other useful but unnecessary tools are the spindle-shaper and the jointer-planer. Of the two, the jointer-planer would probably be the most useful in guitar repair. I use mine in truing surfaces for laminating necks and once in a while for truing an edge in preparation for sawing with the rip fence on my table saw.

This should about cover the most common (and some of the not so common) tools used in repair work. As a matter of fact, if you have all the tools mentioned, you have enough to make guitars as well as fix them. As you may gather if you have read any of the books on guitar making, repairing a guitar can be considerably harder. If you can come up with a tool to make things easier, more power to you.

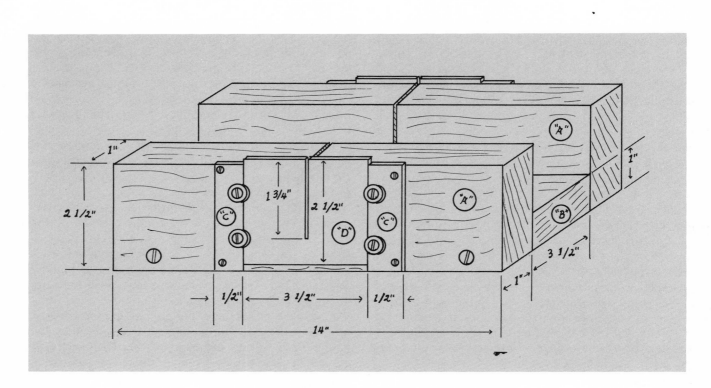

Fig. 12—Adjustable miter box for slotting fingerboards.

ADJUSTABLE MITER BOX FOR SLOTTING FINGERBOARDS

In repairing guitars, you will eventually have to make a fingerboard from scratch. A miter box could be set up to where there is a slot spaced properly for every fret for a given scale length. There are many different scale lengths, though, and trying to set up a dozen boxes could run into time and money, particularly since you may need a given scale once a year or less. The plans shown here are for a single-slot miter box with an adjustable guide on each side to set the amount of depth for a given thickness fingerboard. The box is designed for use with a Model #68 Disston dovetail saw, which may be purchased at almost any hardware store.

Now to the plans. Notice the capital letters in the circles. These denote the different pieces needed for making the box. All corners and edges should be cut as square as possible for maximum accuracy.

To start off with, we need two pieces of hardwood, maple or birch preferably, for cutting the "A" sections. These should be 1" thick, 2½" wide, and 14" or so long. The length doesn't matter, because you can make the box as long as you want it, but I wouldn't make it shorter than 14". Cut one piece of hardwood for "B" one inch thick, 3½" wide, and 14" long. Making sure that the edges of "B" are perfectly square, fasten one "A" to each edge of "B" with three heavy screws, one at each end and one in the middle. Countersink the screws flush. Check with a square again for accuracy. You may glue as well as screw the pieces together if you wish.

Make a mark down the side seven inches from the end for the saw slot and, setting the box on edge and using the band saw miter gauge, saw through the two sides slowly until you contact "B" or the bottom of the box. This completes the wooden part of the box.

Buy some ¾₁₆" (can be up to ¼") high-alloy aluminum plate. Aluminum plate, even aircraft high-alloy type, may be cut with a skip-tooth band saw blade or with a carbide-tipped circular or table saw. Just take it

slow and don't force things. I used my carbide table saw for most of the cuts, because it cuts very smoothly and requires very little sanding to smooth the edges.

Cut four pieces ½" by 2½" long for the "C" pieces. Drill two holes ¼" down from each end and ⅛" from the back edge and countersink for flat-head wood screws to hold these guide pieces to the sides of the miter box. Drill two more holes in each piece, one at each end, down ½" from the end and ⅛" from the front edge and do not countersink. These are for washers and screws to lock plate "D" in position.

Cut two pieces 2½" high by 3½" long for plates "D." Mark 1¼" from the edge of the plate and saw a slot with the bandsaw 1¾" deep. This slot is for the dovetail saw to ride in. The dovetail saw has a back on it. Check to make sure the back of the saw hits the top of the slots before the teeth hit the bottom of the slot. If they hit the bottom, saw the slot deeper.

Another thing to check is *very important*. Make sure your dovetail saw has the same measurement from the edge of the teeth to the back of the saw the full length of the saw blade. Otherwise you may be cutting a tapered slot in your fingerboard.

After the aluminum pieces are made, clamp piece "D" to one side of the miter box with a spring clamp, lining it up square with the slot on the miter box. Clamp pieces "C" on either side snug against the edges of "D." Drill through countersunk holes at the back edges of both of the "C" pieces and install screws. Remove all the spring clamps. Piece "D" should slide up and down snugly. Drill through un-countersunk holes and install round head screws or bolt headed sheet metal screws with slightly bent washers. When these are tightened, gate "D" is locked in position. Install aluminum pieces on opposite side exactly the same way.

These gates "D" can now slide up or down to control the depth of cut with the saw.

To use, set the box on the edge of your work bench, lay the marked fingerboard in the miter box, line the marking up with the saw guide slots, set a block on top

Fig. 13—*Cutting fret slots on fingerboard blank using the adjustable miter box and dovetail saw.*

of the fingerboard, apply a large "C" clamp from under the workbench to the top of the block and tighten to lock things into position. You may now insert the saw in the guide end, if the depth is set right, saw the fret slot out, loosen clamp, shift to the next fret position you have marked on the board, tighten the clamp and saw the next slot. Continue until you have all the fret slots cut. It is fairly slow, but very accurate if you have laid out the fret markings properly. See photo for actual clamping setup.

DRILLING JIG FOR GROVER SLIMLINE TWELVE STRING MACHINE HEADS

The Grover twelve-string Slimline machine head is perhaps one of the best, if not the best, machine head made for the twelve-string guitar. The only problem, as mentioned in the machine head section of the miscellaneous chapter, is fitting them to the guitar. The design of the machine makes the plate very rigid, which is great, but it creates problems as the holes have to be drilled to an accuracy of a plus or minus .010". In other words, a drilling jig is very necessary to do a proper job of installation.

This jig must be machined to very close tolerances as to the location of the $^{21}/_{64}$" peg holes and the $^{3}/_{32}$" holes in each end of the jig. Other measurements than the center to center measurements do not necessarily have to be exactly as I have marked them on the drawing.

To make the jig, a piece of $^{3}/_{4}$" thick by 1" by $6^{1}/_{2}$" long steel is needed. The sides of the jig may be rough, but the top and bottom surfaces must be flat and parallel with each other for layout purposes. Notch out each end of the jig $^{3}/_{4}$" by $^{1}/_{2}$" (see drawing), leaving a $^{1}/_{4}$" flange at each end.

Lay out the centers for the $^{21}/_{64}$" holes first. In fact, I would drill them out, set the machine head into the holes to check the correct fit, and if things fit, fine. I would drill the $^{3}/_{32}$" holes using the machine head as a pattern.

This machine work would best be done at a machine shop with a calibrated cross-feed table on their drill press, because the spacings should be accurate to the thousandths of an inch as shown on the drawing.

To use the jig, center it on either the second or third hole on each side of the guitar head, remembering to turn the jig in the right direction for fitting the right-

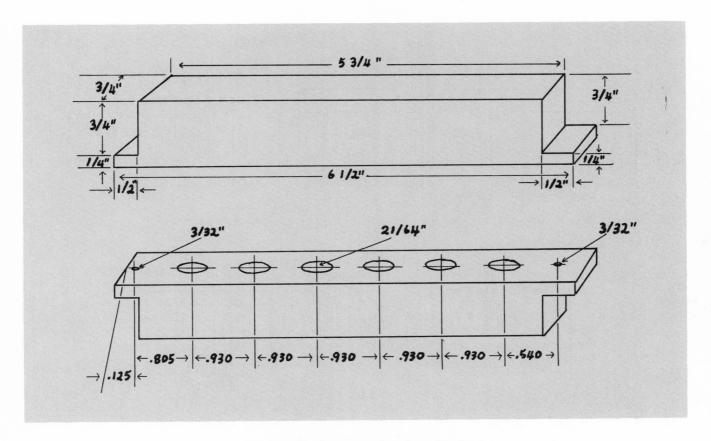

Fig. 14—*Drilling jig for Grover Slimline machine heads.*

or left-hand machine head, and clamp to the head with either a spring or cam clamp. Drill for and install a machine-head screw in each end of the jig. If the holes in the jig don't cover all the original holes, remove the jig, make and install plugs to fill the holes not covered, and reinstall the jig.

Next, take a $2\frac{1}{64}$" drill bit on which the tapered edge of the flute has been ground (see drawing) to a 90° angle with the cutting edge. This will allow you to drill through the wood with hand pressure only. The flute, when left to its natural angle to the cutting edge, usually around 65°, is self-feeding and can really tear things up, especially when coming out the other side of a previously drilled, smaller hole. With the reworked flute drill in a variable-speed drill motor, you can drill clean holes almost every time without chipping or tearing. I grind the flutes on all the standard twist drills I use in woodworking except for the real small ones.

A word of warning on the reground flutes. *Do not* use these on metal now, because they will gum up and burn the edges. Keep them separate from your metal drills.

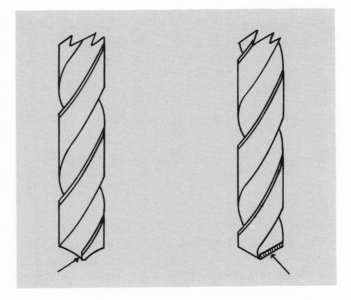

Fig. 15—*Custom sharpening a standard steel-cutting twist drill for use in wood. Arrows and shaded area show where special grinding is done.*

19

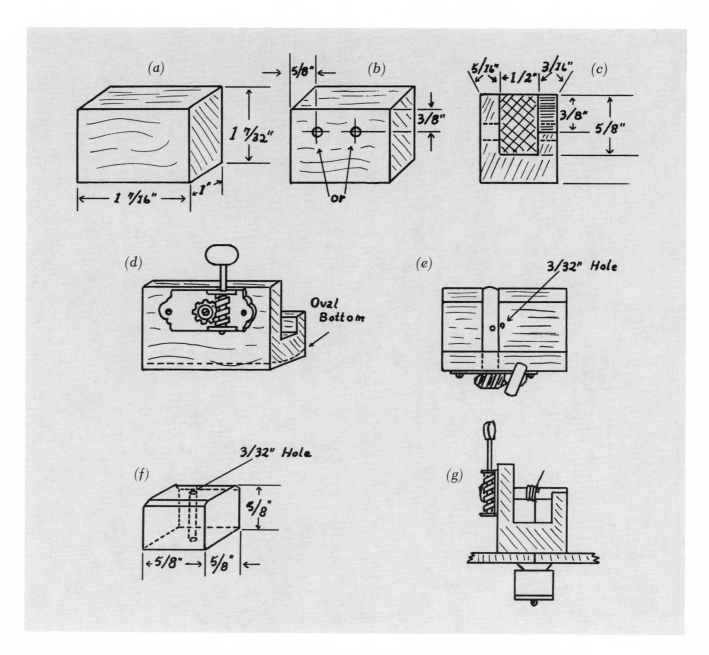

Fig. 16—Cross-patching gadget. (a): Size of individual block. (b): Hole location for machine head. (c): Shaded areas are to be cut away. (d): Oval bottom for use in guitar waist. (e): Hole drilled for string. (f): Patch block dimensions. (g): Gadget in use (cutaway).

CROSS-PATCHING GADGET

This little gadget has saved me a lot of time and has simplified some of the repairs, such as a long split in the side of an instrument that has sprung out of shape. The usual procedure is to remove the top or back so a clamp can be installed from inside the guitar to the outside, forcing the crack back into alignment. With this gadget, the major portion of misaligned cracks may be repaired from the outside and through the sound hole of the guitar.

I picked up the basic idea from Mr. Bill Cheatwood and have somewhat redesigned it to fit my own ideas. At any rate, my hearty thanks for a great idea.

The measurements for making these gadgets are not at all critical. In fact, they may have to be changed a bit to fit your particular machine heads. The measur-

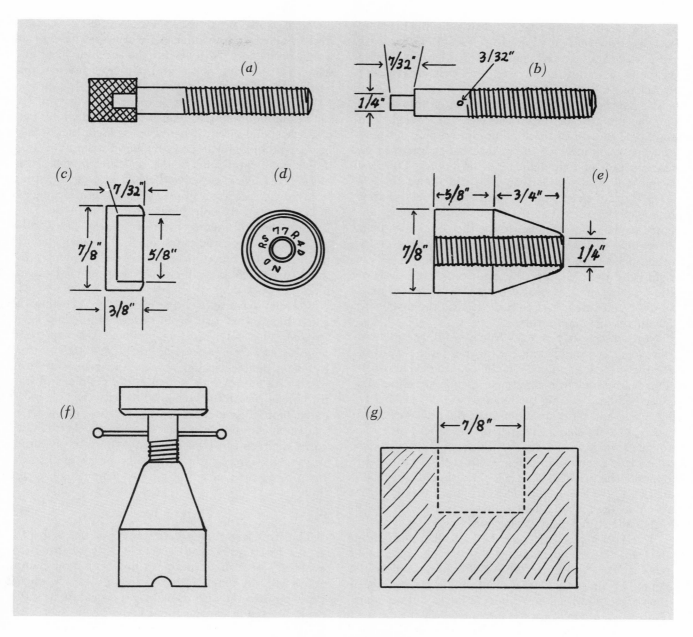

Fig. 17—Strut jack dimensions.

ments I arrived at come from working with a scrap of walnut that I had around the shop. The finished gadgets do the trick, though, and if you want to follow my dimensions exactly, you are welcome.

The wooden part of the gadget should be made of a good quality hardwood. I used walnut, but maple, birch, cherry, rosewood, etc., would work fine. If you have a good friend in a machine shop or have access to a good machine shop, aluminum would be a beautiful and per-

manent material to make the main part of the gadget instead of wood.

I started with a stick of wood 1" thick by $1\frac{7}{32}$" wide and a little over a foot long. It is easier to do the figuring, drilling, and sawing operations on a long piece and trimming to size afterwards. Several pieces may be cut from a long piece then, and they are ready to install the machine heads.

The next step after cutting the long strip is to measure

⅜" down from the top edge decided on for the machine head location. Mark the line the full length of the work piece. Take a square and mark off 1⁷⁄₁₆" lengths, adding on the thickness of the saw kerf (thickness of saw cut) to each piece.

We now have the work piece marked off into lengths and the line marked off on the side. Go through your good used individual machine heads and pick out however many you need for the quantity of gadgets you are making. Left or right hand, it is no bother. The next layout will take care of that. You will notice the two holes laid out in section "B" with the arrows pointing to one or the other. Lay the machine heads out on the board in the order you plan to use them and lay a mark across the ⅜" line, marking ⅝" from one end or the other, depending on whether the machine is a left- or right-hand one. Measure the diameter of the shaft on the machine head used, and using a drill press to make sure the holes are square to the side, drill the shaft holes for all the machine heads.

Next, observe section "C." We are still working with the gadget as a single unit. Set up your table saw, utilizing the rip fence and saw out the "X" shaded area first. This can be done by making a cut the length of the work piece ⅝" deep, setting the fence over ³⁄₃₂", making another cut, and so on until you have the piece cut out to where it looks like a channel or the groove side of a tongue and groove joint. After this part is cut out, reset your blade depth and rip fence and cut ⅜" off the side opposite the machine head side. You should have about half of a hole left on this side to support the end of the machine head shaft. This cutaway will allow you to install the string easily during usage.

The next step is to saw off the individual pieces from the work piece and install your machine heads as in section "D." Notice the "Oval Bottom" marked on the figure "D" drawing. Oval the bottom on at least one of the gadgets with your belt sander or by hand if necessary. This oval-bottomed piece is for working in the curve of the "waist" on the side of a guitar when repairing side cracks. One piece should be sufficient unless you are planning to have more than one cracked side under repair at the same time.

Check section "E" and again set up your drill press with a ³⁄₃₂" drill bit so the hole may be square with the base of the gadget. Center the bit from the sides, butt the drill up against the machine head shaft, and drill through the base. Chamfer the hole very slightly to remove burrs.

Wax the base of the gadget thoroughly to prevent any glue from sticking to the gadget and to prevent gluing it to the guitar, and it is finished.

Another idea that would work, if you could find the materials, would be to make the gadgets out of stainless steel or aluminum channel. All you would have to do would be to drill the holes for the machine head and string, cut one side down, and pop rivet the machine head to the channel.

The patch block is next. I made these out of ⅝" square aluminum blocks. They may be made from brass or hardwood also, but if hardwood is used, they should be waxed thoroughly to prevent glue adhesion. We want just a small cross-patch glued underneath, not a big block. This block prevents the ball end of the string from cutting into a soft spruce patch and provides a good flat surface to help pull things into position.

Using the drill press to insure a "square" hole, drill a ³⁄₃₂" hole through the patch block. You may chamfer the hole on the non-contacting surface to eliminate the sharp edge where the ball end of the string contacts the block.

You may have noticed in section "F," showing the patch block, that two of the edges of the block are beveled. This is for locating purposes. Use a piece of double-stick tape or a piece of tape folded back on itself to give a double-sticking surface, and take your cross-patch with a .018" hole drilled in the middle, and stick it to the tape with the hole lined up with the hole in the patch blotck. Remember which direction the grain of the patch is running in relation with the two beveled edges, and you can then make sure the patch is turned in the right direction by feeling the bevels or checking them by sight by means of a mirror through the sound hole.

Strut Jack

The strut jack shown here was a product of frustration. I had a guitar with a couple of loose struts that could not be clamped into position with cam clamps, and I was just about ready to remove the back when I came up with the idea of making a miniature jack that could be used inside of a guitar body. The jack has been extremely helpful in both the results and time saved.

There is some more machine work involved here, mostly with a small lathe.

The parts needed to make each individual jack are one ⁵⁄₁₆" Allen head cap screw 2¼" long with at least 1½" of threads (18 threads to the inch), a sealed ball bearing with a ⅝" outside diameter and a ¼" inside diameter (this size bearing is available at any bearing supply house in several different brands), and some ⅞" aluminum rod.

Wrap hay wire around the threads on the Allen head cap screw (wrap the full length of the thread to prevent messing up the threads) and chuck the thread end of the cap screw into a metal lathe. Look at the drawing

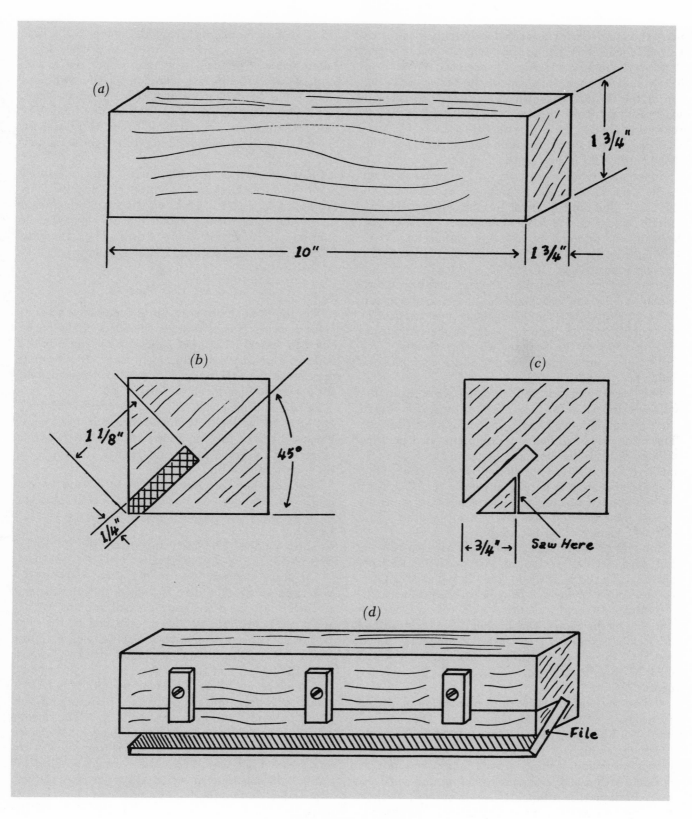

Fig. 18—45° fret-end dresser.

marked section "A." The shaded area of the head is to be machined off. Machine the head of the cap screw down to the dimensions shown in section "B" and drill a 3/32" hole through the shank of the cap screw at the top of the threads as shown. A 3/32" rod (a nail will work) is then fitted to the hole and bradded, or a ball of solder is applied to the end of the bar to keep it in place. This piece of rod should be around two inches long. The screw portion of the jack is now complete.

A piece of the 7/8" aluminum rod is now chucked up in the lathe to make the bearing cup, section "C" on the plans. The dimensions of this cup are not too important, except for the inside dimensions. Use a boring-bar setup and machine the inside dimensions for a .001" press fit over the O. D. of the sealed ball bearing. After the cup is machined and cut off, press in the bearing (section "D") and then press the cup and bearing assembly on the step machined on the end of the cap screw. The cap screw should be about .001" press fit in the center race of the bearing. As the inside and outside measurements of the bearings will vary around 1/2 of .001", mike your particular bearing when machining for a press fit.

The base for the jack is the next step. Here again, the outside diameter and shape are not too important. I used the 7/8" aluminum rod and a 1 3/8" length for the base. This piece may be drilled in a drill press, but I used my lathe to drill the 1/4" hole and to center the 5/16" x 18" tap so it would thread the hole perfectly straight. The shape of my base may be seen in section "E." Cut a 1/4" smooth notch across the butt end of the base, screw the top assembly into the base, and you will end up with a completed jack looking like section "F."

Some large dreadnought guitars are too deep for the jack, even when fully extended, so to make the jack more universal for both shallow- and deep-bodied guitars, make a couple of wooden bases, as in section "G." The measurements aren't too critical here, either, except for the hole in the center, which should fit the outside of the jack base snugly. I used hardwood around 2" square and 1 1/2" thick. Select a drill the diameter of the base used, in my case 7/8", and drill several blocks to various depths.

To use the jack, set it into the proper height base block (if needed), set it under the loose or split strut, and jack into position. Apply a cam clamp to the outside in the same area as the jack and snug down. Check the strut with a mirror and, if things are not in position, shift the position of the jack and cam clamp around until you find a position that will hold them up properly. Remove the jack and clamp, apply glue with the hypodermic needle, and reset the jack and clamp exactly as you had them.

You may be wondering about the notch in the base of the strut jack. Sometimes you have a strut immediately below a problem strut and cannot use a base block. This notch sets very nicely on top of a strut and prevents the base from turning with the screw. That, by the way, is the purpose of the ball bearing head. The head remains stationary and doesn't turn with the shaft, making it much easier to hold in position while tightening.

I have cut notches 3/8" wide and 5/8" deep in a couple of my wood base blocks at the bottom and directly under the drilled holes. This works on the same principle as the notched jack bottom, except that they straddle the strut rather than setting on top of them. These are sometimes necessary for real deep-bodied guitars.

45° FRET END DRESSER

This tool is not a necessity, but it comes in very handy in refret work. It is used along the edges of the fingerboard to dress the frets, not only on a 45° angle, but to make an even edge down the fingerboard. After dressing, the edge of the fingerboard will look like a straight line. It's a nice finishing touch for a refret job.

To make the file block, saw a 1 3/4" square by 10" block out of maple or birch. It should be a very hard piece, because it will be rubbing against the metal frets during usage. Cut the piece so the end grain is running as in the drawing for section "A."

Note the grain direction in section "B" and lay out a 1/4" slot, 1 1/8" deep on a 45° angle. Set your table saw on a 45° angle, and making several passes, cut the 1/4" wide slot.

Check section "C" closely and cut off the 3/4" wedge as marked. The woodworking part of the file is finished.

Cut three pieces of brass or steel strap 1" long, 1/2" wide, and 1/8" thick. Drill a 3/16" hole 3/8" from the end of each strap, bend the strap a small amount so that when the screws are tightened, each end of the clips will contact the wood solidly to lock the wedge against the file. The holes should be drilled about 3/4" down from the top edge of the file block for the clip screws.

I used the 12" Simmons "Hand Smooth" file for the holder, as it has parallel edges instead of tapering towards the point, and it also has one smooth edge. The smooth edge should be the exposed edge so there is less chance of buggering something should you slip up. If you can find "Safe Edge" lathe files, these would be ideal because both edges are smooth and parallel. Get the 12" size and, clamping the file in a vise with aluminum or brass pads protecting the teeth, wrap a rag around the tang and give it a sharp rap with a ball peen hammer, breaking it off just below where the teeth start. Do the

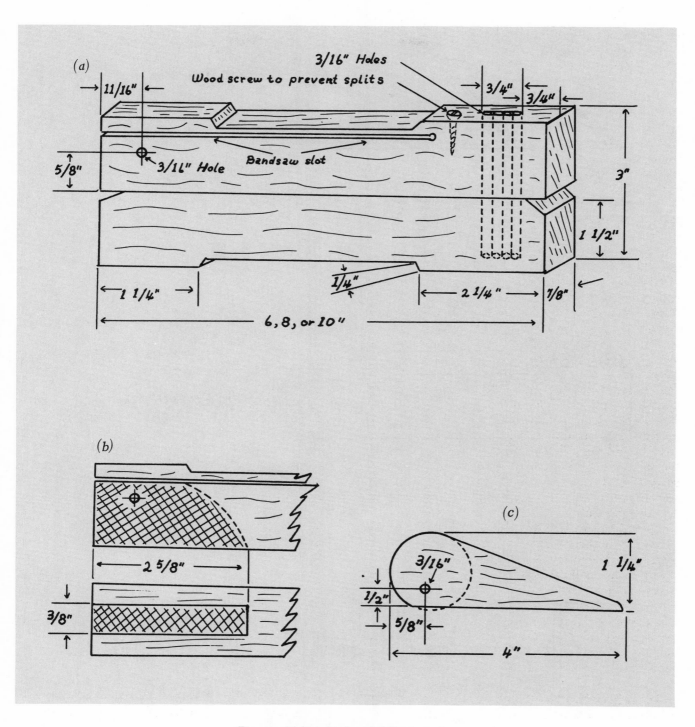

Fig. 19—Making hardwood bridge-cam clamps.

25

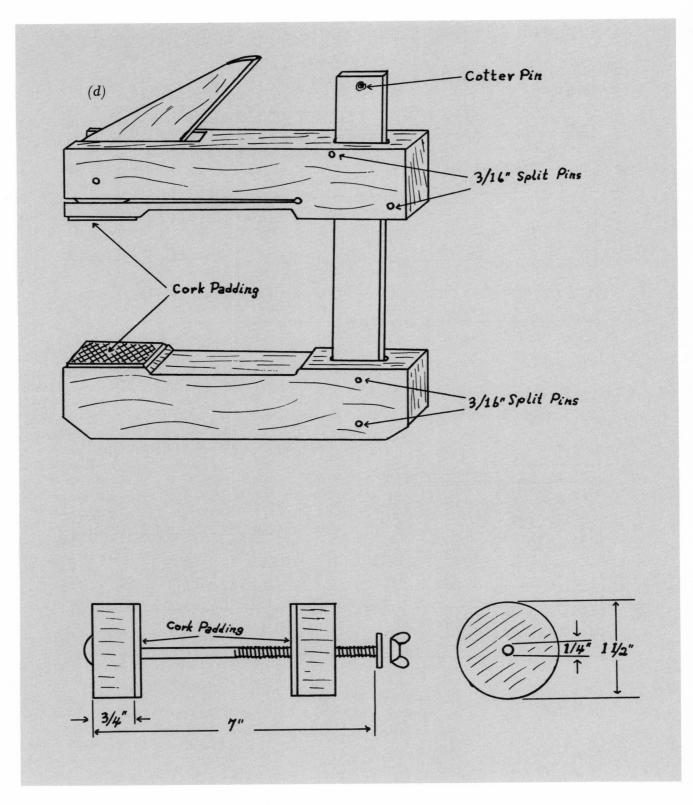

(d)

Cotter Pin

3/16" Split Pins

Cork Padding

3/16" Split Pins

Cork Padding

3/4"

7"

1/4" 1 1/2"

Fig. 20—Hardwood bridge-cam clamp continued. Guitar sized version of violin spool clamp.

same thing on the opposite end, using the rag again to protect yourself against flying bits of high-carbon steel. The stuff shatters like glass. Breaking off the ends of the file gives cutting teeth the full length of the file which, speaking from experience, works much better. Smooth off the sharp ends and set the file in the block, as in section "D." To set the proper clearance for the file, set the block on the edge of a fingerboard and set the file to where it will clear the face of the instrument with a couple of thin cardboard pieces taped along the edge of the board on each side for face protection.

If you get real ambitious, you might make a right and left block, setting the files in opposite directions so you can work both edges of the fingerboard from the head end of the neck. For further description of the usage and a photo of the block in action, see the refret chapter.

Making Hardwood Bridge Or Cam Clamps

These clamps may be purchased from suppliers such as Vitali Import Company, but if you want to try your hand at making them yourself, the job isn't too difficult to do.

As you can see in section "A," the top and bottom jaws are better made as a single unit and split apart after the sawing and drilling operations are finished. The wider work piece gives you more to hang on to, and, the most important reason, it facilitates the drilling of the ³⁄₁₆" slightly overlapping holes for the metal bar slot. Drilling and cleaning out the slot as one piece insures having the bar slots for the two pieces lined up exactly when split apart.

The first job is to lay your hands on some ⅞" thick by 3" wide hard rock maple. The length of the jaws may be any size you wish, but the three lengths 6", 8", and 10", are handy sizes. I use the 6" size most and have more of them than the other sizes. You should have at least two each of the 8" and 10" sizes for bridge work.

Follow the drawings exactly in section "A," laying everything out on one side of the work piece and making all the saw cuts with the band saw, with the exception of the long cut splitting the two pieces. The bevel on each end of the bottom jaw is to help clear some of the tight-fitting sound holes and isn't necessary on the top piece. Cut around ⅜" off for the bevel. The amount isn't too important as long as it doesn't weaken the clamp.

Make sure you drill the hole at the end of the cut marked "bandsaw slot" and set a wood screw in at the end of that to prevent splitting the saw cut on through. This long thin piece acts as a spring on the drilled end and, of course, the cam acts on the other end. Drill the ³⁄₁₆" hole for the cam pivot and then set your drill press very carefully and, using a guide block clamped to the

drill press table and another clamp to hold the workpiece to the guide block, drill the first ³⁄₁₆" hole slowly with the drill set at high speed. Slack off the clamp holding the workpiece to the guide block, shift slightly to line up for a slightly overlapping hole, and slowly drill through again. Do this until you have a ¾" slot drilled out. Clean out the slot with a thin wood chisel and files until a piece of ³⁄₁₆" thick by ¾" wide steep bar stock will slide through freely.

You may now split the two pieces apart and set up for the next step. Check the shaded areas in section "B." Set your table saw depth to where it will cut through the shaded piece without touching the flexible piece. If necessary, slip a wedge between the two pieces to spring the thin piece up out of the way. Set your rip fence so you can cut out a ⅜" wide slot 2⅝" into the end of the piece, setting the fence and making several passes with the saw until you have a ⅜" wide slot centered in the end piece for the locking cam to operate in. Cut a couple pieces of sheet cork and glue them to the contact areas of the jaws, as seen in section "D."

To make the "cam" as shown in section "C," find a piece of the hardest maple you can get. The easy way to lay it out would be to draw a 1¼" circle on a piece of cardboard 1¼" wide and 4" long. You can then locate the center for the ³⁄₁₆" pivot hole and lay out the shape as per section "C." Trim the cardboard template to shape and lay on the hard ⅜" thick maple for the cam. Mark and drill the pivot hole and bandsaw out the cam. Sand it smooth and fit to the locking end of the clamp. If it is tight, sand a little off the sides. It should be snug, not tight. For the pivot pin, you may use a piece of ³⁄₁₆" brass or drill rod with an "X" sawn about ¹⁄₁₆" deep into each end with a razor or jeweler's saw. I would use the steel drill rod myself rather than the brass. Slip this through the hole and center punch the "X" lightly in the center to spread the ends enough to lock the pin in place. Be careful. If you center punch too much, you could split the wood.

The next thing needed is one foot of ³⁄₁₆" by ¾" wide steel bar stock for each clamp. The bar is set into the bottom jaw of the clamp and pinned into place with two ³⁄₁₆" split pins or with drill rod pins as described in the previous paragraph. Check with a square to make sure that the bar is lined up square with the lower jaw before drilling and pinning.

The upper jaw is a bit different, because it has to move up and down on the bar and during usage is jammed against a pin at the inside top and outside bottom of the upper jaw. The easiest way to get the pin location right is to lay the two jaws together as in operation, but with the bar lying on the surface of the upper jaw rather than through the slot. Clamp together with a spring

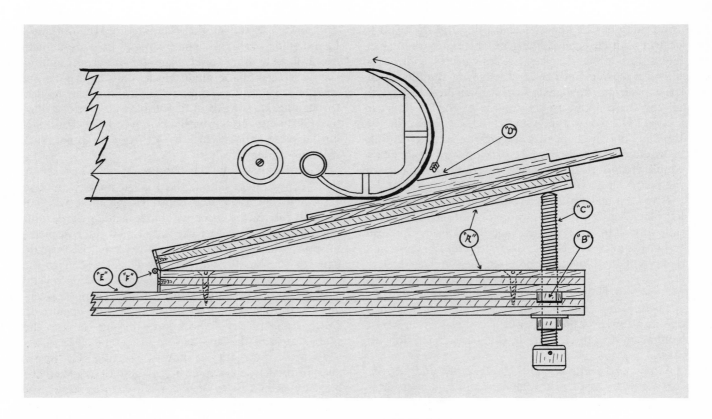

Fig. 21—*Thickness sander for bridge making.*

clamp and, using a $\frac{3}{16}$" bit mounted in your drill press, drill the holes with the bit butted up against the bar snugly. This should, when the pins are in place, result in the top jaw locking up square with the bar when tension is applied with the cam. You may have to cut a little more wood from the front and back edge of the upper jaw slot to allow the jaw to rock back a little bit for adjustment. Install the pins in the upper jaw. Drill a small hole in the upper end of the steel bar, slip it through the upper jaw, install a small cotter pin in the hole to prevent the upper jaw from sliding off the bar, and your cam clamp is ready for use.

You might want to make a couple of the 6" jaws and set them up on a bar 24" long for use in clamping the length of the guitar for light duty repairs instead of using heavy steel bar clamps.

GUITAR-SIZED VERSION OF VIOLIN SPOOL CLAMPS

This type clamp has been used for years by repairmen on members of the violin family, and it works just as well on the clamping of edges of tops and backs of guitars.

Decide on the number of clamps to be made and buy, for each clamp, one $\frac{1}{4}$" by 7" long "carriage bolt" with

a single washer and wing nut. Using a threading die, chase the threads to where you have at least $2\frac{1}{4}$" of clean threads. This will give you enough adjustment to handle most guitars.

Saw or turn out two pieces of wood for each clamp, $1\frac{1}{2}$" in diameter by $\frac{3}{4}$" thick and drill a $\frac{1}{4}$" hole in the center of each piece. The spools need to be faced with either cork or leather to protect the working surface. I used $\frac{1}{16}$" sheet cork, which is available from most gasket companies for a very reasonable price. It's cheaper and less durable than leather, but it is not as hard to work with and is easily replaceable.

Slip the bolt through one of the spools down to the square shoulder and carefully tap the bolt until the head is seated flush with the wood. The square shoulder of the carriage bolt holds firmly and keeps the bolt from turning. Slip the other spool on the bolt, followed by the washer and wing nut, and they are ready for use. These clamps are very strong, and care should be used not to tighten them too tight, because you can collapse a side rather easily with too much tightening.

THICKNESS SANDER FOR BRIDGE MAKING

The illustrated thickness sanding jig makes short work

28

of radiusing and sanding the thickness of the ends of Martin and Martin-type bridges. It gives a clean factory appearing touch to your finished bridge.

It is really difficult to give any explicit measurements, because the jig will have to be set up to fit your particular sander. Also, it should be quickly removable from the sander, should it be in the way of other sanding operations. Again, you will have to work the removability problem out for your own sander. I will give some of the measurements I used on mine, and you can work accordingly.

The two pieces marked "A" and the base piece marked "E" are made from ¾" plywood. The two "A" pieces are 13" long by 5" wide. The base piece "E" I made 8" wide, and the length will depend on how you set the jig up for your sander.

The two "A" pieces are fastened together at the butt with a 5" piece of piano hinge marked "F" in the drawing. Drill four countersunk screw holes, one at each corner, through the bottom "A" piece into the "E" base board and fasten on with a couple of screws temporarily. Mark back from the front edge of "A" pieces the distance of 1" and center mark this. Drill a ½" hole through the bottom "A" and base "E" pieces on this mark for the threaded rod assembly.

Take a piece of ½" threaded rod around 6" long and make a wood knob for one end of it. The shape and size is up to you. Drill and tap to fit the rod, screw on, and pin to prevent coming off. If you like, drill a ½" hole in the knob, mix up some epoxy glue, pour into the hole and set the rod in place. You need to round and smooth off the other end of the rod and acquire one flat washer and two nuts to fit the rod. I used hex nuts, but square ones will do fine.

Set one of the nuts into base board "E" after removing the temporary screws and bottom "A." This may be done with a wood chisel for a really neat job, or you can saw overlapping slots across the base board so the nut will fit flush and be tight enough to keep the nut from turning. Set the nut into place and screw the bottom "A" piece back on the base board with all four screws.

Screw the other nut down the rod assembly, slip on the flat washer, and screw the whole rod assembly up through the base board, and the adjustment part is finished. If you like, you may screw a piece of metal strap under the upper "A" piece where the adjustment assembly contacts, and you may also want to face the upper "A" piece with hardboard or Formica, but unless you are making a lot of bridges, the small amount of wear involved makes facing the piece unnecessary.

To use the jig, set it in place as per your set up, and adjust it to the thickness of the bridge marked "D" in the drawing. Screw the bottom nut and washer up tight

to lock the setting. If you will notice both ends of the bridge drawn there, you will notice one end has the radius sanded in it and the other end is notched out square. This notching is done on the band saw and is cut thicker than the sanded thickness and enough wood is left on the thick part so the radius may be sanded on both ends, leaving the center section the proper size. The notch does not have to be cut out, but it sure saves sanding belts by removing some of the unnecessary wood that would otherwise have to be sanded off.

Another *very important* thing. Notice the arrow curving around the belt sander roller? This denotes the direction of belt travel. It should always cut against you when sanding thicknesses. Otherwise it might pull your work piece, including your hand, into the jig and really make a mess.

Reworked Chisel for Removing Bridge Plates

This tool is designed mainly for one job as described in the miscellaneous repairs chapter, and that is removing the original bridge plates from under the tops of guitars by working through the sound holes. I have also found it useful in removing struts, old cross patches, and anything I can hook it under. The idea for this tool comes from the repair shop of the C. F. Martin Organisation, to which I owe a great deal of thanks for my success in the repair field.

To make the tool, I used an old chisel measuring ⁵⁄₃₂" thick, ¾" wide, and 4¾" long from the butt of the handle ferrule to the tip of the cutting edge. It could be longer, but not by more than an inch at the most, as room inside a guitar is limited. A shorter chisel could be used, but you will have less leverage to work with.

The first step is marking off 1" from the cutting edge. This will be the center of the inside of the bend. Lay out on a piece of cardboard the curvature and angle needed as shown in the drawing. The drawing, by the way, shows the handle cut off at the ferrule. Don't cut it off yet, as the wooden handle gives you something to handle the chisel by while heating it for bending.

The rest of the preparations are simple. Set your vise where the blade of the chisel will slip between the jaws snugly. Fire up your propane torch or whatever you are using as a heat source, and heat about an inch area, ½" to either side of the center mark for the bend. Heat to a bright cherry red, quickly slip the end of the chisel into the vise, and bend until it fits your cardboard pattern. Make sure you bend the tip so the cutting edge is on the inside of the curve.

Allow the chisel to cool off and in the meantime cut the top out of a quart-sized motor oil can and fill with motor oil. Used oil will do fine. Get a piece of burlap

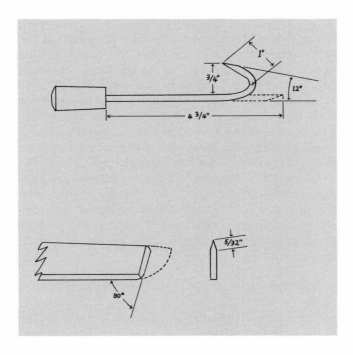

Fig. 22—Reworked chisel for removing bridge plates. Reworked knife for removing fingerboards.

sacking and put it to soaking for emergency use and set everything outside where nothing could be damaged should you have a fire.

Reheat the end of the chisel to a light yellowish straw color and immediately quench in the oil. Should the oil start to burn, throw the soaking wet burlap over things. If you must temper the chisel indoors, it would be a good idea to have a fire extinguisher handy.

Allow things to cool off completely, remove from the oil, and clean off the oil with lacquer thinner. Notice the 12° angle in the drawing? Carefully grind the flat tip to that angle and hone smooth and flat. Cut off the handle about ⅛" above the ferrule and round off smooth. The tool is ready for use.

Reworked Knife for Removing Fingerboards

This knife is reworked for the specific purpose of removing fingerboards as described in the disassembly chapter. I used a stainless-steel electric knife blade to make my tool, but any butcher knife with a blade thickness of 1/32" to 1/16" is usable if it has a "hatchet edge." You can see the type of edge I am talking about in the exaggerated drawing marked section "B."

The blade I used was 10" long and slightly over ¾" in width where it curved up towards the tip. Reworking the tip of the blade is one of the most important steps in making the tool. The dotted line shows the original

tip and the solid lines (section "A") show the change of angle and the resharpened edge. The new edge should be around 80° to 85° in relation to the cutting edge of the blade.

The hatchet edge is important because this causes the blade to act as a thin wedge to separate the glue join after it has been heated with an electric iron. This wedging action rather than a cutting action minimizes the problem of pulling up splinters of wood during removal.

The blade should be kept polished, using a cloth buffing wheel and jeweler's rouge, to prevent glue from building up on the blade and thereby making it easier to use. I highly recommend a stainless steel blade for this tool, as it is easy to polish to a high finish and doesn't rust from handling.

As for other uses, the blunt cutting end of the tool makes quick work of removing struts after a guitar is disassembled. It is also useful in shaping new struts after they have been glued into position.

Bending Iron

This tool is used mostly in guitar construction, but I use it quite often in repairing instruments. Should you have to make and fit a complete new side or curve a patch, the iron is almost a necessity. You can make a special boiling trough, boil your wood until limber, and then clamp it into a mold to form the shape. I find it much easier to soak the wood for an hour or so and shape it over the hot bending iron. I can shape a complete side in a few minutes, and the wood is almost dry from the heat. It seems to develop a better "set" than the boiling method. In other words, it doesn't try to assume its original shape after the clamps are removed.

I have set bending irons up several ways, both horizontal and vertical, tried two or three kinds of gas, and tried several burner systems until I came up with the one shown here. It gets almost red hot and extends out away from the work bench to give some room under it when working with a complete side.

I will describe the support first. This must be very sturdy, because you can put quite a bit of downward pressure on things when bending a side.

I used a 10" by 12" heavy-duty metal shelf bracket, available from almost any hardware store. This piece is labeled "a" in sections "A" and "B." To strengthen this more, I welded a piece of ¾" angle iron from one end to the other. This angle iron is marked "c" in section "A" and the row of x's shows where the welds are located, as you will find in all the drawings of the bending iron. The "V" of the angle is pointed down, and each end where it contacts the shelf bracket is flattened slightly to make a better joint for welding.

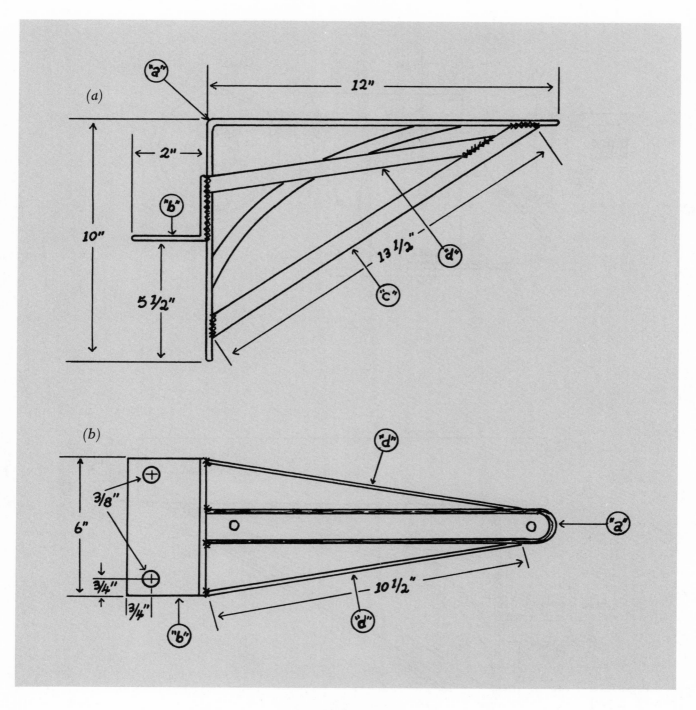

(a)

(b)

Fig. 23—Bending iron.

For the next step, you need another piece of angle iron, 2" on each leg of the angle and 6" long, which is welded to the back of the short leg of the shelf bracket. This is marked "b" in sections "A" and "B" and is the main part of the work bench support. The two ⅜" holes are for bolting it to the work bench.

Notice the straps marked "d" in section "A" and "B." They are made of ½" by ⅛" steel and are sawed on an angle on each end so they may be welded neatly, as shown in sections "A" and "B."

After all the welds are finished, clean off the slag with a wire brush and give the whole support a coat of equip-

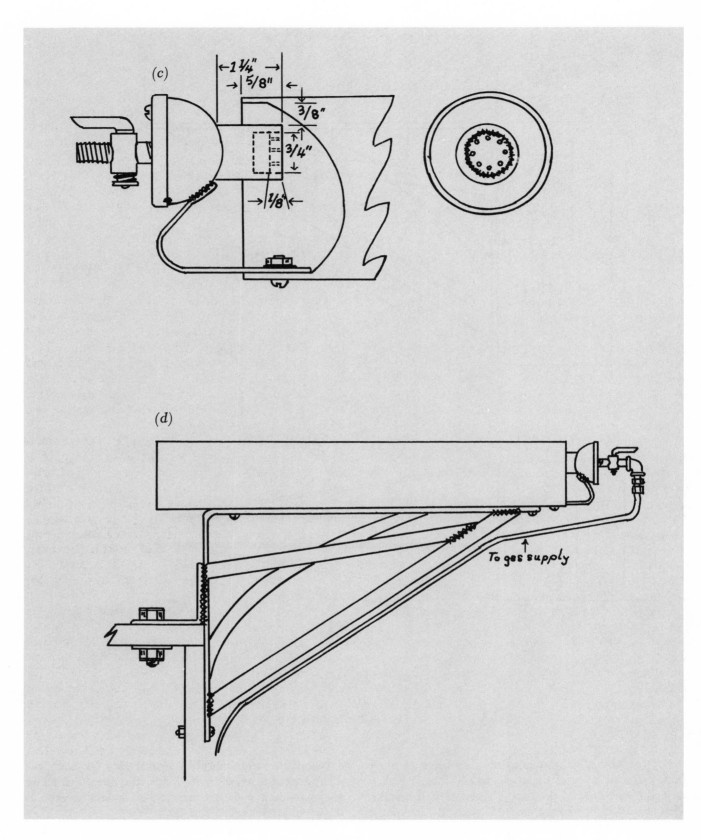

(c)

1 1/4"

5/8"

3/8"

3/4"

1/8"

(d)

To gas supply

Fig. 24—Bending iron continued.

ment enamel or lacquer, and we are ready for the business end of the iron.

The burner was my biggest problem in setting up the iron. I tried several types of long inside burners but just couldn't seem to find a setup that would keep the bending tube hot enough. I finally took the cast iron burner and mixer (that bell shaped piece with the movable cap for controlling air flow is the mixer part) out of a cheap little single-burner bathroom heater and sawed off the burner end, leaving only a 1¼" stub and the mixer as shown in the cut away drawing in section "C." I chucked this up in my lathe and bored the hole out round to a ¾" diameter and ¾" depth. A ¾" in diameter by ⅛" thick slug is brazed in the end of the hole, and 8 holes ⁷⁄₆₄" in diameter are drilled in a circle pattern as shown by the end view in section "D." A piece of strap is also brazed to the mixer so the new burner may be mounted in the heating tube as shown in section "C."

The heating tube for the "iron" is not really iron. It should be made of copper or brass. Iron seems to leave deep burn scars on the wood which are difficult to sand out, so stick to copper or brass. Mine is a piece of copper pipe, ¹⁄₁₆" in wall thickness, 3" in diameter, and 15" long. The pipe is mounted on top of the reinforced base with a couple of ¼" bolts, as shown in section "E." The strap on the burner is shaped so the end sets about ⅝" into the tube and is about ⅜" from the top of the tube and is fastened with a ¼" bolt as shown in section "C."

Now there is another decision to make. What kind of gas are you planning to use? The shutoff valve and jet combination that you can see in sections "C" and "E" is removable by just screwing it out of the mixer. On the mixer end of the valve is a piece screwed into the valve with a small hole in it. This is the gas jet. If you plan to use butane or propane gas, you will need the jet designed for the gasses. They are under higher pressures and burn hotter than natural gas and must be jetted accordingly. If you plan to use natural gas, get the larger jet designed for it. Install the proper jet and run a piece of ⁵⁄₁₆" copper tubing from the valve, under the iron out of the way, and on to your gas supply. I use propane from a camper bottle with a regulator that I picked up second-hand.

You can use the small bottles of propane gas designed for propane torches, but be careful. Open the mixer valve wide and *control the flame with the valve on the torch bottle.*

To check for the proper operating temperature, lick your finger to get it real wet and touch the tube momentarily. If it sizzles, it's hot enough to use.

You may wonder why I chose to have the burner at the working end of the tube. With this burner, the opposite end of the tube from the burner will have flame coming out of it, and it would be very uncomfortable if things were reversed.

Contoured Slot Jig for Tension Rods

Accurately slotting a neck, especially if it is still set in the guitar, is almost impossible to do really well by hand. A router is the best solution to the problem, but controlling the router by hand is not the answer. A relatively simple guide jig can be made from plywood and casting plastic that will not only guide the router in a straight line, but will cut the proper contour on the bottom of the slot and rough out the anchor slot for the end of the rod.

The measurements shown on the drawings and in the text here are for my own jig that is in use in my shop. If you follow the drawings and directions very carefully, you can make a similar one.

The first thing to do is to rework the router base. Install a ¼" rod that has a point machined on one end in place of a router cutter. Set the depth of the point flush with the bottom of the router base and scribe a line across the base as shown in section "A." Mark and center punch two positions on this line, one on each side of the center point 2⅛" from the center. Remove the base from the router motor and drill and tap the two holes for a #10 x 32 thread.

The next job is to make, or have made, the two pieces for the slot guides. These may be made of aluminum or brass and should be ½" in diameter and ½" in length. Do not use steel for these unless it is stainless steel because rust can cause problems sliding in the jig. They should be center drilled for a ³⁄₁₆" hole and counter sunk for a #10 x 32 countersink head machine screw. Screw these to the drilled and tapped holes in the router base (marked "A" in sections "A" and "B"), reassemble the base and motor, and we are ready to start the wooden part of the jig.

Section "C" shows the top and side view of the jig. It should be made from a good solid piece of ¾" plywood. At one end of the drawing in section "C," you will notice a ¼" by ¾" batten that is used to fasten the butt of the jig back together after the slot is cut the length of the board. Cut out this notch now and fit the batten in place with a couple of small screws and then remove it. This will be reinstalled later.

Very carefully lay out the slot and cross slot at the head of the jig and cut this out with the band saw. This slot should be a snug, but not tight fit for the guides on the router base. After cutting the slot, glue and screw the batten in place at the butt of the jig and let dry.

Notice the 10" slot marked "a" in section "C"? This is cut just under the first ply and should have a small amount of wood from the second ply on the top piece.

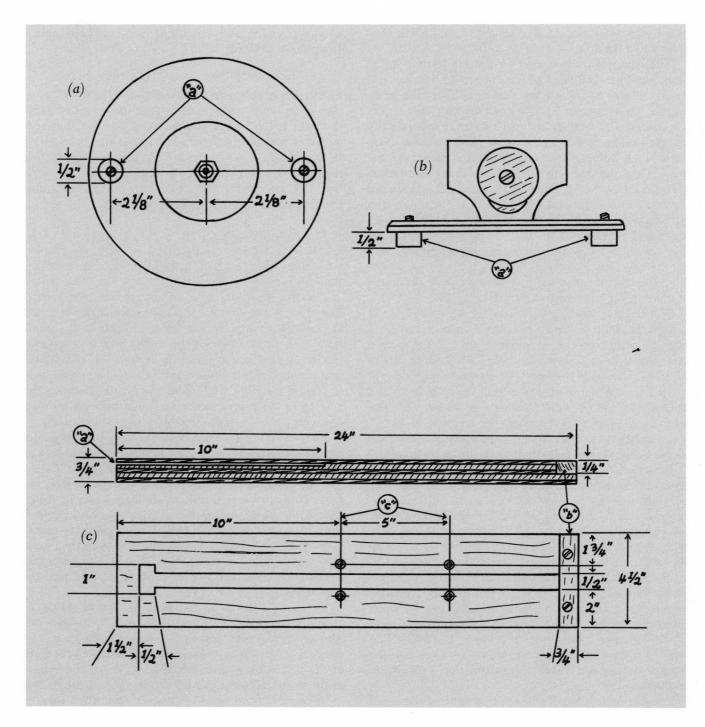

Fig. 25—Contoured slot jig for tension rods.

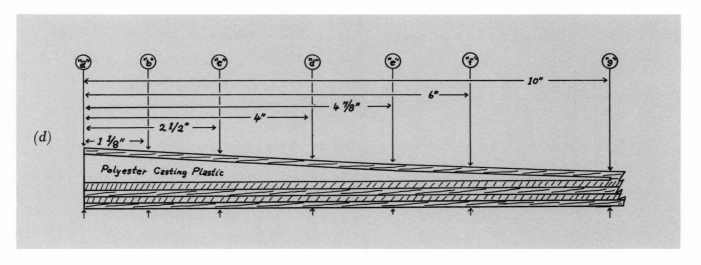

Fig. 26—Contoured slot jig for tension rods continued.

Don't cut it too thick, as this thin piece has to be springy.

After sawing this slot, check the layout measurements in section "D" and lay out the six lines designated by the letters "a" through "g."

Cut some small pieces of wood about the size of ice cream sticks (as a matter of fact, ice cream sticks would do fine) and about an inch long. Wedge the end of the thin piece to where you have a thickness of $1\frac{3}{16}$" at point "a" and stick three or four of the small sticks on the end with a few drops of glue and let dry. When they are dry, we have to get the rest of the letter thicknesses right. If you are lucky, they will be very close. If they are not thick enough, a wedge will open things up, and, if too thick, tape may be used to close it down. At any rate, as you get each dimension set, glue a couple of the small sticks in place to hold it before going on to the next dimensions.

As I mentioned before, the thickness at "a" should be $1\frac{3}{16}$", at "b" $1\frac{1}{16}$", at "c" 1", at "d" $\frac{15}{16}$", at "e" $\frac{7}{8}$", at "f" $1\frac{3}{16}$", and at "g" we are at the original thickness, or $\frac{3}{4}$". Take it slow and get these measurements right, because the curvature of the tension rod will depend on your accuracy.

After all the pieces are glued to the jig, double check your measurements, and if they are off, do the job over until they are right. If the measurements were right, we get ready for the next step. Wrap masking tape carefully around all the spread area on the inside of the slot as well as the edges of the jig, including the cross slot at the head of the jig. Allow the tape to overlap quite a bit and make sure it is stuck down good. The only area not taped off is the end with the $1\frac{3}{16}$" measurement. After the taping is finished, set the jig in your wood vise with the untaped

portion at the top. This will act as a type of funnel for the next step.

I used regular casting plastic, a polyester to which a catalyst is added to make it set up. This plastic may be purchased in quarts with the hardener from most hobby shops. The plastic resin for fiberglassing boats may be used, although you may have to work fast if you get a drop or two too much hardener in the mixture. Any of these catalyzed liquid plastics will do the trick.

Mix the plastic and catalyst and stir *thoroughly* until you know that the catalyst has mixed completely with the resin. Carefully pour the mixture into the cavity and allow to harden and cure. If some of the plastic leaks out, you might have to mix a second batch. Do this as soon as the first batch jells and, if necessary, add more. About six ounces should fill things up.

After the plastic has cured for approximately ten to twelve hours, remove the tape and clean off all the excess plastic down to the wood. Clean out the slot with files and sandpaper until the router and guides slide up and down the slot freely. Sand everything smooth and round all sharp corners slightly with sandpaper.

Now refer back to section "C" in the drawings. You will notice the four holes designated by the small "c." These are drilled and countersunk for the small screws that will hold the jig to the guitar neck surface while the slot routing is taking place.

The last step is to coat the whole jig with a liquid plastic finish to prevent humidity changes from warping the wood and to provide a smooth, hard, chip- and wear-resistant surface for the jig. Spray cans will work for this.

To use the jig, scribe a straight line down the center of the neck and, centering the slot of the jig with the

35

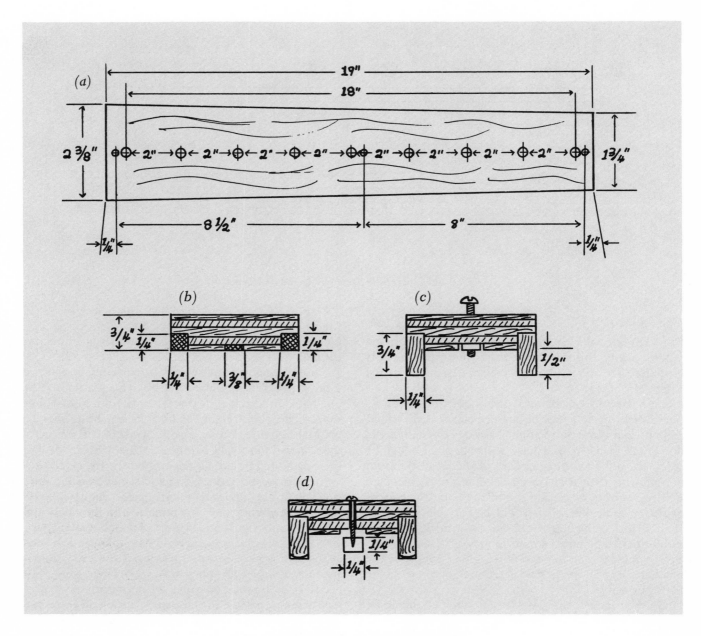

Fig. 27—Universal three-point clamping caul.

center line marked on the neck, fasten the jig down with the four small screws. The jig must be positioned so that the line marked to designate thickness "d" will be where you plan to have your anchor at or near the head of the guitar. If you are using the hidden anchor with the rod adjustment at the butt end of the neck or under the guitar face, the anchor slot should be at least ⅛" under the head end of the fingerboard. To be absolutely accurate, set the router on your jig and mark the position of the cutter blade across the jig at the front and back edge of the cutter. The router should, of course, be at the end where one of the guides will slip back and forth in the cross slot. If you are in doubt, set the jig on the neck with a couple of clamps and set the router on the jig without starting it and see just where it will be cutting and shift the jig until it is positioned right. Then screw it down. In fact, it is a good idea to do this anyway.

If you are planning to have the anchor at the butt end of the neck and adjust it from the head end, cut the anchor slot with a chisel. After doing the job several times, you will get the hang of it. It would be a good idea also to try the setup on a piece of junk the first time to get the feel of things.

See the chapter on neck reinforcements for further information and drawings of various tension rod setups.

Universal Three-Point Clamping Caul

This caul is designed to apply pressure at three points on a curved fingerboard and has an adjustable center section so it may be used on just about any curvature fingerboard. I put mine together out of aluminum plate, but as most shops will not have the equipment to do this, one made of plywood and hardwood will be satisfactory.

You will notice in section "A" that the ¾" piece of plywood is tapered from 1¾" to 2⅜" in width. There are nine ³⁄₁₆" holes starting ½" from either end and spaced on 2" centers. These are for the ³⁄₁₆" by 24-thread by 1" long round-head stove bolts. You will notice three other holes, one located ¼" from each end, and one near the center. These are for three wood screws which will contain and line up the center adjustment section. Lay out and drill all these holes after cutting the ¾" plywood to the shape shown in section "A."

Now, refer to section "B." You will notice three shaded areas. Set your table saw on ½" depth and your rip fence on ¼" width. Saw out the ¼" sections on each edge of the caul back. Reset your rip fence and set your blade depth on ⅛" or whatever thickness *square* nuts you bought with the stove bolts. The width of the ³⁄₁₆" by 24 nuts will usually be ⅜". Using repeated passes and settings of the rip fence, saw the nut slot, centering it so the nuts will be a snug fit when the stove bolts are slipped through and screwed into the nuts. Install all nine of the bolts and nuts with a few drops of epoxy glue to hold the nuts in position when the bolts are loosened. The bolts should be waxed so that glue will not stick to them and the nuts should be washed in alcohol or other solvent so the glue will stick to them and hold them in place.

Put this back to dry and, using some scraps of real hard wood such as maple or birch, saw out two pieces ¾" by ¼" by 19" long and one piece ¼" square by 19" long. The last piece should be very hard, preferably ebony if you can find it, but maple or birch can be used if the grain is right. This piece can be replaced easily, as it is held by only three screws and is movable.

Glue the ¾" by ¼" sections in place with epoxy glue, giving you a piece looking like section "C" from the end view. Clamp carefully in place. Any discrepancies can throw the whole jig off.

Section "D" shows the ¼" square piece in place, hanging loose from the three supporting wood screws.

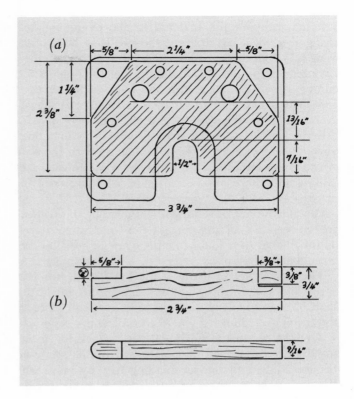

Fig. 28—Jigs for Moto-Tool.

The screws should be long enough to allow the center piece to hang low enough so the bottom of it is nearly level with the bottom of the two legs. The bottoms of the two legs should be rounded slightly, as in section "D." This may be done carefully with a small block plane, but be careful not to get the bottom edges off true. If you do, sand the whole bottom with a belt sander or hit with a jointer lightly to true up the bottom and then try again with the plane.

The caul is now ready for use as described in the disassembly and reassembly chapter, unless you want to use some sort of plastic finish over the wood to seal it off from humidity changes.

Jigs for the Moto-Tool

I have found that making a smaller and redesigned base for the #229 Dremel router makes it much easier to work with for cleaning out fret slots, inlay work, and using with the reworked edge guide for cutting binding and purfling slots.

The new base plate for the base may be made of Plexiglas, brass, or aluminum of thicknesses from ⅛" to ³⁄₃₂". The ⅛" is closer to the original plate thickness.

Remove the original plate and use it for the drilling

pattern, clamping the material to the original plate. Using a ⅜" drill bit, drill out the two large holes and, using a ⁷⁄₃₂" drill bit, drill out the four remaining holes. Countersink the four ⁷⁄₃₂" holes so that the original retaining screws are flush with the bottom of the new plate. Lay out the line under the two large holes shown in section "A" and lay out the rest of the plate from this.

Before you go to the trouble of laying everything out, however, check to see if the holes line up with the rest of the router attachment. If you were accurate with the drilling and the clamps didn't slip, it should drop in place.

Lay out the rest of the shape as shown by the shaded area in section "A" and cut out the base. Smooth and polish all edges and make sure there are no burrs on the bottom of the base plate.

The original plate had a cutout 1¼" wide for the cutter area and, as you won't be using cutters any larger than ½", the smaller cutout gives more support plate in the cutter area, allowing you to control things easier.

Save the old plate, and if you need something to do someday, make a small table and inset the old plate in the top flush with the surrounding top. By mounting the parts back on this plate, you have a small spindle shaper to play with.

In sections "B," "C," and "D" you can see the cutter guide that I use for cleaning out purfling and binding grooves around the edges of guitars. I would normally use a full-sized router in cutting these out from scratch, but this setup works beautifully cleaning out or reshaping the original grooves. In a pinch, it may be used for cutting the complete grooves from scratch, if you take it slow to avoid overheating the cutter burr and/or the motor.

I made my guide out of aluminum with an adjustable end (see the chapter on disassembly and reassembly for photos), but this is not necessary. Make two or three of them with a different height notch in the ends. Making them from hardwood such as maple or birch simplifies things, and since they are for occasional and not production usage, they should last for a long time.

To make, cut two or three pieces of hardwood ⁹⁄₁₆" by ¾" by 2¾" long. Saw a slot ⅜" down from the top and ⅜" into the end. This slot should be at least ¹⁄₁₆" so it will slip onto the router edge guide. You can see the slot location in section "B." The other end has a notch cut out of it. Cut back ⅝" and the other dimension designated by the "a" can be several different heights. I would suggest making three guides with three heights, ⅛", ¼", and ³⁄₁₆". If you should need any other sizes, you can make them later or rework one of the three already made.

Round the end carefully to keep it uniform. It has to

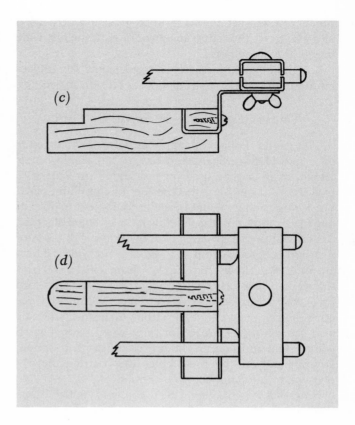

Fig. 29—Jigs for the Moto-Tool continued.

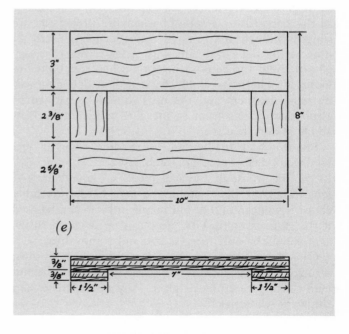

Fig. 30—Jigs for the Moto-Tool continued.

Fig. 31—Using the Dremel and bridge slotting jig to cut deeper saddle slot in a guitar bridge without removing bridge.

be larger than the cutting tool so that you don't cut deeper in spots should you not be able to keep the guide at a 90° angle to the cutting area. If the cutter were larger than the tip, it would be almost impossible to cut to a uniform depth, especially when working with curved sides. I'm speaking from experience on this, because I almost ruined a guitar once.

On the router edge guide, you will find a notch cut into the metal to allow you to back the cutter into the notch for a shallower cut. This notch is where our guides fit. At the back of the notch, a hole must be drilled for a screw to fasten through the guide and into the end of the wooden guide piece. Center each piece of the wooden guides in the metal part and drill for the screw (sections "C" and "D").

The jig may now be assembled and set for action. To play it really safe after setting things up, I recommend cutting a notch of the intended size into a piece of scrap

wood and fitting the binding and/or purfling to that notch. If it fits, cut the guitar, if not, reset the guide until it cuts the right size notch. It's just too easy to mess up here, so precheck first.

The jig showing the top and edge view in section "E" is one I designed to use the Moto-Tool and router bit to deepen saddle slots on oval-topped bridges to get a flat bottom on the saddle slot. This jig may be made 6" longer, or 16" so it may be clamped to the top of the guitar with cam clamps from the back edge, or made short like mine and clamped from through the sound hole with short cam clamps. I prefer the shorter one because the guitar tops have a certain amount of bow or bellying up instead of being flat. The shorter guide is easier to handle for me in this situation.

This jig is designed for use with the 2⅜" router base shown in section "A." The ¼" edge guide rods are slipped into their holes on the router base body after

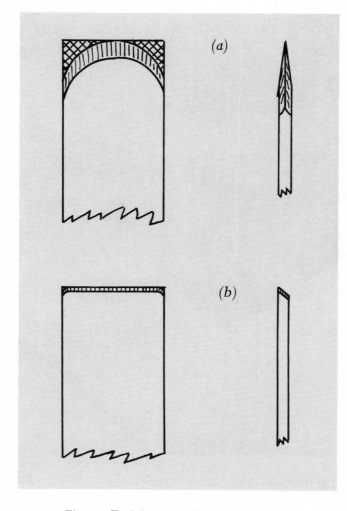

Fig. 32—*Tools from putty knives and spatulas.*

full length of the slot, but without sloppiness. It should be snug but moveable.

To use the jig, set it in place over the bridge of the guitar. Use the router bit in the saddle slot to line the jig up. On steel-string models, the jig will set slanted because the slot is slanted. Clamp with cam clamps and check for alignment. If it is in line, set the router bit to the depth required and rout out the slot. I find this a very quick and accurate method of doing the job with the bridge on the guitar.

Another handy gadget I find useful in cutting sound hole purflings or round slots of any kind is the Dremel #82923 trammel point set. Set one of the ¼" edge guide rods in the router base and lock in place. Slip the trammel point on the other end and measure the distance you need from the center of the point to the cutter and lock the trammel point on the rod with the lock bolt. Set the point in the center of the required circle and go to work.

There are many more uses for the Moto-Tool, and you will probably find some of your own and maybe design some jigs to suit some of your own techniques. As you go through this book, you will find a few more uses brought out.

Tools from Putty Knives and Spatulas

There are several very handy tools that may be made from putty knives, spatulas, or artist's palette knives. Some are similar in looks but different in operation because of a slight variation in sharpening the edges.

I will start with section "A." This tool edge design is for two purposes. The first one is made from a couple of cheap wooden-handled, carbon-steel putty knives. The knife originally had a square end, but the "X" shaded area shown in the drawing was ground off. It was then ground on a long tapering slant like the edge view in section "A." I worked over two of these to be used with the knife heater seen in use in the disassembly and assembly chapter. The round wooden handles make them easier to use because they don't get hot like metal handles or melt like plastic ones. The blades are rather short on these, but they work fine for melting a glue line between a back and side.

I grind this same kind of edge on the end of a long spatula or palette knife and cut the handle off at the blade. It works better for slipping under a pick guard or bridge during removal, and without the handle you can work almost flat with the top. Polish off all rough edges where you will be handling it to make it easier on the hands and/or wrap a couple of turns of tape in the handling area.

In section "B," we use a different type of putty knife. Buy one with the metal tang extending all the way

removing the edge guide. The guide is removable from the rods by loosening a wing nut and sliding the rods out. The rods are then slipped into their holes on the body with equal amounts extending out from either side. The jig should be made to where the base of the router drops between the two 10" pieces and is prevented from going on through by the rods resting on the two boards. I put Formica on mine for a smooth sliding surface. To see the guide in action, see photo.

To make the jig, cut from ⅜" plywood two pieces 1½" by 8" long. Cut one piece 3" by 10" and another 2⅝" by 10". Glue them together as shown in section "E." Make sure everything is square and that the critical measurement, the 2⅝" wide slot is right. You can glue on one of the 10" pieces and use your router base to position the other, making sure the base slides freely the

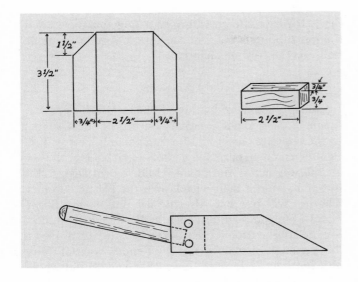

Fig. 33—Super pooper scooper.

knife off on the top edge of the scoop. It sure saves a mess.

To make the metal part of the scoop, I cut the side out of an old lacquer thinner can. I laid out the pattern on a piece of cardboard and cut the tin out around it. Bend up the sides and that part is done.

Cut a piece ¾" square by 2½" long out of any scrap wood you might have on hand. Set it in the back of the scoop and, using carpet tacks, tack it in place with a couple of tacks on each side and four or five along the bottom. Section "A" shows the dimensions I used, but you may make it any size you want.

Section "B" shows the scooper tacked together and with a handle installed. A piece of ⅜" birch dowel rod makes a good handle. Drill an angled hole as shown in section "B" and set the handle in place with a few drops of glue.

While we are on the subject of stripping paint, find one of the frosty looking plastic bottles that rubbing alcohol comes in these days. The plastic these are made of seems to be unaffected by paint stripper and, when cut down to about one third its height, it makes a nice small pot to hold the stripper while you are painting it on the back of a neck or on the side of a guitar. It's much better than trying to pour it out of a can and still control the mess on small surfaces.

REWORKED END-NIPPERS AND PLIERS

End-nippers, when properly reworked, make a fine tool for removing frets from a fingerboard. They come in many sizes, but I like the 6" size best for fret pullers. They are fairly wide on the jaws and do a pretty good job of pulling the frets without pulling too many chips. The cutting edge of most nippers is not flush with the end of the tool, so this has to be ground off. The angle of the jaw inside the cutting edge usually has to be changed also. You will notice in the two drawings in section "A" that the left-hand one has not been reworked. I have drawn two lines on each jaw showing the material to be removed. The right-hand drawing shows the finished tool.

I have gone through several sets of these in the past ten years, and I find the best way to grind these is to use the disk sander. It's very hard on disks, but you get a good smooth job. Just keep some water handy and don't overheat or burn the edges while grinding.

The pliers in section "B" are a pair of cheapies. If you will look at the left-hand side, you will see what they normally look like, and on the right-hand side the jaws have been modified. One jaw has an oval notch across the face of the jaw, and the other has a small slot cut in it with a hack saw. You can grip a fret with these and

through the handle, as it will be used with a plastic hammer. Hitting the handle on a short tang, one will eventually split the handle. You will notice in the edge view of section "B" that the edge is ground on around a 45° angle. Also, notice the flat view of section "B." I have rounded the corners of the blade off slightly. This is to keep from scratching the finish with the sharp corners while removing a bridge.

After all the grinding to shape is done, hone the edge carefully to remove any burrs and to leave a razor edge on the tool. To see a photo of the tool removing a bridge, check the disassembly and assembly chapter.

The next putty knife can be another cheapie. Do *not* buy one with a plastic handle, as this knife is used for stripping paint and the stripper will remove the plastic handle with the greatest of ease.

Grind the edge in the same fashion as the knife in section "B" with one main exception. Instead of rounding the corners, leave them square. After honing this one, deliberately hone the cutting edge off dull. Don't dull it too much, just enough to where you can't cut yourself. This will allow it to remove the paint without gouging up part of the wood or scratching things badly.

SUPER POOPER SCOOPER

This little scooper cuts the stripping time of a guitar by a good third, and it helps keep from getting stripper all over everything. If you will check the finishing chapter, you will find a photo of it in use. You just use the dulled putty knife and push the stripper and loosened paint right into the scoop, and you can wipe the putty

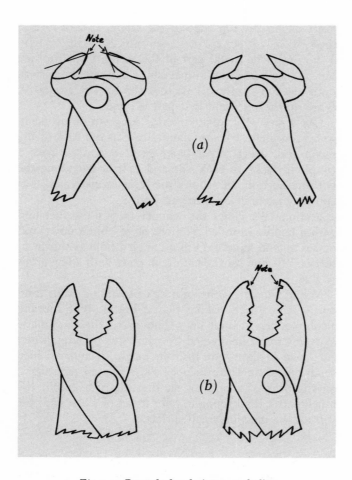

Fig. 34—Reworked end-nippers and pliers.

shape them to the curvature of a fingerboard without the fret slipping around in the jaws. For more information, see the fretting chapter.

Nut Knocker

Saw up a couple of hardwood blocks ¾" thick and 2" square. Sand a slight concavity on one of them similar to the opposite curvature of a fingerboard. This will set right down on an ovaled fingerboard and contact the nut all the way across the board. Hold it firm against the nut and give it a light whack with the plastic hammer. The nut will pop out. Use the flat one on flat fingerboards. On some guitars, such as the Fender products, use the knocker from both sides tapping lightly until it is loose enough to remove. On the Fender, you will probably break more during removal than you get out whole. There just isn't much meat to work with there.

4

On Stocking Materials and Hardware for Repairs

The materials and parts you stock would depend largely on the kind of repair work you plan to do. For relatively minor work, you wouldn't be needing to stock wood for making new tops, backs, sides, fingerboards, etc. If you plan to do heavy repairs or to make a guitar once in a while, then you would need enough different kinds of materials to build the instrument. I keep enough wood on hand to make at least ten or fifteen guitars so that it can age and acclimatize to this area. I buy most of my wood on the West Coast and, since I don't know how well cured it is, I try to keep enough ahead so I can have it around for at least a year (preferably several years) before using it.

The main woods you will probably be needing are: spruce for tops, ebony and rosewood for fingerboards and bridges, and some Honduras mahogany to make necks. Very seldom are the back and sides of an instrument damaged beyond repair, so all you need there will usually be small scraps of rosewood in as many grain patterns and densities as possible in both Brazilian and East Indian types, Honduras mahogany in various grain patterns, maples of several types, and maybe some walnut. These scraps may be used for repairing holes from impact damage. Become a pack rat when it comes to saving *all* exotic wood scraps when making fingerboards, bridges, or for that matter, a whole guitar. The scraps are worth their weight in gold if one of them matches a repair job.

In selecting spruce for guitar tops, look at the end grain of the pieces first of all. It should be as near quarter-sawn as possible. This means that the grain runs up and down at a 90° angle to the surface of the wood. There should be from around ten or twelve lines to the inch on up to eighteen or twenty lines per inch. The closer grain seems to give more response in the treble range, while the coarser grain favors the bass end of the scale. Thump on the wood with the knuckle while holding it lightly by one corner with the fingernails. It should have a clear, resonant boom. You can feel it sort of "shivering" in your hands. Tap it with the fingernail and it should have a good crisp ring. The sound should

be nearly the same over the complete pair of pieces for the top. If you check a few dozen sets of tops, you should begin to understand what I am trying to explain. A luthier friend of mine, Lorenzo Pimentel, who has been making guitars for years in Albuquerque, says that some people have a feel for selecting wood and others don't. I'm inclined to agree with him.

To find a source of old spruce for repairing old tops and wood for making and replacing struts on old instruments, one good place to check would be piano repair shops. A lot of times they will junk out an old piano for the hardware and discard the rest. While the spruce used for sounding boards is usually glued up out of narrow strips, the struts can be cut up for making guitar struts.

You could possibly use the sounding board itself for making a top for a guitar, but you would have to settle for around a five-piece top, as the boards used are seldom wider than four inches. I just don't like the idea of that many glue seams in the top of a guitar.

Another wood I have been playing around with for making struts is good clear white pine. It should be well cured, with no resin streaks, fairly tight grained, and be cut perfectly on the quarter. One of the best sounding guitars I have ever made (my own personal instrument) was assembled with white pine strutting as an experiment. As a result, I won't hesitate to use it again when spruce isn't available.

Selecting wood for backs and sides is not quite so difficult. The grain selection is not as touchy here as in the tops. Some prefer straight grained materials, while others use figured woods. I have made several guitars from various types of woods, both fancy figured and plain straight-grained and I have had excellent results with both.

On selecting wood for fingerboards and bridges, you should look for as near quarter-sawn, straight-grained, and dense a rosewood or ebony as you can find. The straight-grained, quarter-sawn wood adds strength to a neck when used as a fingerboard and transmits the

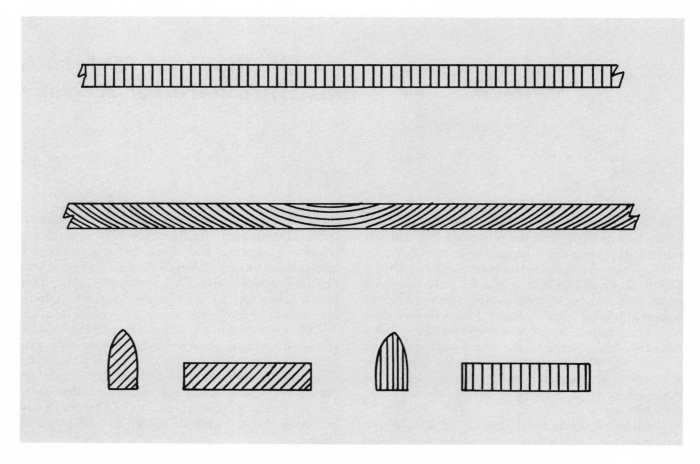

Fig. 35—*Quarter-sawn wood acceptable for tops should have the grain running as in the top drawing. Wood sawn on slab as in middle drawing is unacceptable. To get comparable strength the wood would have to be much thicker, resulting in more bulk with the resultant loss in sound. End view of strut grain on the left is unacceptable for the same reason. Bridge blank on the left could be used, but it should be like the strut and bridge blank on the right for the best results.*

string vibration cleanly to the top of a guitar when used as a bridge as well as adding strength to the top.

Keep in stock a supply of binding and purfling materials, both in wood and in plastic or celluloid. Anytime you rebind or repurfle a guitar, save the old binding and purfling for later use on repairs.

You can buy some pretty fancy wood purflings, such as herringbone, etc., from some of the supply houses. These are sold in straight lengths and cannot be bent as purchased. There are a couple of ways to get around this problem. One is by boiling them for a few minutes to soften the glue and separating the sides from the center section and quickly fitting it to the guitar, being very careful not to lose any of the pieces while everything is sliding around.

The method I use is a bit slower, but you do not run the risk of losing any of the pieces. I use my knife heater

and specially reworked putty knives. Heat the knives and run one of them along the glue seam between the center core and the outer edge. Alternate the knives so you will always have a hot knife and remove both sides from the core. This reduces the stiffness and allows you to bend all three pieces around a pretty sharp curve. Whichever method you use, the pieces should be glued on all at the same time along with the binding to hold it in place while the glue sets. Gluing the binding and purfling on at the same time helps to eliminate any gaps between the pieces.

A stock of fret wire is a necessary item if you are doing fret work. You get by far the best price when you buy in bulk rather than enough for one instrument at a time. I buy by the pound and keep two sizes in stock. I buy a small wire for banjos, mandolins, and electric guitars and a standard wire for the rest. This small wire

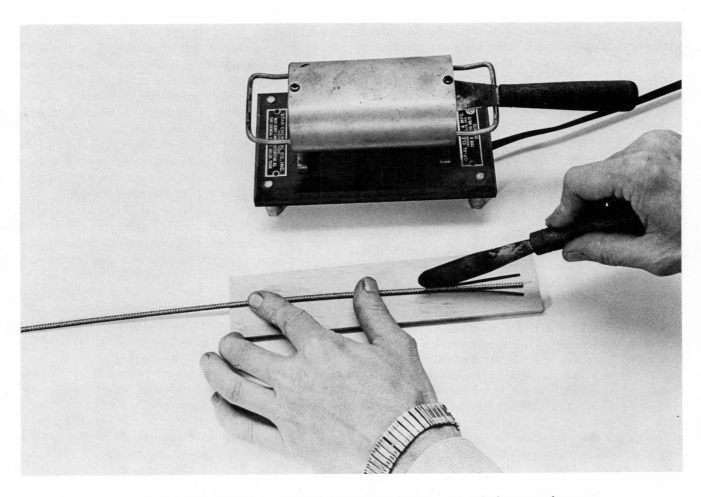

Fig. 36—*Separating the sides from a purfling strip with hot knife so it may be bent around a curve without breaking.*

is not the tiny stuff you find on old mandolins and banjos, but is about .015" narrower than the standard-sized wire. The extremely small wire, while looking more "traditional," is much harder to play on, and if you are using the instrument constantly, the slightly larger wire is a lot easier to fret.

On some instruments, you will find an extra large wire being used. It has been my experience that you will get a little better accuracy in the intonation with the standard wire and better wearability since the large wire seems pretty soft. When going through a dozen pounds of fret wire a year, you learn a lot about frets. The hard nickel-silver-type wire is the kind to buy. Stay away from the soft wire unless you are planning to refret only classic guitars, and skip the brass wire except as a last resort. The price difference is not all that much, and silver looks much classier.

I rework and replace many bridges, most of which I build from scratch, and replace many plastic nuts with ivory. In making new nuts and bridge saddles, ivory or bone is the best material to use because it is hard enough to wear well and still be worked easily. It also transmits sound readily to the instrument. Most plastics just will not stand up under constant use for nuts and saddles. The strings cut into the plastic, binding in their slots, causing tuning problems, and problems with rattles. The plastic pieces are also prone to break. Good ivory or bone is getting scarce and expensive but should be used if available. Some of the supply houses such as Vitali Import Company can still supply ivory most of the time.

Carry a few sets of machine heads of various price ranges. The best moving ones in my area seem to be the Grover Rotomatics. The German-made Schaller is another good one and is similar to the Rotomatic. These are, of course, for steel-string instruments, but both companies carry lines for classic or nylon-string instruments.

For twelve-string guitars, the Grover Slimline machines are probably the best going. The peg heads have to be jig drilled to very close tolerances, and you will find a drawing in the special tool chapter on making a jig for this.

The Kluson Deluxe is a pretty good inexpensive machine, and there are a few others, both American and foreign makes, that are worth stocking. Experience will tell which ones will move and which won't.

Stock a few good lines of strings for various types of instruments. Don't go overboard here, as you can build your inventory up in a hurry with all the strings on the market. I handle mostly the Darco line, a part of the C. F. Martin Organisation. I have a few other brands, such as Savarez nylon strings, La Bella and Vega for banjo strings, and a few sets of Gibson strings for electric guitars and mandolins. Again, experience will tell you what line will move well in your area.

Most guitars coming into a shop can use new strings. If the strings are bad, tell the customer so and ask if he would like new ones installed when you work on his guitar. If you decide to invest in a Strobotuner, this instrument can show the customer the bad strings and can make a difference in the decision whether to buy new strings or not. You can move quite a lot of strings that way, and the customer doesn't have to put the strings on himself, and you don't have to mess with fighting the old ones. It works out both ways here.

In areas where there is quite a lot of humidity during the summer and cold during the winter, or during a change from a humid climate to a dry one, many guitars develop cracks. During the winter when the heating systems are being used, the air becomes very dry and causes cracking. Stock a line of guitar humidifiers, such as the Goya #355, and push them during the fall and winter months. About seventy five percent of the cracks could be prevented with the humidifiers. I for one don't particularly like to work with cracks, and this can crack down on the cracks in a large percentage of the cases.

Music stores in these areas should invest in a good humidification system. They can be set up to work with their heating systems and can prevent a large amount of in-the-store cracking of instruments if they could be set to keep the humidity at around 40 per cent. This goes double for repair shops, because you sure don't want a guitar to crack while it is in your shop for repairs.

As you get settled into the repair work, you will get a better idea of the parts and materials you will need to stock. There is no need to try to stock everything in the book, because the overhead can eat you out of your profits. Work in co-operation with the music stores in your area. Most of the time they will work with you if you do good work and can help in obtaining brand parts for some of the brand instruments. Some of the guitar companies will sell only to franchised dealers, and you will have to buy parts through them.

Get a good bookkeeper or accountant to handle your records and books and keep them straight so you will avoid trouble with the tax people. You will need to get a sales tax number and charge sales tax on parts sold. A good accountant can keep you straight on this and will be deductable as a business expense. Since just about every state has its own setup on sales tax and records, an accountant in your general area will know what has to be done in getting a tax number and where and how to pay the sales tax. On self-employment-type jobs, it is customary to pay your income tax on a quarterly estimated basis. This way you don't have a big lump sum staring you in the face at the end of the year. This can get pretty involved, and an accountant is the best way to handle this situation unless you understand these things.

5.

Glues Used in Guitar Repair

There are many types of glues used in guitar making and repair. The most commonly used glue up until recently (fifteen years or so) was animal or fish glue. This glue was applied hot, and it required some pretty fast work to keep the glue alive until all the clamps were in place. In fact, a pot of hot water and a thin-bladed knife could usually be found along side of the hot glue pot. You used the hot and wet knife to keep the glue sticky until clamped. If this sounds like a lot of trouble, it was. At the time though, this glue was the best available. It usually held very well unless subjected to heat and/or high humidity, in which case it promptly let go. Of course, it was a relatively easy job to disassemble a guitar glued with one of these glues. The shear strength was fairly low, and a thin blade slipped into a joint would sometimes pop the whole joint loose. If that didn't work, a little water mixed with a small amount of alcohol applied to the joint would soften it enough to loosen it. A few drops of Kodak Photo-Flo or other wetting agent (detergent) added to the water and alcohol sometimes worked even better.

One advantage of the animal glue that I have found is the fact that it doesn't seem to darken spruce. Most glues have a tendency to darken spruce or any light colored woods. Sears stocks a hide glue in liquid form that works pretty well. It also has a chemical in it to inhibit the formation of the molds that have a tendency to destroy the glue after a few years. I have used this glue at times and once in a while get real lucky and make a top repair that is almost invisible.

Most of the instruments assembled in the last few years use the polyvinyl resin glues. These are the white glues you see under so many different trade names. The one I use here in Oklahoma is the brand "M & D" polyvinyl resin. It is made by the Macklinburg Duncan Company and is an excellent glue. The only complaint I have about it is the problem in lifting of the finish over a glue line. This seems to occur with most of the white glues. It is an excellent inside glue, though. This glue is soluble in water and also can be removed with heat. One

hundred and sixty degrees is usually enough to cause it to turn loose. This is one of the reasons that guitars left in hot cars often assume weird shapes after an hour or so. A car left in the sun on a summer's day may get as hot as 200° or more inside, and this is enough to soften any kind of glue used in instrument making.

Another type of glue available is the powdered plastic resin glue. I have used these to laminate woods for guitar necks and have never had one turn loose. They are a powder and are activated by being mixed with water. Once they are set up and cured thoroughly, they are waterproof. They are rather brittle.

One of the best of the water soluble glues I have found is made by the Franklin Glue Company and is called Titebond. It is an aliphatic resin glue and is quite a bit stronger than the white glues. It is a light yellow in color and does have a darkening effect on light colored woods. In other words, repairs in spruce tops will show perhaps a little darker than a white or hide glue. It, unlike the white glues, does not seem to lift under a glue line and doesn't seem to gum up as bad on sandpaper while sanding. I really like this glue and have almost entirely settled on this glue as one of the best all around types.

I do use an epoxy glue for certain jobs. I use epoxy for seating frets while doing a fret job, for mixing with colored dyes in filling cracks with small chips missing, and for setting loose necks where a lot of the wood is missing in the dovetail or where the wood is rotten. It can be mixed with saw or sanding dust and used as a non-shrinking wood filler or used where a join is not perfect, such as gluing an old fingerboard back to the neck after removing for repairs. It is almost impossible to get it to lie down exactly as it was before because of the different shrinkage rates of the woods used. Also, it is usually necessary to use heat to remove a fingerboard and this can cause shrinkage. To use one of the evaporative-type glues would leave gaps as the glue dried and shrank. The epoxy, being a chemically catalyzed glue, does not shrink and can fill these gaps nicely. I have used several brands of epoxies including the rapid-dry types and have always come back to one particular brand. The Borden's or "Elmer's" epoxy is the one best suited to my experience. It stays a semi-paste while curing and does not run all over the place like some of the brands. Some of these are almost as thin as water as soon as the chemical reaction starts and can run out of a joint before it has a chance to set. The Elmer's epoxy, regardless of the advertisement, does not dry clear. It has a light yellow or amber color. You have about fifteen or twenty minutes to work with it before it starts to jell, depending on the temperature. The warmer it is, the quicker it sets. But this should be plenty of time if you have pre-checked the fit. Before gluing with any kind of glue, you should pre-fit everything, even to the extreme of clamping it. This way you will know just what clamps will be required and can have everything laid out and ready when you mix the glue. Epoxy is a very strong glue when mixed properly. Most of the poor results obtained with epoxy can be traced to improper mixing or insufficient mixing. You should mix *equal* amounts from each tube on a *glass* or *plastic* mixing surface. Some people use cardboard and wonder why they get poor results. Absorbent type materials can soak up some of the chemicals from the glue resulting in a poor mixture. The glue should be mixed for around a minute or until the whole mixture becomes a light creamy color. The glue is now ready to use. You should not get any of the glue on your skin if you can keep from it. It has been known to have a toxic effect on some people. The glue may be removed with alcohol, naptha, or lacquer thinner while it is still a paste. After it is set up, use a chisel or sharp knife.

While we are on the subject of glue, I will let you in on a real sneaky trick. Say you have a loose or split strut on the back or under the face of a guitar and want to glue it without removing the back and with a minimum of work. The split or loose area is just loose enough to cause rattles or vibration and you want to get enough glue into the crack so you can clamp it back into position. The question is, how to get the glue where you want it without getting it all over everything else? The easy way to do this is to acquire a hypodermic syringe with a twenty-one gauge needle. Hone the point off blunt, so that you won't be sticking it into the wood instead of following the crack. The next thing is to find a small-diameter piece of electronic wire with a plastic coating. Cut a piece of the plastic coating long enough to cover all but $3/16$" of the hypodermic needle, slip the plastic off the wire, and slip it on the needle. You may be able to find some electronic "spaghetti" the right size, but the wire is usually easier to find. Fill the syringe with Titebond and fit the plastic-covered needle to the barrel. You can now reach the syringe in through the sound hole, and by feel, insert the tip of the needle under the loose strut. It will go about half way through and stop

because of the plastic covering. You know you are getting the glue under the strut instead of squeezing it out the other side. Give the plunger a little squeeze, move it over a small bit, and give her another squeeze. Keep doing this until you have covered the complete loose area. Reach in there with a thin spatula made from a used razor saw blade, spread the glue out a bit, and you are ready for the clamp.

I keep two of the hypos full of glue all the time, one with the spaghetti and one plain for reaching into deep cracks when I can see what I am doing. The twenty-one gauge needle is about as small as you can get glue through efficiently without thinning the glue down. This size needle is plenty small enough for most jobs. Do not try to use epoxies through one of these needles, because they are just too small. If you have to use epoxy, use one of the standard glue needles available from most hobby shops. These are too big to use in cracked struts, though. I understand that it is illegal in some states to own a syringe unless you are a diabetic. In that case, I don't know what to tell you unless you have a good friend who is a doctor or pharmacist and will get them for you. Sometimes you can get used ones from doctors if they know you and know that you are not going to abuse them by using them for some illegal purpose. If you get the used ones it is a good idea to soak them in alcohol for a few minutes before handling them. You never know what might be on the needle and if you should stick yourself handling them, you might catch something. Keep a couple of small rubber stoppers handy to stick the needle in when you are finished with it. This will keep the glue from drying out and you don't have to clean the needles all the time. If the needle should plug up, a guitar treble E string will ream out the hole.

There are some other types of glue that can be used for special purposes, such as gluing plastic and celluloid bindings. One of these is DuPont's "Duco" cement. This has the property to melt the plastics slightly and cause them, when clamped, to bond together. This can be used to bond the plastic to the wood also. I usually scratch up the binding with a razor saw blade and use epoxy, the scratches giving something for the epoxy to bond to.

Last but not least, when working with heavily resined woods such as the rosewood family, or if you have handled the glue contact area quite a bit with your bare hands, wash the contact area with a solvent such as alcohol or lacquer thinner to remove surface resins and/or body oils so the glue may bond with its maximum strength.

This should be enough to give you a general knowledge about some of the available glues. I will discuss some of these further on in the book, and there will probably be a rehash of some of the things written in this chapter.

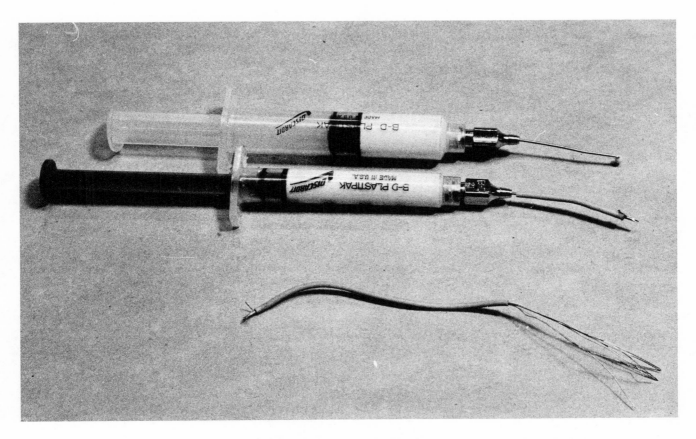

Fig. 37—Hypodermic syringes showing bare needle, needle with sleeve, and plastic coated wire from which sleeve was made.

6

Body-Crack Repairing Techniques

The repairing of cracks is one of the most frustrating jobs in this business. There are so many types of cracks and different procedures for repairing them. There are the weather cracks caused by the lack of humidity; age cracks caused by the gradual drying out and shrinkage due usually to years of storage and neglect (antiques stored in very dry attics, closets, etc.); stress cracks caused by undue stress such as too heavy gauge of strings, poor initial design, and unequal shrinkage of various materials used in manufacturing the instrument (for instance, high shrinkage of celluloid pickguard material glued directly to slower shrinking spruce tops causing cracks in the spruce at either upper or lower edge of the pickguard); and one of the main causes other than neglect, impact damage. An impact of any type can start cracks in highly stressed areas. The top or sounding board is stressed very highly, particularly in the bridge area, and a bump or blow here can split the top very easily. Impact damage to the sides or ribs of the instrument can cause dramatic results. I have had guitars in my shop split end to end like a ripe watermelon. A high proportion of these badly split sides however, could have been prevented as they usually started with a small impact crack or weather crack. If they had been repaired then, they would not have spread, but with the tension of the strings, continued playing, and neglect, they just gave up and split.

The techniques used in repairing cracks vary, depending on the location, type of wood, whether the crack is flush, or if stress has pulled it out of alignment, if it is a tight crack, or if it is an open or spread crack.

I will start off dealing with cracks in the spruce tops. There are very difficult to repair due to one fact; it is *almost impossible* to repair a crack in spruce, or for that matter in any light colored wood, that will not show the repair. You have to explain to your customer ahead of time to expect to be able to see the crack, and if you get a good, almost invisible repair, you will have one happy customer on your hands. If it is a tight hairline crack and not out of alignment, you are in luck. If the wood is age darkened, you can use either epoxy or Titebond to glue the crack, but if the wood is very light in color, the Franklin or Sears hide glue may be used to keep from darkening the wood so much. At any rate, the seam will be noticeable upon close inspection.

To keep from having to clean up a big glue mess, I apply ¾" masking tape along either side of the crack, leaving the crack just barely showing. I then slip my hand inside the guitar under the crack, apply some upward pressure to spread the crack slightly, and work glue into it with a small flexible spatula made from a worn out X-acto razor saw blade. I keep working glue into the crack until it comes through to the underside of the top. Then release the pressure, making sure you have not caused a misalignment. Wipe the excess glue off the inside of the guitar with a small dampened rag (dampened with alcohol or naptha if epoxy was used) and run down the crack lightly on the outside with the spatula, spreading the excess glue "squeeze-out" over on the masking tape.

The crack should be cross-patched to prevent opening again or spreading on past the repair area. The cross-patching may be done either before or after the glue is set. On the spruce top, use spruce for the cross-patch, as the patch should match the wood type it is being applied to. This is to prevent the later possibility of the patch coming off due to a different expansion and shrinkage rate of dissimilar woods. The size and the shape of the patch vary with different repairmen and the particular application. In the belly or main sounding area of the top, the patch should be kept as small as possible so as not to affect the tonal qualities of the instrument. Around the sound hole area and back towards the neck in the less resonant area of the top, I prefer a heavier patch for rigidity. I use from around a ³⁄₃₂"- to ⅛"-thick material for the patches.

If you apply the cross-patches after the glued crack has dried, sand the area flat to allow full contact of the

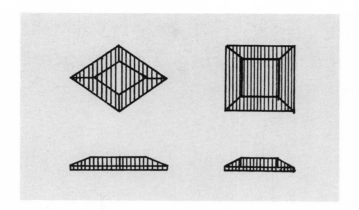

Fig. 38—*Commonly used cross-patch shapes. Size and materials used depend on size and location of crack.*

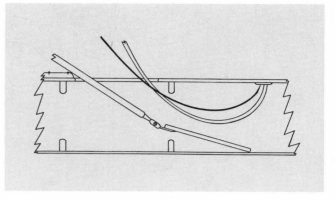

Fig. 39—*Using sharp and blunt pointed rods in combination with mirror to place cross patches in position through sound hole of guitar.*

patch. Since we are working through the sound hole of the guitar, it is necessary to see what we are doing and this has to be done with a mirror. I find that a mechanic's inspection mirror with the collapsible handle (available at most auto supply houses) is the very thing for this job. As I mentioned in the chapter on tools, you keep finding other tools necessary all the time. The mirror is one I didn't mention. There will be others as we get into things farther. For instance, a small high intensity light on a flexible gooseneck can be aimed at the top of the guitar in the crack area and around two or three inches above the face. The light will shine down through the spruce and the glued crack will usually be visible in the mirror underneath as a shadowish looking line. In some cases, such as with an extra dense or thick top, or in the case of plywood tops, you may not see anything. In this case the lamp, such as the one I use, can be inserted through the sound hole inside the guitar. The lamp I use has a double-shielded shade 3" in diameter and is on a wall mounted, flexible gooseneck, 18" long. It works inside rather nicely, and, with the double shade, the heat radiation is cut down somewhat. Still, it is not a good idea to leave the lamp inside for more than a minute or two at a time. A small swivel-head flashlight or flashlight with the flexible gooseneck extension can be used, but it doesn't furnish nearly as much light, although it has the advantage of not heating up much. I prefer the high intensity light.

Now we have solved the vision problem. Next, the problem is to get the cross-patch to the proper area and applied. One way I have used is to straighten out a heavy coathanger, form a handle on one end by doubling the wire and twisting it together, sharpen the other end to a fine point, and bend it in a long shallow "U" shape so that you can insert it into the sound hole of the guitar.

It should be shaped so you can bring the point up to where the repaired crack is and where you are applying the cross-patches. Do you begin to get the picture? Now make another handle from ¾₁₆" brass or mild steel rod shaped the same way, except that instead of a sharp point it should have a blunt end. It wouldn't hurt to make two sets of these handles, one set around 18" long and one around 10" or 12". Using bendable materials, you can reshape them for a particular job, reaching side cracks, back cracks, etc.

Now stick one of the cross-patches on the sharp-pointed handle, making sure that the grain of the patch is running so as to be across the grain of the top when applied. Apply glue to the patch and insert the handle inside the guitar, watching in the mirror to see where the patch is going. This may be a little awkward at first, because you are seeing things backward in the mirror. Bring the patch up against the top and hold it while you bring the blunt-tipped, stiff handle up against the patch. Hold this tight and wiggle the sharp point out of the patch and remove the mirror, etc., and turn the instrument face down so the glue can dry without the patch falling off. You may clamp the patches in place, but this usually is not necessary if the patch fits flush. It can be difficult to reach some of the patches to clamp them anyway. Some of them, you can reach with the long wooden bridge or cam clamps, but on others it may not be possible.

On these patches that are inaccessible by these means, or on cracks that are out of alignment, other means have to be devised. A friend of mine, Bill Cheatwood, had this problem with a lute one time and came up with a beautiful solution. The gadget he showed me was kind of rough, but it sure did do the trick. It used a used machine head of the individual type to pull a guitar

Fig. 40—*Closeup showing the solder ball, patch block, and cross patch threaded on the guitar string.*

treble E or B string up through a cross-patch, through the crack, up through the gadget on the machine head shaft. When tightened, it pulled the patch up from underneath against the crack, holding the patch in position and realigning any misalignment in the crack.

I have played pretty free with this idea and redesigned it quite a bit. The principle is the same, though. I use a small block under the patch to prevent any splitting of the patch as it is pulled up tight and also to prevent the string pulling through the soft spruce patch. I made the blocks of aluminum, but brass or hardwood could be used. Hardwood blocks should be waxed with a hard non-silicone wax to prevent sticking so they may be removed easily.

When using these gadgets, I have found certain procedures work better than others. Instead of trying to thread the guitar string through the block, patch, and then trying to feed it through the hole from the inside by feel, I drill a small hole .018" through the crack where I want the patch, feed the string through from the outside, and pull it on through the sound hole, mak-

ing sure that I don't pull it all the way through and have to start over again. I drill the same tiny hole through the cross-patch, the drill, by the way, being held in a pin vise, as .018" is too small for the normal drill chuck. I insert the string through the patch and through the block to which I have applied a small piece of double-stick tape to hold the patch to the block without shifting. You will notice in the drawing on how to make the cross-patch gadget that I have beveled the edges on one side of the block. Remember which direction the grain of the patch is running, and when you are guiding the patch in place with your hand, you can tell by feel if the grain is in the right direction by feeling the bevels on the block or looking at them with a mirror and light.

We now have the string running through the patch, tape, and the block, but since we started the string through from the outside there is no way to prevent it from pulling it right back through. Get your soldering iron out and heating up while you take your needle-nose pliers and wrap a couple small turns of the string around the end of the nose. Be sure that you protect the finish of the guitar with paper or something and apply a ball of solder to the string where it is rolled up. Let this cool and you have a stop as good as the original end on the string. If the area cannot be reached with your hand, leave some of the string hanging past where you make the solder ball and tie it to another string before pulling it into place.

We are ready to start the gluing. I use the masking tape trick again, and then work the glue into the crack with the small spatula mentioned earlier. I apply glue to the cross-patch and pull it into position checking to make sure the grain is running right and is positioned properly. I hold the string tight with one hand and slip the gadget over the string. Run it down the string as close as you can and, still holding it tight, take a couple of turns through the machine head shaft. Now lift the machine head up to hold the patch tight and tighten the string up on the shaft, pulling the gadget tight against the face of the guitar and pulling the patch up against the underside of the face with the subsequent pressure from both sides aligning the crack back to its original position (hopefully). If you are working with epoxy such as the Elmer's brand, you have enough drying time to set two or three of these gadgets in place to align a long crack. When you get used to using the gadgets, you can get a couple in place using a faster glue. Just get your wires and patching blocks and patches set up for two or three gadgets at a time instead of one. It's a bit of a mess to keep track of more than two at a time if you are in too big a hurry, so don't try more than two unless you use the epoxy. Let the glue dry thoroughly.

To remove the cross-patch gadgets, unwind enough of the string to get your dikes underneath to cut the string. Then reach inside the guitar and pull the remaining string and block out or pull it out with the long string if you used this method. You will have a small hole the size of the string left to fill. This can be done with a little daub of glue unless you used a pretty big string. Pull the masking tape off, and then, using a sharp chisel or knife, clean up the glue line over the crack. I then scrape it with a knife point slightly to get the glue slightly below the level of the original finish so that you can build up with lacquer. If you leave the glue level with the finish and touch it up, you will go through to the glue again if you try to level the touch up work with the rest of the finish.

On some of the tops, particularly if they have many cracks, you may not be able to align all of them. The thing to do is line them up as best you can and then sand and refinish the whole top.

Some cracks, on the top in particular, are spread open. I've seen gaps as much as 1/16" wide in some of the worse cases. This type crack is usually caused by one of two things, an extreme lack of humidity or poor curing of the wood used in construction with the resultant shrinkage of the different woods at a different rate. The top, being spruce in most instances, shrinks much more and ends up with wide gaps trying to shrink to its stable point.

In the first case, restoring some of the moisture may close up the biggest part of the gaps. I keep my shop in between 40 and 50 per cent humidity and I will hang one of these guitars for a couple weeks, allowing it to acclimatize. If the cracks remain open, you have trouble.

There is another reason for cracking also. Guitars that have been exposed to extremely high humidity or freak conditions, such as being floated down a creek after being blown there by a tornado, will invariably swell and warp. Most, if not all, of the bracing and glue joints will be ruined because the glue, in most cases, is water soluble. When the instrument dries out the joints will usually open in many cases. If they are dried out slowly and carefully, they may survive without too many cracks and will be reparable.

Now for the technique of repairing open cracks. If the edges of the cracks are out of alignment, the cross-patch gadgets are brought into use, applying patches about 2" apart. Try to keep as much glue out of the crack as possible by applying glue to the ends of the patch, leaving the center directly under the crack free of glue. The glue squeezed into the crack will have to be removed for the repair. This is the reason I usually do not cross-patch until the repair is completed, except when there is misalignment.

Now, the next step is to clean out the crack. I keep several used saw blades handy from which I have removed the stiffening backs. The razor saw cuts around .010" to .015" wide cut depending on the sharpness, and the small guitar maker's saw blade from .025" to .030". Use the thinnest blade possible to clean the crack out the same width the full length, being careful not to saw through the cross-patches if already applied. Angle the ends of the crack at a 45° angle away from the end of the crack.

The next step is to find a scrap of spruce as near the same color of the top as possible. The dark lines in the scrap should be close to the width of the cleaned crack, and the scrap should be about the same thickness or thicker than the top and slightly longer than the crack. If you will look at the end grain, you will see the dark lines running up and down, preferably at a 90° angle to the surface. These dark lines are the hard portion of the grain and give the spruce its strength. The light colored part is considerably softer. What we have to do now is to split *one* of these hard grains of spruce off the scrap. This is done with a sharp, rounded end X-acto knife. You may have to try a couple times to find out which

Fig. 41—*Cleaning open crack with thin saw blade in preparation for inserting grain filler piece.*

direction the wood will split properly. Run the knife down the center of the soft wood between the grain wanted and the one next to it, leaving some of the soft wood on either side of the hard part. If it didn't come off clean but split across the hard grain, try again on the next one, working in the opposite direction. I have found it almost impossible to split off a hard grain clean by itself, so I don't even try. It is much easier to clean off the soft wood later. When you finally have a grain off in one piece, you will have to deal with the soft wood. Again working carefully on one end, clean the soft wood down to the hard grain. If you split on through it, work the opposite direction. Rough most of the soft wood off,

turn it over, and working in the opposite direction, clean the other side. By looking closely, you can tell when you hit the hard grain and you can feel it if you have a delicate touch with the knife. Now, scrape the grain carefully to finish cleaning off the soft wood and check it in the crack. It should be scraped until it is a snug fit the full length of the crack. Cut the ends on a 45° angle to match the angle at the ends of the cleaned out crack. The grain should be slightly longer so it will fill the length of the crack completely with a small amount sticking over. If it does not fit properly either work with it till it does or start over and make another filler. This method will come as close to hiding a crack in spruce

55

Fig. 42—Splitting grain from scrap piece of spruce with knife for making crack filler piece.

as any one will, if you fit things properly. Fit everything and double check it before gluing anything.

Now, tape either side of the crack with masking tape, apply glue to the crack and filler and slide it into the crack. Press down carefully, working from one end to the other, to seat the grain, wipe the excess glue from each side of the grain with corner of spatula, and let dry thoroughly. Remove tape, trim excess carefully, working with the grain of the filler, and if minor touch-up is scheduled, scrape until slightly below the surface of the finish on either side of the repair.

If you have not cross-patched, clean underside of the repair with sandpaper and reinforce with cross-patches. If you came out with a level, smooth, close-fitting repair with no gaps, congratulations.

Cracks in the back of a guitar are easier to see from the inside of the guitar. Better than 50 per cent of the back is visible from the sound hole and the rest is visible with the aid of a mirror and light.

Minor back cracks are repaired in much the same fashion as the top cracks. The cross-patching gadget is a big help here because the extra stress of the compound curvature of the back usually forces cracks out of alignment except for the smaller ones. All back cracks should

Fig. 43—Cleaning soft wood from hard grain with razor-sharp chisel.

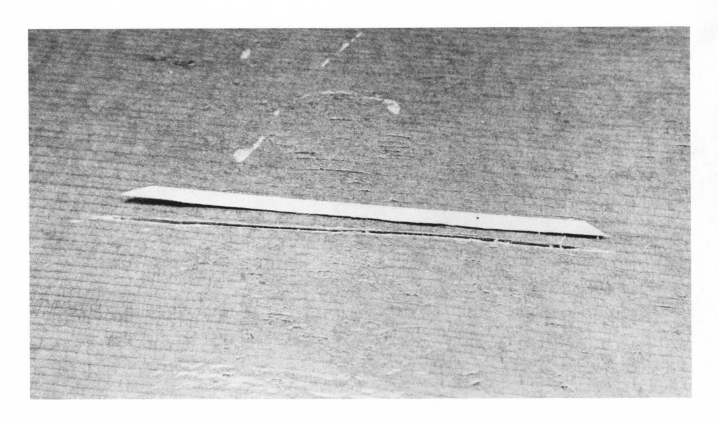

Fig. 44—Grain cleaned off with ends tapered for filling cleaned crack.

Fig. 45—Grain filler in place, with glue spatula sized for cleaning excess glue off on masking tape.

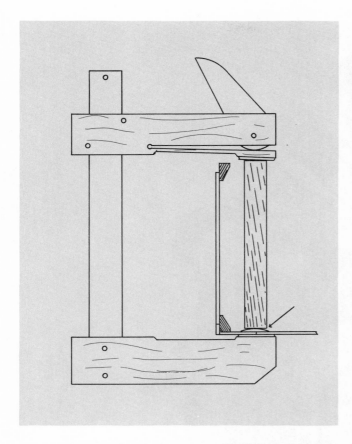

Fig. 46—Cross patching back or top crack with back and top removed. Arrow points to cross patch held in position with block set in place on top and length of cross patch so cam clamp can be used to align the crack and hold the patch firm until the glue dries.

inside surface is perfectly smooth and flat for the patching strips.

These strips should be ¾" wide and made of the same material as the back. These strips should also be clamped carefully so they maintain contact with the back for their full length. The wooden bridge or cam clamps are best for this job.

I recommend epoxy to glue both the crack and the reinforcing strips. The epoxy used to glue the back crack may be dyed with a small amount of powdered alcohol-soluble aniline dye (Star's Match-O-Blend stain powder kit) to the same color as the bare wood, but remember that the dyed glue will dry and finish darker after it cures. This step (dyeing) will save touch-up time, particularly when repairing small cracks on a dark finish.

On touching up the cracks, the same procedure described in top cracks is used. Before applying finish, apply a small amount of alcohol with an artist's brush and check the color. You may have to add a small amount of stain to get the color match close.

If you are waiting for me to tell you how to remove the back to repair it, be patient. We will get to that later on when I will tell you how to disassemble a guitar from one end to the other. We have more cracks to deal with, and I would rather get as much instruction on crack repair in one chapter as possible, even though some of the side repairs will necessitate removing the back. Speaking of side repairs, they are next.

Side cracks are usually a bit different from other body cracks. The strings, being fastened to the top of the guitar and the neck at the machine heads, are trying to pull the top up and toward the neck. The neck, being fastened to the upper bout, is trying to pull upwards. Thus the heel or bottom of the neck is trying to pull the back off. The stress from the two directions is trying to separate the guitar at the sides. When you get a crack in the side and ignore it, you have a kind of twisting force at work. The usual result is a crack the full length, or at least from the waist to either the neck block or the butt block, depending on which bout the crack started from.

On some guitars, on Martins in particular, you will find cloth tape running down the side from under the notched lining at the top to under the bottom linings at spaced intervals. These are to prevent spreading of side cracks in the event you get it clobbered or something. On quite a few instruments, you will find nothing. On the dozen guitars I have built, I have usually reinforced the sides. It is good insurance. I have used both cloth strips and wooden strips and am satisfied with both.

Our problem here is to repair the damage after it has occurred. If it is a small crack and has not sprung out of alignment, the repair is simple. Tape off outside, work

be cross-patched because of this stress. Unless the crack stops at a strut, a patch should be placed at the extreme end of each crack to prevent further splitting of damaged grain. A patch should be spotted at least every two inches along the split. In fact, on very long cracks extending the length of the guitar, I have found the only way to do a really satisfactory job is to remove the back and strip the crack the full length just like the center seam of the back. The crack will, in a lot of cases, still work, even when stripped the full length. This shows up as a raised line in the finish visible to the eye and noticeable to the touch. On some instruments, particularly the aged ones, you can almost predict this will happen.

This is why I recommend removing the back on these. If the crack is clear across the back, you can separate the pieces, wash the edges several times with lacquer thinner and alcohol to remove old waxes and polishes, and use an edge-clamping setup to close the crack while gluing. You can also clean the excess glue easier and make sure the

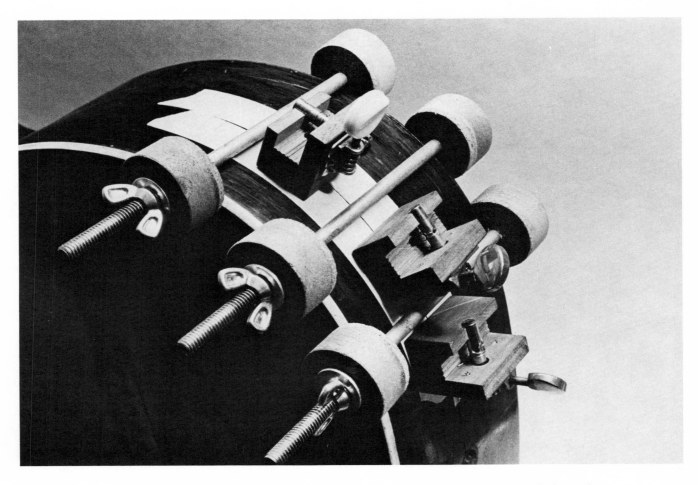

Fig. 47—Cross-patch gadgets in place to align the side crack and spool clamps to pull the crack together.

glue through the crack, attach a couple of the spool clamps from edge to edge, compressing the crack together, and cross-patch on the inside, one at each end of the crack and about every two inches in between. All my jobs should be so simple.

It's when the cracks have spread enough to cause misalignment that the fun begins. If the crack is not too badly out of line, it may be pulled back into alignment with the cross-patch gadgets and spool clamps, working on a short section at a time. I usually work a 4" to 6" area, allowing the glue to set before working another section. This way, starting at one end of the crack, it is possible to align almost perfectly the side and get by with a minor touch-up job on the finish.

If the guitar is split through the butt block or badly warped out of position, it may be necessary to remove the back so the crack may be clamped from both sides. These badly stressed out of shape repair jobs should be stripped the full length on the inside, like the back cracks. The short wooden bridge or cam clamps may be used with a 2" or 3" long by ¾" square block wrapped in wax paper between the jaw surface and the side. These may be taped to the guitar or to the clamps to make the handling easier as the clamps are applied. These are to keep the sides flush and square at the crack. Tighten just tight enough to keep the clamps from falling off and set the spool clamps on the edge, tighten down to close the crack and tighten the others until the sides are square. Check for alignment and if everything is true or as close as possible, remove the clamps, apply glue, and set her up again. Again I stress checking all clamping setups before gluing. Sure saves a mess if you have to make a change in the setup. Allow glue to dry, clean up the mess, and strip inside of the crack. Instead of wood stripping, nylon or fiberglass tape may be used for this job. I prefer to use the wood cross-patching, as

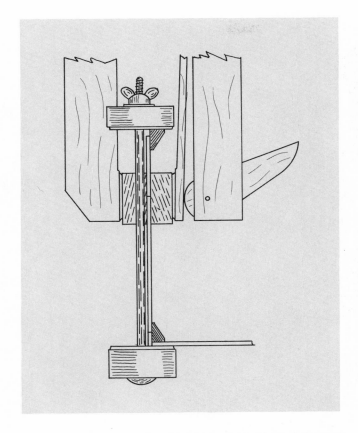

Fig. 48—*Using small blocks on either side of side crack in combination with cam clamp to realign the crack and spool clamp to pull the crack together. This setup is used with either the top or back removed.*

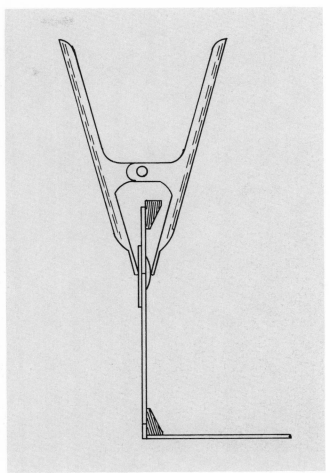

Fig. 49—*Using spring clamp to hold cross patch in position on inside of guitar. Notice the pad on the outside of the crack to prevent the clamp from marking the wood. Again we are working with back off. Cam clamps may be used for this job if the spring clamps won't reach the area of the crack.*

I have seen the tape give way on one job and I had to do it over. Luckily I was able to reach the spot through the sound hole and re-repair the spot with wooden cross-patches. On these back-off jobs, should the butt block be cracked through as I have seen on so many oldies, glue and clamp, carefully aligning the block. Start at the block surface where the back was glued and drill ¼" holes in at least two places through the area of the break at least an inch past the break. Glue maple dowel

pins down in the holes and the block is as good as new. Well, almost.

I hope this chapter has given enough information to start you on your own. The different types of woods and other factors involved make it impossible to tell you exactly how to do it on your particular problem, so you will have to use your head and figure it out yourself. Good luck.

7.
Disassembly and Reassembly
of Guitar Bodies

Disassembly of a damaged instrument must be done with extreme care. When the guitar was constructed, extra material was left during assembly and trimmed to size afterwards. We have to take the extra care, because we have no such excess. The instrument must be re-assembled exactly as we took it apart, or as nearly so as possible. If any wood is lost, we have to replace it, hopefully in such a way that it won't be noticeable when the repairs are finished.

Should an instrument be damaged so badly that the repairs cannot be done working through the sound hole, the decision has to be made as to whether we will remove the top or the back. In most cases, it is easier to remove the back, with the exception being, of course, the complete replacement of the top. To remove the top entails removing the fingerboard, or at least the part of the fingerboard over the face of the top. Since the top is made of spruce, a very soft wood, it is much easier to damage than the hard woods used in the rest of the instrument. The logical solution, therefore, would be to remove the back.

The instructions for removing the back or top are very similar, so instead of repeating twice, I will cover both at the same time, adding anything extra required for one that may not be required for the other.

The first thing to do, of course, is to remove the strings and hardware that might be in the way. If the guitar is to be refinished, remove the machine heads, pickguard, bridge, strap buttons, and butt peg, as these are not to be finished. One exception here: the C.F. Martin Organisation does finish over their pickguard. It is sanded thin around the edges to blend into the top to a certain degree and is finished along with the rest of the top.

To remove this guard and almost any glued down guard, a thin pancake spatula or artist's palette knife sharpened around the end is forced under the edge of the guard and worked on back to remove it. Work a little ways and lift the guard slightly to see if any wood is coming up with the guard. If so, start from the oppo-site end of the guard and work back. Removing anything from the top should be done with the grain, or you will end up with problems such as deep splinters to glue back, and should they pull far enough, they will show after refinishing. Remember also that since the top is almost invariably book-matched (single board split and folded out like the pages of a book and edge-glued), the grain will run in *opposite directions* on the opposing sides. Should you start a splinter, glue it down immediately. If you should catch it on something, you might really tear things up.

Removing the bridge may be done with the spatula in somewhat the same way as the pickguard, remembering that the bridge is glued to both sides of the top, and, as mentioned in the preceding paragraph, the grain changes directions as we cross the center glue line, so work accordingly.

Another method of removing a bridge is to take advantage of the shearing weakness of the glues used in most construction. This works well on the older models in particular, where the glue has had a chance to age and become brittle. Use a common putty knife with a narrow, flexible blade. The blade is sharpened on a bevel from the top edge to the back. The long edge is placed against the face of the guitar at the base of the bridge. The blade is then sprung so that it lies flat against the face, but with the handle angling up. This is given a sharp rap with a plastic hammer. This is done around the bridge in several places, working carefully, to prevent the loss of wood by working against the grain. If the bridge shows signs of coming up with splinters, use the thin spatula, inserting it under the bridge, and cutting the splinters loose from the bridge.

Some repairmen use heat, such as applying a large soldering iron against the bridge, starting at one end and heating hot enough to soften the glue before moving across the bridge, wedging under the starting end with wooden wedges. I really prefer one of the first two methods, as they are much faster and do not discolor the wood as heating often does. Also, some classical-type

Fig. 51—*Using spatula to remove a bridge.*

Fig. 50—*Removing pickguard with specially sharpened spatula or palette knife.*

Fig. 52—An alternate method of removing a bridge using a reworked putty knife and plastic hammer.

bridges are finished instead of waxed or oiled, as most steel string bridges are. Heating hot enough to remove these will destroy the finish. This is fine if you are going to refinish, but it is just extra work otherwise.

Since we are working with the top of the instrument so far, we will continue with the top removal. The technique for removing the back is identical to removing the top anyway, with the exception of removing the bridge, pickguard, and the fingerboard problem.

There are two ways of dealing with the fingerboard problem. The first is the complete removal of the board. The second is the pulling of the fret immediately above the edge of the top at the neck join, in most cases the twelfth or fourteenth fret, and sawing through the fingerboard to the face of the instrument. The latter is the most accepted practice, except when the board needs replacing or when something needs to be done to the reinforcing of the neck, as when installing or replacing a tension rod or T-bar.

The tools I use for the complete removal of the fingerboard are an electric flatiron, a reworked electric carving knife blade, and a couple of ⅟₁₆″ by 4″ by 6″ pieces of asbestos. Cardboard may be used if asbestos is not available, but care should be taken not to overheat the

Fig. 53—Sawing through fingerboard with razor saw at joint above edge of body after removing fret in preparation for removing end of fingerboard for top removal.

finish underneath if it is to be preserved. The electric flatiron can be either the standard size or the smaller travel size. The travel size is easier to handle. It should be set to linen temperature, or as hot as it will go. The knife is reworked at the point end. The point is ground on a slant, angling away from the cutting edge at about a 70° angle and is sharpened down to meet the regular edge. It should be sharpened to a hatchet-type edge instead of a long tapering edge because the blade, being about $\frac{1}{16}$" thick, works as a wedge instead of cutting.

The asbestos or cardboard is laid on the face on either side of the fingerboard while the iron is heating. Make sure that it doesn't slip out of place because it doesn't take much heat to blister the lacquer. The iron can then be placed on the fingerboard on the area over the face. You may either set the iron directly on the board or use a piece of aluminum foil if you are using your wife's or mother's iron. Rosewood, in particular, has the bad habit of staining the bottom of the iron and transferring this stain to anything else the iron touches. Personally, I prefer to leave the frets in the board at this time, as the tang of the fret seems to transfer the heat very rapidly to the glue line. It takes less heating time to do the job and does not dry the fingerboard out as badly as when you really cook it.

Fig. 54—*Using an electric iron to heat fingerboard for removal. Notice the cardboard to protect the finish on the face of the instrument.*

We will be working the fingerboard a section at a time, starting over the face. Heat for a couple minutes and then try to insert the end of the knife under the end of the board. If it lifts slightly, the glue is getting soft. Work all the way around the board until it is free of the face and you can slip the knife all the way through from side to side. If you have heated the board properly, it should have come up without taking any of the face wood with it. Well, very little, if you were lucky. If it still gives trouble, apply some more heat and work at it some more. After you have freed up the end of the board from the top, slip a wooden shim under the end to wedge

the end to prevent the glue from sticking again and to place a little strain on the part not yet loose. Heat the next section and work the knife further, or until you can grasp the knife blade on both ends. Wrap a rag around the sharp end so you won't carve a finger, stick the head of the guitar in your chest and grasp the knife with both hands. Work the blade towards you, pulling first on one side of the blade and then the other, stopping to heat the next section as you get through the soft glue, until you have the board completely free of the neck. After practice, or when you have removed as many as I have, it usually takes only ten minutes or so to remove one. If

Fig. 55—*Using reworked blunt edge knife to remove the fingerboard after the glue is softened with the iron. Notice the wedge under the end of the board to prevent the glue from rebonding as it cools off.*

you are removing only the stub end to remove the top, it takes even less time.

Often, you will either leave a little of the fingerboard wood on the neck surface or pull up a little of the top or neck wood on the fingerboard. A small sliver on the contact surface doesn't matter unless it is exposed on the edge, in which case, it should be glued where it belongs. Larger pieces should be replaced, period.

Also, in heating the wood hot enough to soften the glue, you will usually blister the finish on the edge of the board. This is normal and will have to be touched up after reassembly, unless of course, you are doing a

complete refinish. The fingerboard will also be bowed from the heat, so turn it over on a couple blocks and weight it slightly over straight while it is cooling off. If necessary, you can heat the back of the board with a propane torch while applying weight to handle excessive bowing or warpage.

After the removal of the fingerboard, or part thereof, you can progress to the removal of the top. The next step in removing the top or the back, is the removal of the body binding to expose the glue seam where they join the sides.

If you are trying to save the finish as much as possible

69

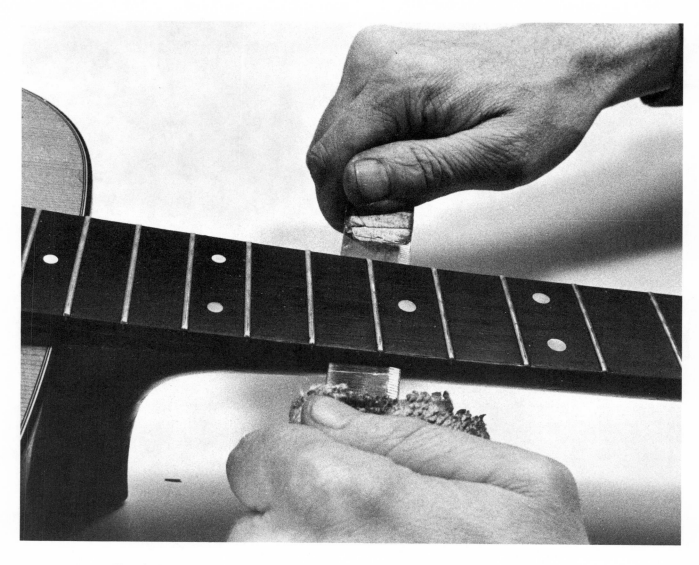

Fig. 56—*Using both hands on the knife after working clear of the body. Notice the rag to prevent slicing your hand.*

to get by with just a touchup (hopefully), the next in-structions should be followed very closely. Of course, if you are going to refinish, this step isn't necessary. Take a sharp knife or wide wood chisel and scrape through the finish very carefully, a small amount at a time, at the join between the binding and the wood. Take it slow, because if you scrape too deeply at one time, you will chip the finish. Scrape until the seam is exposed all the way around the top or back. This step, if done properly, will just about eliminate the chipping that always follows the next step.

Take an X-acto knife or other sharp, thin blade and cut along the line separating the bottom edge of the binding from the side all the way around. Make sure you cut to the depth of the binding thickness. With a thin blade, this is not too difficult and is done to elimi-nate pulling splinters from the side while removing the binding. Now, check the butt end of the guitar to see if the binding has a join there. If so, we will start the re-moval from there. Some makers use one-piece bindings, and there will be no join at the butt, and on these I usually start at the waist because it gives you some slack to work with after the removal is started. If you are leery of trying this, you can always use the razor saw and cut a

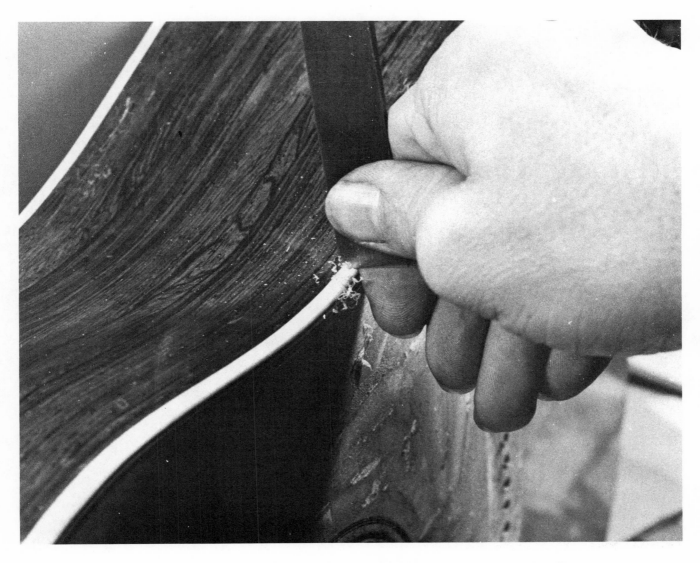

Fig. 57—*Scraping through the finish over the body binding joint to prevent chipping the finish on removal of the binding.*

joint at the butt, in line with the center seam. Anyway, after cutting around the bottom edge of the binding, I take a rounded-end X-acto knife and insert down the glue line behind the binding, popping it loose. Continue, working with the curved, sharp edge of the blade in the direction of removal. I work with a rocking motion, inserting the blade with the handle angling away from the direction of removal and rocking it forward. Keep checking the bottom edge of the binding, making sure it is cut free and isn't pulling any of the side wood with it. If you should get a sliver, glue it back immediately so it won't be lost, leaving a gap to hide on reassembly.

On some instruments, particularly the Spanish and Mexican imports and most of the handmade classic guitars, the bindings are made of wood. This can be a problem. To remove this, scrape all the finish from the bindings down to the glue line. Take a large soldering iron as a source of heat and, working carefully, trying not to scorch the wood too much, heat the binding and use the knives as on the regular bindings. In a majority of the cases, the grain of the wood will splinter up on you, leaving you with several pieces instead of a single one. I usually just cut the bindings around the bottom edge and chisel it off in pieces, cleaning the notch out square as I go. When it comes time to rebind, I just

Fig. 58—*Cutting through the body binding joint with X-acto knife to free the bottom edge of the binding.*

make new wood binding. It seems easier for me that way.

After we have removed the bindings one way or the other, we are ready for the next step, removing the top or back itself. There are several methods of doing this. Which method I use depends on the age of the instrument and the condition of the glue.

If the glue is very dry and brittle and coming loose, such as on an old guitar or one that has been wet and dried out, merely slipping the sharp thin spatula into the exposed glue seam will often pop the top or back loose. Many times, I have had the top or back practically fall

off in my hands. Anyway, the main problem you will run into on these is the area where the top or back is glued to the neck or butt block. Start with the butt block, after working the sides loose all the way on both sides of the blocks. Slip the spatula into the joint, working it in slightly all the way across the block area, and then do it again, working it in farther. If it shows no sign of coming loose, try again, and if it still doesn't pop loose, fill a hypo or eyedropper full of a solution of one part alcohol, three parts water, and a few drops of Photo Flo or other detergent and inject it into the seam and

Fig. 59—*Working through the top edge of the body binding joint with knife to remove the binding. Purfling can be removed the same way if it is to be reused.*

let stand for a while. Try the spatula again, and if it still doesn't come loose, give it some more solution. When you get this end loose, prop it up a couple of inches with a block. This will put pressure on the neck block joint. Working with the spatula through the gap to the inside joint of the neck block, try to work the top or back loose. Sometimes on the old ones, this joint will part, and the top or back will go flying from the tension we have put on it with the block, so be careful. If it is still stubborn, use the solution to soften the glue until it does come off.

Another method of removing tops and backs is with a hot knife, either wet or dry. Some shops keep a pot of boiling water for heating the parting tools, but I find that the tools dry off pretty fast if things are hot enough to melt the glue. I prefer to use dry heat and apply the water alcohol solution with a hypo or eyedropper to the seam. When the hot knife hits the wetted wood, steam is generated, loosening glue and parting the joint.

The setup I use for this is one of Star Chemical Company's knife heaters, the Type "K" to be exact, and a couple of reworked putty knives. I grind the blades of the knives to a round end instead of square and then

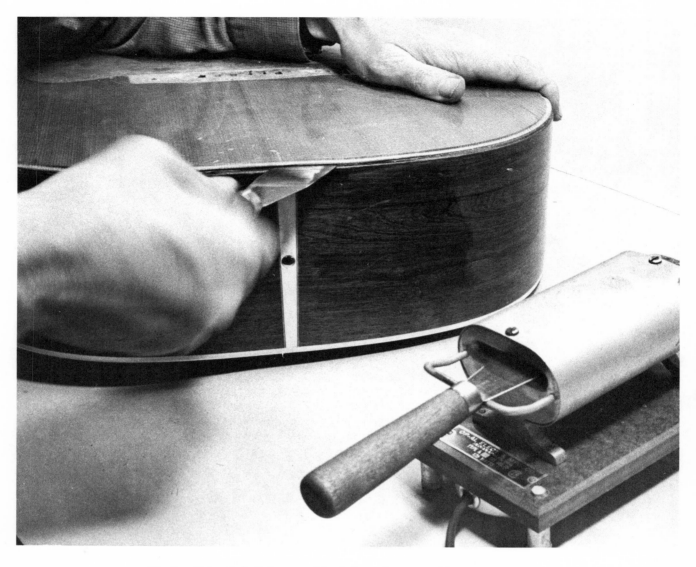

Fig. 60—*Using the knife heater and hot knives to loosen a stubborn top to side joint.*

sharpen to a thin edge. The edge should be ground so that it is tapered from both sides equally instead of the usual square edge found on new putty knives. The knives can be inserted in both ends of the heater, and while you are working with one, the other can be heating. This way, you can keep moving without having to wait so long for the same knife to heat up.

In most cases, water will not be needed, as the hot knife melts the glue on contact. If you have to use the water, be sure to allow plenty of drying time before trying to reassemble things. If too much water is used, it may cause warpage, so use sparingly. If it gets to other glue seams, we may end up with things loose we hadn't planned on.

The hot knife method probably is the best method to use for the newer guitars assembled with the polyvinyl resins or white glues. If a guitar has been assembled with the plastic resin (water-mix powdered glue), water will have little effect and will probably turn loose with the first method mentioned in this chapter. Experimenting around will usually find the correct method or combination thereof to do the job. With the procedure described in the preceding pages of this chapter, and plenty of experience, you should be able to handle just about any

Fig. 61—*Top glued into place and held with cam, spool, and strapping tape clamps.*

back or top removal. It is not possible to describe every situation you will run into, and you will have to use your own judgment on these.

Another thing I will mention here. It is better not to take both the top and back off of a guitar at the same time. One should be left glued to the sides until the other is reglued. It can then be removed if necessary. The reason for this is that if both are removed, the sides will spring out of shape and be almost impossible to line up in the original shape. By removing one at a time, the remaining back or top, as the case may be, will hold the sides in alignment reasonably well.

Reassembly of the parts is the next step, after doing all the necessary interior repair work. This takes a lot longer than wrecking one out.

Realigning and regluing the top or back is a very touchy business. Clean all the old glue from the mating surfaces and try the top or back for fit. Use a couple of wooden bridge (cam) clamps for clamping over the neck and butt block areas. Use wooden blocks the size of the butt and neck blocks to protect the wood from the clamps and to spread the pressure over the blocks evenly. Using either the wooden cam clamps or the spool clamps, spring the sides in position and clamp. If everything fits

Fig. 62—*Dremel setup with edge guide for cutting the binding and purfling slots. This guide is made from metal with a bearing, but the wooden guide shown in the special tool chapter works equally well.*

properly, remove the clamps, remembering the order and positioning of the clamps and blocks, apply glue, and re-clamp. If things do not fit, rework and refit until they do. The substance of the next sentence will be repeated more than once through this book, as it is *very important and should not be forgotten.* By checking everything and fitting all parts and clamping them before gluing, you will eliminate most errors, and the time spent prefitting will, in the long run, save you money by saving you the time it may cost you to correct a mistake, that is, if it is possible to correct.

If the top or back should fit well enough that clamps over the neck and butt blocks and at the waist on either side will hold the rest close, short strips of filament tape may be used in place of the regular clamps. Be sure they pull things down good and tight, or go back to the cam or spool clamps. When you have the top or back glued on and cured, pull the clamps and clean off the excess glue with a sharp chisel, checking to make sure you don't cut so deep as to cause the binding to fit badly.

At this point I will digress slightly. Sometimes on old antique instruments, the body has caved in to some ex-

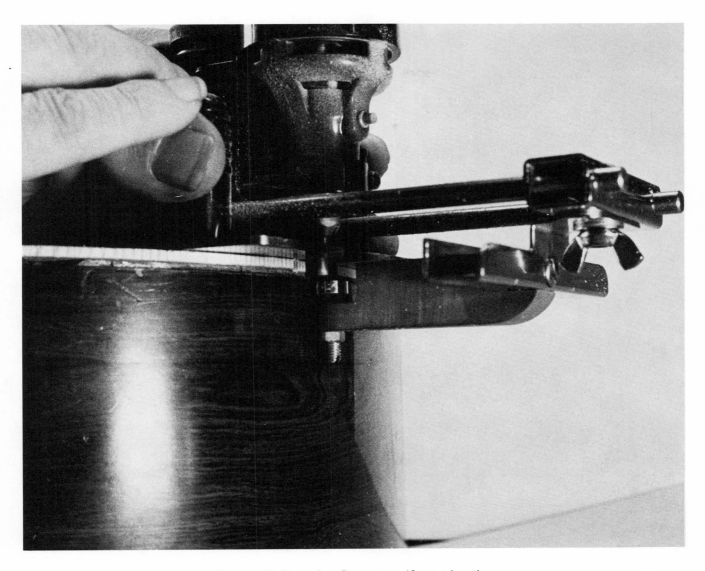

Fig. 63—Binding and purfling cutter-guide setup in action.

tent where the neck joins, and when sighting down the neck, you see an abrupt change in the neck angle at the body join. This can be caused by several factors, usually by uneven shrinkage of the different woods used in construction. Also, some people will use too heavy a string on these old timers and pull them up that way. On these instruments, the problem can sometimes be corrected by removing and resetting the neck at a slightly different angle, or, if you have the back off, you can try a trick I have used successfully quite a few times. I simply clamp a straight thick board to the neck or fingerboard surface, forcing it into a straight line. When you fit the back, you will find that the edge near the neck area will overlap slightly, or in case of a bad angle, maybe as much as $\frac{1}{16}$" or so. You will have to trim off the ends of the back struts slightly, and tuck the sides in a small amount, allowing a small overlap as far down as the waist of the instrument. After checking the fit of the back, apply clamps and remove the heavy block from the fingerboard surface. Sight down the neck. The neck should set true with the body, or at least reasonably close. Any small discrepancy left, if not more than $\frac{1}{32}$" or so, can be

77

Fig. 64—*Gluing the binding and purfling on at the same time using masking or strapping tape to hold it in place until the glue dries.*

taken care of later by planing and refretting the board. If the neck is straight within reason, reclamp the heavy board back to the fingerboard, remove the clamps holding the back in place, apply glue, and reclamp.

After the glue is set, remove the clamps, and we are ready to retrim the binding notches or grooves. This may be done by hand with a sharp chisel, but, being naturally lazy, I have reworked the Dremel shaper guide and, when used in combination with the number 115 Dremel cutter, it makes short work of cleaning up binding grooves. In fact, I use this guide and cutter for removing glue whether or not I have overlapped the back. The cutter can be set up or down and the guide in or out to cut any size or depth groove you are likely to run into. On tops, you usually have some purfling inside the binding to provide a contrast line between the binding and light

colored top wood. Should this have to be replaced or changed, this Dremel and guide setup will handle most of this with ease. You will have a small amount up close to the neck to do with chisels and knives, but the time saved with the Dremel can be considerable. It is usually more accurate also. This tool works well when cutting around a headstock for fancy binding of the guitar head.

If the guitar was bound with celluloid or plastic binding, as most are today, you should have been able to save the bindings by careful removal. Clean the old glue from the contact areas, and check the fit by taping to the guitar temporarily with masking tape. The chances are, you will have a gap from $\frac{1}{16}$" to $\frac{1}{8}$" wide left, as the bindings will have shrunk a small amount. This is normal. Celluloid is particularly bad about this, and it is also the most commonly used material for binding pur-

78

Fig. 65—Bending a dulcimer side with the bending iron. Guitar sides, wooden binding strips, patch material, etc., may be bent also.

poses until the past few years, when some of the companies changed to different types of plastics. These new plastics shrink very little, if at all.

When you have the bindings cleaned and fitted, the contact surfaces should be roughed up to provide something for the glue to bond to. I use a razor saw blade for this purpose, scraping it sideways down the binding contact surfaces. You can use one of the modern plastic glues, such as Duco cement, and eliminate this step. The Duco tends to melt into the plastics, providing a molecular bond. Allow plenty of time to dry, six to ten hours, depending on the temperature. I usually use Titebond. If the fit is poor and wood is missing and there are gaps, I will use epoxy dyed the color of the wood.

At any rate, tape off the wood on both edges with masking tape to collect any glue squeeze-out, apply the glue, and hold in place with either filament or masking tape. Cut a small piece of scrap celluloid the size of the gap left by shrinkage, and insert to complete the binding. Allow glue to dry thoroughly, usually six to eight hours, depending on the temperature and glue used. Even with evaporative-type glues such as Titebond, the drying time is slowed down by the plastics, which act as a vapor barrier, and extra time should be allowed for curing thoroughly. Next comes cleaning up the excess glue.

The top edge of the binding can be cleaned off by filing with a small mill bastard file, working off excess glue until you hit the edge of the masking tape. Pull the tape and you have just a thin line of glue left. I then use a cabinet scraper held at a slight angle and scrape the bindings and glue until flush with the finish of the inside edge. The sides of the binding may be scraped

79

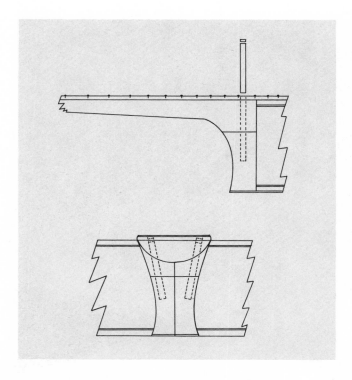

Fig. 66—*Top: Dotted line shows hole drilled through fingerboard to take maple dowel and plug to repair separated joint on laminated heel-neck construction. Bottom: End view shows dowells and fingerboard plugs in place (dotted lines) for permanent repair of separated joint or cracked heel.*

with a large sharp wood chisel held between the thumb and forefinger, using the finger as a guide to keep from scraping down too far and getting into the finish. Remove masking tape and finish leveling the glue line with the finish. Using the cabinet scraper again, round off the sharp corners of the bindings, sand or steel-wool them smooth, and they are ready to touch up or finish.

Now, we get back to the wood-bound instruments. If, by some miracle, you were able to get the wooden bindings off in a usable condition, clean off the old glue, tape off the guitar, and glue back the same way as the plastic bindings. You may skip the scraping with the saw, as the glue will bond to the wood without this step.

If you were not able to have the original wood bindings, new ones must be cut and bent to fit. The type of woods used will determine the procedure used for shaping and fitting them.

For white bindings, white holly is an excellent wood and very easy to work with. Just soak it in hot water or boil for a few minutes and you can form it right to the guitar. Tape into position with glue under it (Titebond or

other water-soluble glue), and allow to dry thoroughly.

There are other light colored woods suitable for bindings, with white maple the closer to being white after the white holly. The dark woods used for this purpose may be rosewood, walnut, or pressure-dyed maples. There are a few other woods used, but the above are the most common.

These hard woods are a little harder to work with. They will have to be bent to fit the guitar by one of several methods, the most common being either to boil and clamp over a jig until dry or, the method I use, to soak for an hour or so and bend over a bending iron, fitting the wood to the body as you go.

Measure the distance from the center of the upper bout of the guitar, around the body, to the center of the waist, and then measure the same distance from the center of the lower bout. Add together, and you will have the length to cut the bindings. When you saw them out, allow a couple of inches in extra length to play with, as you may not be able to bend to exactly the right fit. Mark the location of the center point of the waist, allowing one of the spare inches on each end, and put to soaking. Start at the waist, bend over the hot bending iron, checking against the guitar as you go for fit, and, when finished, tape to the guitar until cool. The binding will usually be dried out pretty well from the heat of the bending iron and will be ready to trim and install as soon as it has cooled and set for a couple of hours.

This chapter on disassembly and reassembly of guitar bodies would not be complete without a description of how to remove and reset guitar necks. I shall have to be fairly general with the description of this job because there are so many different neck setups, each with their particular problems.

The main problem with the Spanish-type construction will usually be the parting of the joint between the neck proper and the piece glued to the bottom to make the heel. The block on the inside and the neck and heel are made as a unit and are not separable. If this joint parts, the thing to do is to inject glue with a hypo as far into the joint as possible and clamp back into position. To insure that it stays, I drill down through the fingerboard from two directions, about ½" to either side of the center line of the fingerboard, down into the heel through the joint, and insert birch or maple dowel pins with glue into the holes. I cut the dowels short by about ¼" and force them down below the level of the fingerboard. I then machine a couple of plugs the diameter of the hole and of the same material as the fingerboard and plug the holes. If the holes are on one of the main position frets, such as the twelfth, you could use pearl dots, but

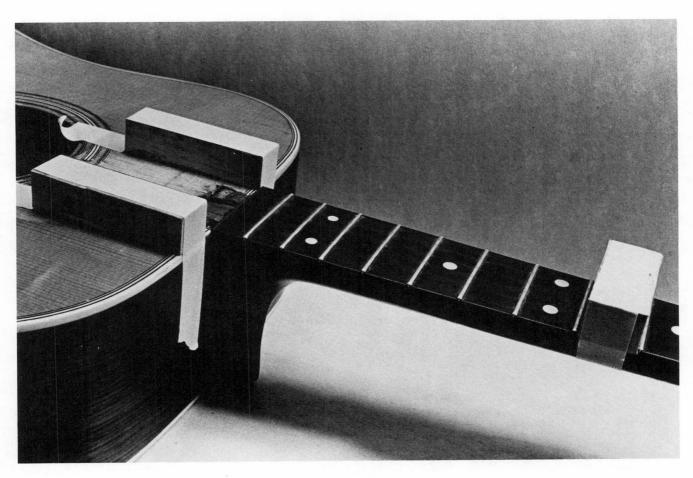

Fig. 67—Blocks applied to the guitar body and neck with tape so the neck may be clamped out.

I prefer to use the wood plugs. These, when selected for color carefully, are hard to spot when trimmed flush with the board and waxed or oiled. I have used this method many times to repair the Japanese necks. Although they are almost always dovetailed into the bodies, they are usually made with the heel grafted to the neck, and in appearance they resemble the Spanish construction. The reason I say to drill on either side of the center line is that you will usually find a tension rod or metal reinforcement of some sort in almost all of the Japanese models, and I have found a steel bar more than once in the Spanish and Mexican models. Drilling from one side will insure missing these reinforcements and prevent damage to same.

If the neck is one of the dovetailed models and has become loose enough to move around with the hand, it is usually fairly easy to remove. I use the spatula to work the fingerboard loose over the face of the body and see if I can wiggle the neck out. If it doesn't come out, tape a couple of blocks to the face on either side of the fingerboard, over where the neck block lies, turn the guitar face down on the edge of the workbench, place another block under the fingerboard down near the nut end, and apply a padded clamp from under the workbench to the bottom of the heel. Be sure the heel is padded to prevent damage, and apply pressure with the clamp. If the neck is very loose, it should pop out. If it is stubborn, shift the clamp to the back of the neck as near the heel as possible and, using a padded block, give the heel a sharp rap with a plastic hammer. Don't do this more than once or twice, checking the wood near the bottom of the heel for compression damage. This will show up as lines in the finish. If you see these lines, cease and desist. It will usually come out with one of the two methods mentioned so far, if the neck was loose to start with. If not, you have trouble. Use the method mentioned next.

Fig. 68—Inverted guitar lying on blocks and clamp applied to remove neck.

Fill a hypodermic syringe with the water, alcohol, and detergent mixture mentioned earlier in this chapter and inject it into the joint, using a long needle to get it back into the dovetail. Allow to set for awhile and then set up again with the blocks and clamp over the workbench and apply pressure. It should come right out. If not, use more water mixture, allow to soak, and try again. After the neck is apart, clean off the old glue while it is still wet and allow to dry thoroughly before trying to reset.

If the neck must come out, and it is still set solid, such as in a replacement situation or on a guitar that may have been hot, causing the neck to shift and reset when cooled, a completely different procedure must be used.

Either remove the complete fingerboard or remove the fret above the join, saw through the fingerboard, and remove the end of the fingerboard over the face of the instrument, as described earlier in this chapter. This will expose the upper portion of the dovetail joint.

In most cases, there will be a gap between the end of the neck and the block where the dovetail was cut out. Take a broken hacksaw blade which has been sharpened to a long angled point leaving the teeth side intact, insert it into the gap, and clean out as much of the old excess glue squeeze-out as possible. Blow or shake out all residue possible and fill with the water solution. Let stand for an hour or so, to wet things good and deep. Some people use scalding water here instead of water at room temperature, but I have my reasons as you soon shall see. Leave the alcohol out of this solution.

Take a piece of asbestos and cut a rectangular slot approximately ¼" by 2½" and lay this down on the guitar with the slot exposing the dovetail slot. A piece of cardboard may be used if asbestos is unavailable. The idea is to protect the finish from heat damage. I now

Fig. 69—Cleaning out the end of the dovetail slot with a piece of broken hacksaw blade ground to a taper on one end.

take out my secret weapon, a one-piece design, stainless-steel table knife that I have narrowed and thinned the blade on. I insert the thin blade into the dovetail slot, with the heavy handle sticking up above the top of the guitar and surrounded by the heat shield. Are you getting the picture? Make sure the dovetail is filled with the solution, and heat up your trusty propane torch, applying heat directly to the heavy handle of the table knife. The handle will absorb a large amount of heat and transfer it right down the blade into the dovetail slot, bringing the mixture there to a rolling boil and

almost a superheated condition where the water has soaked up the end grain of the neck. It usually takes just a few minutes of this treatment to loosen things up. Add more water as it boils away or leaks out. Sometimes the water will leak badly at the bottom of the dovetail before the rest of the glue is softened, and in such cases I stuff a small amount of tissue paper into the slot, packing it in place with a thin blade. Be careful in removing the table knife. Use a pair of pliers to handle it, and put it where it won't scorch anything when you are done with it. Anyway, keep adding water and heat to the knife

Fig. 70—*Using reworked table knife and propane torch to remove stubborn neck. Notice the shield to protect the face of the instrument.*

until you can move the neck slightly in the dovetail. Remove the knife and heat shield, turn the guitar over to drain out what water is left, tape on the blocks as described earlier, and apply the clamp. The neck should slide right out with a minimum of pressure. Clean out all the glue while everything is still wet, and set it all back to dry for a couple of days at least.

If the described methods will not remove the neck, it is probably fastened with screws or bolts concealed with wooden plugs or from the inside of the neck block. Another reason may be that the neck was epoxied, in which case it shouldn't have to be removed anyway, unless

irreparably broken. An epoxied neck is usually solid as one piece of wood. In the cases mentioned in this paragraph, the solution would be to saw the neck off as close to the body as possible without damaging the side finish and chisel the dovetail clean, as a preparation to installing a brand new neck assembly.

To reset the neck, make sure that everything is perfectly dry and that all old glue is removed from the neck and block dovetail surfaces. Slip the neck into the body and check the fit. It should seat down to where the fingerboard surface (not the fingerboard *fret* surface) joins the neck surface and is level and on the same plane as the face of the top. In other words, you should be able to lay a straight edge along the surface of the neck and the face of the guitar up to the sound hole without having any gaps under the straight edge. The neck should also fit snugly, and not move around when set to this level. If it is loose or fits too low, shims of wood may be used to keep the neck from setting so deep. If it sets too high, some wood must be removed from the contacting surfaces to allow it to seat down.

If the neck sets at an angle, either up or down, the angle of the dovetail must be changed slightly to make the neck set level. The contacting surface on either side of the dovetail that contacts the sides of the instrument must be shaved on a taper from bottom to top, or top to bottom, depending on the angle to which the neck has to be corrected. Be sure to trim the same amount from each side to keep the neck centered with the center seam of the body.

The other aspect of the neck you should be checking, as you are getting the correct angle and depth, is the centering of the neck with the body seam or, as in quite an alarming number of cases, the string holes of the bridge. I have found the bridges set as much as $\frac{1}{4}$" off the center of the guitar. These were evidently offset originally to compensate for a badly set neck, and they would have to be set back the same way. Anyway, determine where the neck should center to, either the center seam of the guitar or to the bridge. When you have everything fitted, remove the neck and shims, laying the shims out carefully so you won't forget the order they have to go back in, and apply glue (after taping off areas that might get excess glue on them) and slip neck and shims back into the dovetail. I then usually apply a piece of wax paper over the dovetail joint and lay a straight, thick block over the face from the sound hole to the nut area of the neck. I clamp with one clamp and block under the face through the sound hole to the top of the big block, and then I add one block with padding behind the neck about midway down and clamp the big block to the neck with the steel clamp. Then, with a large "C" or cam-type clamp, apply pressure from the back of the guitar (bottom of neck block) to the long straight block above the joint. Allow to dry thoroughly, remove clamps, pull tape, and clean up the glue mess.

The quick and dirty method of doing this is to fill the dovetail joint with epoxy glue and align with the large straight block and let the epoxy do the filling instead of shimming things. Sometimes, on some of the real cheapies, people don't want to spend much, and this is the only way you can do it inexpensively and get a job that will last. At least, it is the only way I trust it not to happen again. Some of the cheapies, if the neck has pulled away from the body but can be pushed back with

little pressure, can be fixed with another quick and dirty way. Drill a hole, starting from the back of the guitar, into the dovetail cavity and, using a hypodermic syringe without the needle, force a syringe full of epoxy into the cavity. Apply a bit of masking tape to stop up the hole, turn the instrument over so the glue will settle to the bottom, clamp to pull the neck back against the body, and allow the glue to set up. Remove the tape, and touch up with a spot of stain and lacquer to hide the hole. The hole, by the way, should be drilled as small as you can get the syringe tip into. In fact, the tip of the syringe where the needle fits may be tapered with a sharp knife or sandpaper so that the hole drilled may be smaller.

Now, if the fingerboard has been removed we have to reinstall it. I use several tricks on this job to make things easier and to align the board to a gnat's whisker and hold it in place while gluing and clamping. The tendency is for the board to move around on a clean smooth surface when the glue is applied. In fact, it is almost impossible to prevent this moving around, at least a small amount, when the clamps are applied.

A real sneaky trick I came up with one day, after fighting a board for a couple of hours, is the use of small removable metal pins through the fingerboard and into the neck surface. Since I always remove the frets before gluing a board down, I drill six $\frac{1}{16}$" holes through the fret slots to take $\frac{1}{16}$" pins. When the board is refretted, these holes will be covered with the new frets. I drill the holes one third of the way across the board on each side, in fret slots under one, six, and either ten or twelve, depending on whether the neck is twelve or fourteen frets to the body. The holes are drilled, angling slightly away from the neck, rather than straight up and down, as this helps in preventing any movement of the board during clamping. I make my pins out of $\frac{1}{16}$" soft iron wire (hay wire to me, being from the farm), which is available from most hardware stores in small rolls. Whatever you make the pins out of, they should fit reasonably tight. I punch the wire into a block of beeswax, and slip into the drilled hole. The beeswax is to prevent the glue from sticking to the pin, so it may be pulled out easier when the glue has dried. The pin should extend at least $\frac{1}{8}$" into the neck and cut off about the same amount above the fingerboard.

After pinning the board into position, tape along the edge of all glue lines with masking tape, pull the pins up slightly with pliers until they are free of the neck, and we are ready for the next step.

The next step is another problem: how to get a good firm clamp setup that will provide equal pressure the length of and across the fingerboard. This can be difficult, remembering that we have alignment pins protruding from the surface and that the majority of guitar fingerboards have an ovaled or convex shape from edge to edge. One way is to tape a ³⁄₁₆" rod the length of the board on either side of the pins, place a long flat block on top of these, and clamp. This gives us pressure the length of the board but only in two places on the board, both edges. This is better than just clamping down the middle, but a three-point contact would be better.

I have designed and used a universal clamping caul that provides a three-point contact. It is tapered to fit most widths of fingerboards and has an adjustable center piece to compensate for different shaped boards. Since the caul back is above the board surface, with contact points at the edges and center, it doesn't interfere with the alignment pins.

The rest of the tool setup requirements are as follows: four 4" steel "C" clamps, three wooden blocks 1½" by 2¼" by 1" with one side concave for fitting to the bottom of the neck, one wooden block cut to fit under the face of the particular guitar you are working on (this block is to spread out the clamping stress in this area and help the clamp clear the face strut), and, of course, the clamping caul.

As mentioned before, make a dry run with all the clamps and jigs in place, just as if you had the glue under things. Check along the joint to see how well the fit is. The fit will determine the type of glue I use for sticking it down. If there are no missing splinters or gaps in the contact area, I will use Titebond, but if the fit is rough, I usually use epoxy. The epoxy does not shrink, as it is a chemical cure-type glue, and as a result, it will fill gaps and give you a solid joint. What if you have to take it off again? Well, I have removed epoxied-on fingerboards with the flatiron technique. The Elmers epoxy seems to turn loose at about 180°.

This is the procedure for using the clamping caul. Of course, the first time, do it dry to check the fit, and the next time apply the glue to the fingerboard surface, lay the board on the neck, and push alignment pins into place. The board should not scoot around after the pins are in place, so we can concentrate on the clamping setup. Place the caul on the surface of the board and center it. The center adjustable piece should not be making contact. Take one clamp, clamping block, leather piece, and cardboard piece, lay the leather in concave area of block (leather may be glued in with glue), lay a piece of cardboard over that to prevent the leather from sticking to the finish, slip under the neck near the middle, apply clamp, and snug down. Apply the block and clamp to the sound hole area and snug it down. Apply the other two blocks, pads, and clamps, and tighten everything down pretty tight. Not so tight as to compress the wood on the back of the neck though. Take a large

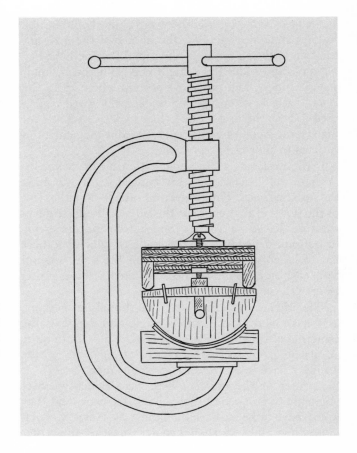

Fig. 71—Cutaway drawing showing three-point clamping caul in position, removable fingerboard alignment pins, and contoured neck clamping block with pads clamped with "C" clamp.

screwdriver and, starting at the middle of the caul, tighten the screws controlling the adjustable center piece down snug. After they are all snug, go back over them and tighten them down tight. Go over the main clamps to make sure they are still tight and clean off the excess glue with the glue spatula.

After the glue has cured, remove the clamps and pull the guide pins out of the fingerboard with pliers. Remove the masking tape and clean up the rest of the excess glue. If the guitar is to be refinished, forget about touching up the edge of the fingerboard. Otherwise, this has to be done. Sand lightly along the edge of the board to smooth things out and brush several coats of finish lacquer on with a fine artist's brush. Sand lightly, hit with some rubbing compound, and the board is back in place.

The guitar is still without frets, though, and the fingerboard surface is invariably out of plane after removal and replacing, either with a new one or the original board. It will have to be trued and refretted. For this job, see the chapter on fretting instruments.

This just about has the guitar back together, with the

exception of the pickguard and the bridge. The regluing of the bridge will be discussed in the chapter on bridging.

On regluing the pickguard, if the guitar is to be refinished, I finish over the area where the guard sets. I then carefully tape off the outside edge of the guard area, scuff up the finish with coarse sandpaper, clean off the celluloid or plastic guard, and scuff up, apply Weldwood Contact Cement to both surfaces, let dry for fifteen minutes, and press together. Line up carefully, because once pressed together, you cannot shift the guard without removing it again.

If the guard is to be replaced "as is" over the bare wood, as on some models, I advise applying one coat, let set for ten or fifteen minutes, and apply another coat over that. The first coat will soak mostly into the wood.

The reason I use contact cement is because in the case of the pickguard the difference in the expansion rate between the spruce top and the plastic or celluloid guard is so different, that it can cause cracking in the guard area of the top. The contact cement holds well and does have some elasticity, allowing some minor movement during expansion or contraction of the top, owing to climatic changes, etc. Should the guard come loose, it is not much of a problem to replace with this glue. If done properly with a good brand of glue, the chances of it coming off are pretty remote.

8

String Action and Tension Rod Adjustment

There are many factors involved in the setting of string action or height of the strings above the frets. When the strings are too high, the instrument is not only hard to play, but also usually does not note out properly. The intonation is off because the strings sharp too much when fretted. The higher the strings, the higher the pitch when the string is fretted. To make the instrument note out properly, we have to correct the action. For that matter, if the strings are too low, the strings will not sharp enough, and can cause the intonation to be flat as we go up the neck. We will work with the high action first and figure out how to correct it.

Guitars, when sent out from the factory to the dealers, have a compromise action set on them. If the guitarist wants the strings set higher or lower, the responsibility of this is on him. The factories cannot set an action that will please everybody, and they don't try. In most cases, the strings will be too high.

After a guitar is played for a while, and has been around through several years of seasonal changes, there are changes in the instrument. The wood drying out, not having the neck adjusted periodically, or at least checked, changing to different gauges of strings, and normal stress changes, can all cause the action to change, usually to make the strings higher.

When lowering string actions, whether working with a new guitar or one with a few years on it, there are certain procedures to be followed to do a satisfactory job.

Check the guitar over thoroughly to determine if it is too high at the bridge, at the nut, if the extra height is caused by a slight or bad forward bow in the neck, if the neck is pulling up at the body, or a combination of any or all of these factors.

The first thing to check would be the neck. There should be a small amount of forward bow, noticeable by placing the head of the guitar alongside one's cheek, and sighting along each edge of the fingerboard. It should have a very slight bow from the nut end of the neck towards the middle of the neck.

Another way of checking this is to place a finger or, if you're lazy, a capo behind the first fret, and then hold a string down at the twelfth fret. There should be a small amount of clearance between the bottom of the string and the top of the seventh fret. This should be around .010" to .015". You can check this with a common mechanic's feeler gauge or, after you've set a few string actions, it comes naturally by eyeball and feel. I can tell by tapping the string and listening to the sound it makes when it hits the fret. The clearance mentioned above is ideal, but if you have a bit more, it is not too much to worry about, if it is between the nut and the middle of the neck. If it is between the middle of the neck and the body of the instrument, or if the fingerboard has a hump in it at the join to the body, or over the face, you have problems.

Practically all instruments these days have a metal reinforcement of some sort in the neck. Some of these are adjustable and others are not.

On the ones with adjustable necks, the excessive bow, if between the nut and midpoint of the fingerboard, can usually be adjusted out. The proper wrench or nut driver to fit the tension rod should be used. Never attempt to adjust one of these with pliers, as this can chew a nut up to where a wrench will not fit properly and may even strip it to where it cannot be adjusted, period.

Perhaps I should mention here the many different adjustment types, and location of the adjustment features.

The first place to check is the face of the peg head. If there is a small plastic or metal plate, retained with from one to three screws, the adjustment will be there. It usually takes a deep-well socket wrench or nutdriver to adjust these or, in the case of several foreign instruments, a small round bar which is inserted in holes drilled in the side of an internally threaded sleeve which acts as a nut. There are a couple of American makes and several foreign makes that use an adjustment requiring an Allen wrench. The wrenches required will be both American and metric, depending on whether the guitar is a foreign or domestic product.

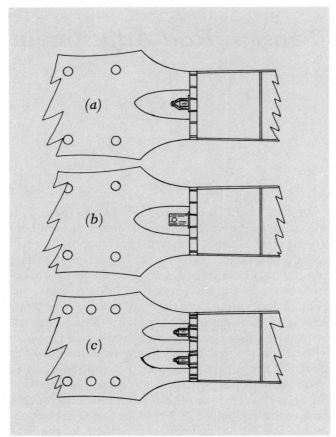

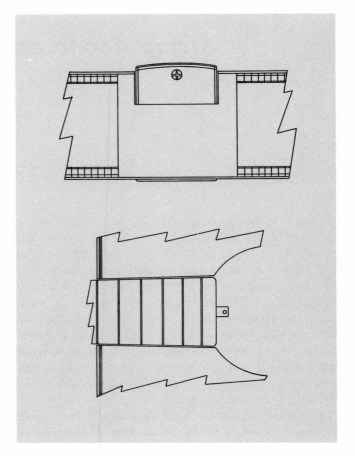

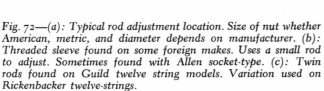

Fig. 72—(a): Typical rod adjustment location. Size of nut whether American, metric, and diameter depends on manufacturer. (b): Threaded sleeve found on some foreign makes. Uses a small rod to adjust. Sometimes found with Allen socket-type. (c): Twin rods found on Guild twelve string models. Variation used on Rickenbacker twelve-strings.

Fig. 73—Top: Fender rod adjustment located at body end of fingerboard. Very latest Fenders adjust at head end of fingerboard. End of board adjustment can be spotted by screwdriver slot. Bottom: Some foreign instruments adjust at body end of fingerboard using small round rod. Some adjust here with metric Allen wrench with socket in end of sleeve instead of hole in side.

Some of the instruments will have an adjustment at the body end of the fingerboard. The Fender adjustment is located there, as are those of several imported instruments. The Fender uses a screwdriver, preferably a Phillips type, but a standard one can be used with care. Most of the imports, when located at the end of the fingerboard, use the small rod setup to adjust. A couple of domestic instruments, the Mossman and the NBN, adjust under the face, using an Allen wrench slid through holes drilled in the struts under the fingerboard, or with a socket and extension wrench through the same area. This is not visible from outside of the instrument, but can be seen with a mirror and light placed inside under the fingerboard area.

All of the various types of adjustment setups I have run into so far adjust the same way. If the neck is bowed forward or up, tighten the nut clockwise, if bowed backwards, loosen counterclockwise.

These adjustments should be made in small increments. My experience says around one sixth turn at a time. After tightening the nut, grasp the neck firmly at the nut with one hand and near the body with the other and wrestle the neck, attempting to twist the neck first one way and then the other. This tends to work the neck and rod, helping to settle the neck into its new position.

Anyway, check after each adjustment until the neck is properly straight. Also, you should almost always adjust the neck with the tension of the strings up to the normal pitch. Otherwise, you are just guessing at the amount to adjust and may have to tune up to pitch several times to get the neck set right, when you could have done it the first time with the strings up to pitch.

An exception to this would be the neck with an exceptionally abnormal bow. In this case, it would be better to make most of the initial adjustment with the

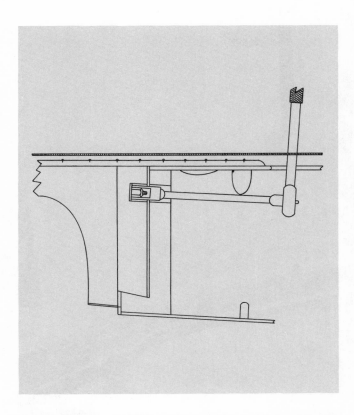

Fig. 74—Location of hidden adjustment feature designed by this shop for my own instruments and those of S. L. Mossman. A variation is used by the NBN factory, using an Allen wrench for adjustment. The hidden feature is ideal for use in straightening necks of older instruments to retain the original appearance.

strings relaxed. Adjust most of the bow out and then tune up to pitch for the final setting.

One trick I use for badly bowed necks with adjustable rods is to place a notched block on the fingerboard surface at the first and the twelfth frets. The notches are cut so that the block contacts the fingerboard and clears the strings. I then lay a heavy block across the top of these, place a clamping pad under the neck at the seventh fret position, and apply a cam clamp from under the neck to the board over the blocks. Apply only enough pressure to give the neck a slight backward bend when sighting along the edge of the fingerboard. Tighten the tension rod nut down pretty tight, relax the tension of the cam clamp, and sight the neck again. If the forward bow is still too much, repeat the procedure, using more pressure on the cam clamp. For the best results, the strings should be up to pitch with this method also.

I highly recommend this clamping setup when adjusting the Harmony line of instruments, as it is relatively easy to break the tension rod when trying to adjust for excessive bow. I will go into the replacement and installation of various tension rod setups in another chapter and

will discuss the performance of the various types and the way they work.

The Baldwin line of guitars uses an adjustment at the base of the neck. It is adjusted with a special key and, judging from the operation of the rod, probably operates on a worm-gear principle. I've never had one apart, but I have adjusted a couple. Again, use only small amounts of adjustment at a time.

If all of this jacking around on the tension rod did not correct the bow in the neck, or if the neck did not adjust uniformly and ended up wavy, or in the case of the necks without adjustments, please refer to the chapter on planing and refretting for the procedure to correct this.

In most cases of high string action, adjustment of the rod will lower the strings to a playable level. If the neck is set properly, with just a small amount of forward bow in the proper location, and the strings are still too high, we must look elsewhere for the trouble.

The thing to check next would be the scale length, in other words, the length of the vibrating string, or the distance between the inside of the nut to the inside of the bridge saddle. Actually the "scale" would be the distance from the inside of the nut to the center of the twelfth fret doubled. The actual distance is longer from the twelfth fret to the bridge to allow for the amount you sharp the strings when you fret them.

Anyway, the scale has a lot to do with the string action or height, as the longer the scale, the higher the strings must be set to keep them from rattling against the frets. How hard a person plays also has a direct bearing on this, as the heavy-handed guitarist must settle for a higher action than one with a light touch.

On the steel-string standard guitars, we find quite a few different scales being used. For general purposes, we will lump them a little closer together. Most of the smaller guitars, and a few of the larger bodied ones, use a scale of around $24\frac{9}{10}$". This is the Martin standard scale for the ooo and smaller (one exception, their twelve-strings use the short scale) instruments. This will vary with other brands, from $24\frac{3}{4}$" to $24\frac{7}{8}$". For simplification, we will stick to the $24\frac{9}{10}$" scale. On the larger Martins and some others, a $25\frac{4}{10}$ or thereabouts scale is used. I shall call them the long scale and short scale.

In a lot of cases, just setting the height of the strings at the nut will correct the action, but first the bridge height should be checked.

The easy way to do this is to place a capo behind the first fret. In doing this, we are eliminating the nut as a determining factor in the action. I make all my height measurements at the halfway point, normally the twelfth fret, but in this case the thirteenth fret, remem-

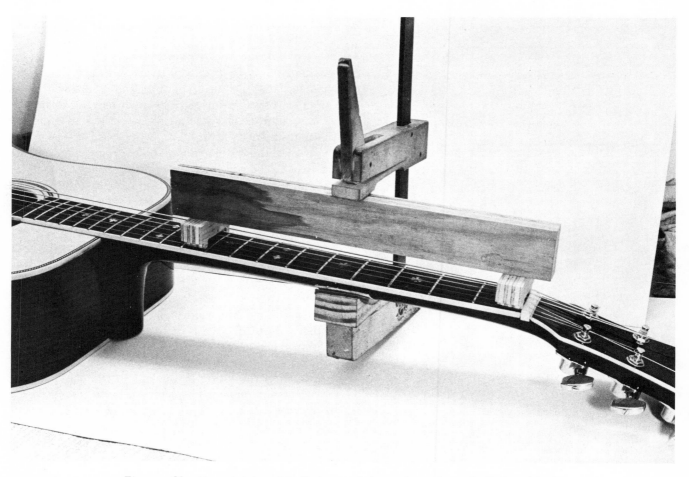

Fig. 75—*Clamping setup to assist adjustment of the tension rod on a badly bowed neck.*

bering we have eliminated the nut with the capo, making the first fret the actual nut.

For a normal string action on the short scale, the height should be ³⁄₃₂" from the top of the first string to the *top* of the thirteenth fret. It should be around ⁷⁄₆₄" from the *bottom* of the sixth string to the top of the thirteenth fret.

On the long scale instruments, the measurement should be about ³⁄₃₂" from the bottom of the first string, and ⁴⁄₃₂" from the bottom of the sixth string, to the top of the thirteenth fret.

You will notice that the bass or sixth string is set higher than the treble or first string. This is done on purpose, as the slower vibrations of the bass string and the extra weight of its windings, cause it to swing farther, and it needs more clearance than the higher pitched treble string. The strings in between the first and sixth are set according to their pitch also, with the second string a little higher than the first, the third higher than the second, and so on up to the sixth.

Now, these distances are approximate. As I have mentioned before, each instrument has its own personality. Some with very sensitive tops may be set lower and still play clean, while others, though identical in appearance, may rattle badly and have to be set at a higher action.

If a person plays real hard, you might have to raise the strings by ¹⁄₃₂" or so, and on others you might get by with a slightly lower action. I usually have the owner of the instrument play for me while I watch his or her style, and I set the instrument's action accordingly.

Also, remember that we are talking about the flat-top, round-hole, steel-string guitar. If you are setting the action for an electric guitar, you may lower the height by about a third less than for an acoustical instrument. We won't get into that too deeply, as this book is primarily concerned with acoustical guitars.

The other types of flat-top guitars would be the classical and flamenco instruments with nylon strings. The scales on these usually vary from 25⅛" to 26½" on some models.

92

With these long scales, the strings have to be set pretty high to keep them from rattling. Another factor here is the fact that nylon strings vibrate quite a bit farther than the steel ones. The normal action height for the classical guitar at mid-scale is in the area of $\frac{3}{16}$" from the top of the first string to the top of the fret and from the bottom of the sixth string to the fret. Depending on the guitarist's style and the type of strings, this may be less.

On the flamenco guitar, the nylon strings are set low enough to rattle deliberately. This is part of the sound for this type of music, and strings must be set to the guitarist's taste and style of playing. The best way to do this is to set him or her down to try the guitar out after adjusting and vary the height a small amount at a time until they are satisfied.

Another important factor to remember is coming up next. If the strings are too high or too low, how in the world do we figure the exact amount that must be added or subtracted from the bridge saddle to bring the strings to their proper clearance? The answer? There is a simple formula that is foolproof for determining this.

Look at the strings as the radius of a circle. The machine head, where the string fastens, is the center of the circle, with the distance to the nut as the first radius and the distance to the bridge saddle as the longest radius we have to deal with. We have eliminated the machine head and nut factor by the use of the capo, which, in effect, makes the first fret the center of the circle. When we raise or lower the strings, we are transcribing an arc or small portion of a circle.

Now, the formula. I make my measurements for the string height at the thirteenth fret (center of scale with capo on), which breaks the radius at the halfway point. Since the bridge is *twice* as far from the center as the thirteenth fret, if we raise or lower the strings $\frac{1}{16}$" at the thirteenth fret, we will have to raise or lower the bridge saddle *twice* as much, or $\frac{1}{8}$". This is the secret of setting the height right the first try. By using precision tools, the vernier calipers and the steel $\frac{1}{32}$" graduated rule, getting the height right the first time is the rule rather than the exception.

After the bridge action is set to the proper height, checking out the nut is the next step. The string height here is important also. If the nut is set too high, the fretting of the strings for the first few frets can literally raise blisters on the fingers or make them so sore that you cannot play. Also, the intonation will be off, particularly for the first couple of frets.

Remember the formula for figuring the bridge saddle height? Well, we run into a similar situation here also. Any amount we can lower the strings here is doubled at the twelfth fret. Suppose we could lower the strings at

the nut by .020". This would lower the strings at the twelfth fret twice as much, or .040". This applies only when the string is played open or not fretted.

Perhaps the easiest way to set the proper nut height is to put the capo back on behind the first fret. Take a set of mechanic's feeler gauges, which are graduated in thousandths of an inch, and check the clearance between the bottom of the strings and the top of the second fret. Since we set the strings higher on the bass side than we did on the treble side, the clearances will be different with each string. Slip the feeler gauges under the strings, determining the clearances of each string, then add .010" to each of these measurements. This will give you the proper height to clear the first fret. Cut the string slot down with the razor saw, or use jeweler's needle files on the wound string slots, until you have the clearance set. Again, you will find guitars that you can set a little closer or that you will have to set higher than others. It just depends on the particular guitar and the playing style used.

If you cut the notches too deep and end up with a rattle on maybe one string, you can shim under the nut with a piece of hard plastic or shim stock. Try around .010" and if it is still too low, the best thing to do would be to make a new nut. They may be shimmed more than that if necessary or if a new nut blank is not available. You should keep a good supply of ivory (preferably) or bone nuts and saddle blanks in stock, because setting string actions will be one of the most often repeated jobs you will be faced with. So many of the manufacturing companies, particularly the imports, use plastic for the saddles and nuts. These generally do not last too long before they need replacement. It is getting harder all the time to find good quality ivory or bone pieces for this job too.

Should you decide to make a new nut, the old one can normally be used as a pattern. Using the calipers and belt sander and the old nut to measure from, it takes only a few minutes to rough one out. It can be done by hand with files and sandpaper, but the belt or disk sander takes all the work out of it.

Should the nut be missing, or if the spacing is off and has to be redone, I have a simple technique for figuring the spacing. I rough the nut out and set it in place. I then install the first and sixth strings, positioning the strings the proper distance from the edges, and marking each one. I then cut the string notches for the first and sixth strings. Next, I take the vernier calipers and measure from the center of the first string to the center of the sixth string. Take this distance and divide by five. The answer will be the center to center measurement for all six strings. Set the calipers to this measurement, and mark the rest of the string positions.

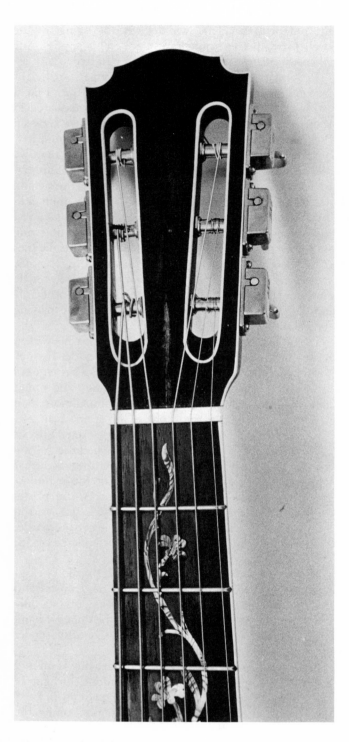

Twelve string guitars are a little more tricky. You have to set the first and sixth *pairs*, then determine the center point between each pair. Measure this, divide by five, and use the answer to determine the center of the other pairs. Then space the pairs accordingly from the center lines.

After the spacings are figured and marked, the notches are rough cut and the strings are installed. The notches should slant down slightly from the front edge of the nut, and should angle slightly towards its adjusting peg. The string slots towards the middle of the neck will, of course, angle more than the ones on the outer edge of the nut. This slight angling of the slots seems to give a smoother adjustment while tuning the guitar.

After the strings are fitted and set to the proper depth for correct action, the strings should be loosened and the nut removed for the final cleanup. Sand the top of the nut down to where the small strings are level with the top of the nut and the wrapped strings are halfway above the level of the nut. This makes a neat looking job, and the wrapped strings will have less chance to bind in their slots than if they were set deeper. Sand all corners smooth, apply a couple of drops of glue under the nut, string it up, and the guitar should now be ready to play.

If you have time, it is best to let the guitar settle down for a day and check the settings again to make sure everything is still all right. If the action is right and the guitar still doesn't note out properly, see the chapter on bridging to correct this.

Fig. 76—Photo shows slots in the nut angled towards their respective machine heads. Author's personal instrument.

9

Truing and Refretting an Instrument

The refretting of an instrument can be a most difficult and exasperating job. When I first started in the business, I used the traditional method of driving the frets into the fingerboard.

I immediately ran into problems, such as cleaning glue from the slots of bound fingerboards without removing the binding; chipping of the fingerboard surface even when using a soldering iron to heat the fret and specially reworked end-nippers to pull the frets out; getting the proper width on the fret slot so it will not expand the wood too much when driven into the fingerboard with the resultant and unpredictable backward bow in the neck, causing problems in setting the proper string action; the working out of frets driven into an old, deteriorated, or rotten fingerboard, even when driven in with glue; and not seating all the frets down to the same level and having to file a fret or two heavily, and having to reshape the crown as a result. These are just a few of the problems I ran into with the traditional method.

The traditional method is the most practical under factory conditions, where they use the same saws and the same size fret wire all the time under controlled conditions. This method is also faster, production-wise.

In a repair shop such as mine, with all the different types and ages of instruments involved, with many different types of materials and sizes of fret wire involved, I decided there just had to be a better way to do the job, one that would work for all kinds of fret work, from an antique with a rotten fingerboard to a brand new one, and one that would be almost foolproof. I found it, too! There are a few areas where mistakes can be made, and I will point them out as we come to them.

By following the instructions I am laying out here very closely, you should be able to do a fret job that will be as good as the best, and better than 75 per cent of the factory jobs that you will run into these days, with all the cheapies hitting the market. Some of the name brands aren't all that good with the fret work either.

In fact, since I have started using my method, the demand for my fret work has increased to the point where it consists of about 30 per cent of my total work load. Many are on brand-new instruments, too.

The equipment required is considerably more than for the driven-in fret job. With the proper tools and practice, the actual working time for the job runs from an hour and a half to about two and a half, depending on the condition of the neck and fingerboard. The actual time for the instrument down time is about ten hours, counting the drying time for the glue.

I will list the tools needed as we go through the steps of my fretting technique, and you may refer to the pictures also, for a look at their particular application.

The first thing to do is to remove the strings, nut, and, in some cases, the machine heads. I use the sandpaper file for working down the fingerboard, and if the pegs of the machines protrude above the level of the board, they should be removed to prevent damage to them from the sandpaper.

While this is going on, you should have your soldering iron heating. You will be using this for heating the frets to soften the glue used to help retain the frets in the board. This is usually a white glue of some sort. I use epoxy glue to retain the frets, and the soldering iron will soften this also to the point where they may be pulled easily.

Check the drawing of the end-nippers and you will notice that the end is ground to where the cutting edge is flush with the end. This allows the nippers to be placed flush against the fingerboard, with a jaw on each side of the fret. When squeezed together, the sharp edge, being flush to the wood, will slide under the fret. The inside angle of the jaw pulls the fret up, and the outside remains relatively flat against the wood, hopefully to minimize the chipping as the fret comes out.

Before you do this job with the nippers, take the hot soldering iron (file a shallow groove on one side to set over the fret), place on the fret near the edge of the fingerboard, heat for a few seconds, move it over towards the middle of the board, and, maintaining contact

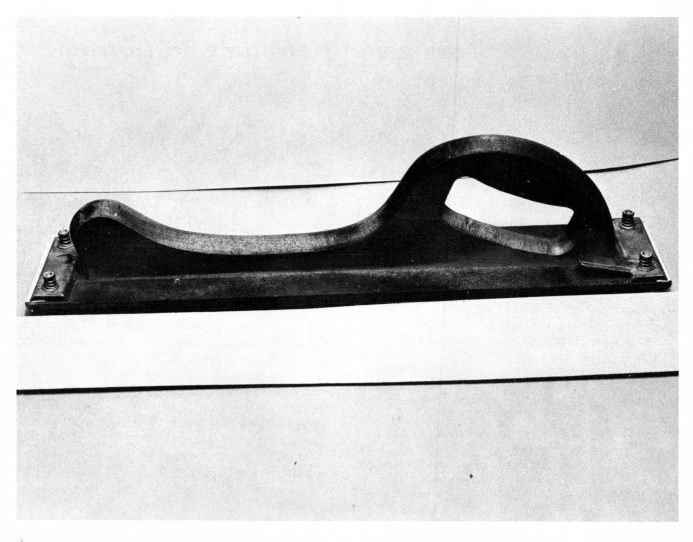

Fig. 77—Sandpaper file and pre-cut paper may be purchased from most auto body shop supply houses.

between the soldering iron and fret, slip the nippers under the end you just heated. Squeeze together, and the fret should lift a small amount. Now, this is important. Do not lift the fret with the nippers yet, but shift them over a small amount and squeeze again. Keep moving the hot iron across the fret and following it with the nippers all the way across the board. The fret should have come up with very little chipping. You will almost always get some small chips, particularly with an ebony or antique fingerboard.

Should you run into trouble and remove a few large chips, reglue them immediately, before they get lost or mixed up with others. I keep my hypodermic glue syringe handy for this purpose. If you can get the chip before you pull it all the way off, you can run the needle under the chip, squirt a drop of glue under it, and press it down to dry.

Another thing. If you should be removing the frets from one of my fret jobs, you will not have the chipping problem, as my system practically eliminates this factor. I have one professional guitarist who goes through frets about once a year, and I have refretted his guitar three times so far, with no problems.

Now, all the frets are removed and all the chips are glued back in place and dry. If the neck is one of the kind with an adjustable tension rod and is relatively straight, with no problems except the worn frets, we are ready for the next step. Tape some cardboard to the face of the instrument on either side of the fingerboard to protect the finish in case of a slip.

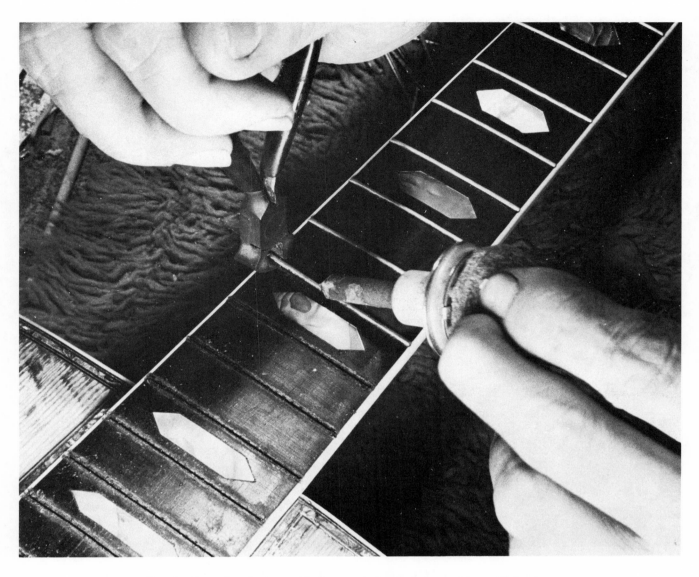

Fig. 78—Removing the frets with the reworked end-nippers and hot soldering iron.

Take the sandpaper file with an 80-grit piece of paper and sand the fingerboard until it is smooth and shows new wood the full length and width of the board. Check the neck with a straight edge from time to time to make sure you are keeping it straight. The tension rod may be backed off a small amount if the neck bows backwards very far after the removal of the strings and frets. Sand carefully if the board has an oval or convex surface, as most steel-stringed instruments do, being sure to take the same amount of wood off all the way across to insure retaining the original contour of the fingerboard. After doing a few of these oval surface boards, the technique becomes automatic.

Sand only enough material off to clean up the surface and get it straight. Make sure you have an accurate straight edge to check this with, and use it.

If the neck will not adjust properly, leaving some waviness, or if the board has a hump, or is kicked up at the end, or if the neck does not have an adjustment and is bowed, drastic measures are called for.

Lay your straight edge the length of the fingerboard and check the low spots. If the neck has a tension rod, adjust it so the low spots are at a minimum. You may either use a razor-sharp block plane or, my preference, the sandpaper file with 40-grit paper on it for fast cutting.

The reason I prefer the sandpaper file is the fact that

97

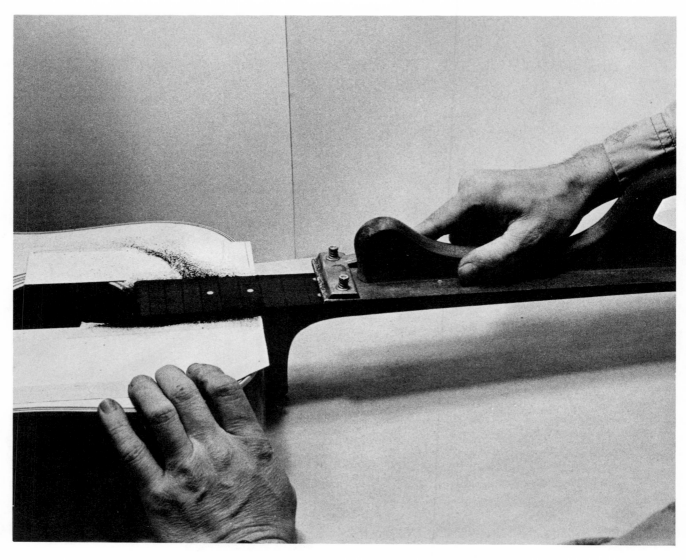

Fig. 79—*Dressing the fingerboard with the sandpaper file to true or clean it up. Notice the cardboard taped to the guitar top to protect the finish if you slip.*

some fingerboard inlays are made of plastic, and even a razor-sharp plane will tear chunks out of these, whereas the sandpaper merely sands them off. The 40-grit paper cuts about as fast as the plane, as the plane must be set very shallow to prevent chipping and gouging.

If the string action is high on the guitar before you started working with it, sand most of the wood off the nut end. If the action was pretty fair, split the difference between both ends of the board and work it down, checking periodically with the straight edge until you have it straight. If the neck is non-adjustable, sand a slight backward bow in the board from around the seventh fret towards the nut end. This should be a rounded

bow and not a straight, flat, backward angle. This can be achieved by leaning on the sandpaper file slightly harder at the end of the stroke over the nut area. The amount of backward bow sanded into the neck should be the same as the forward bow was, so that when the strings are pulled up to pitch again, the neck should be straight.

After roughing the board off with the 40-grit, switch to the 80-grit paper, and sand just enough to smooth out the scratches left by the 40-grit. I then sand by hand with 150-grit finishing paper, and we are ready for the next step.

Purchase a good *non-silicone* paste wax (I use Star

98

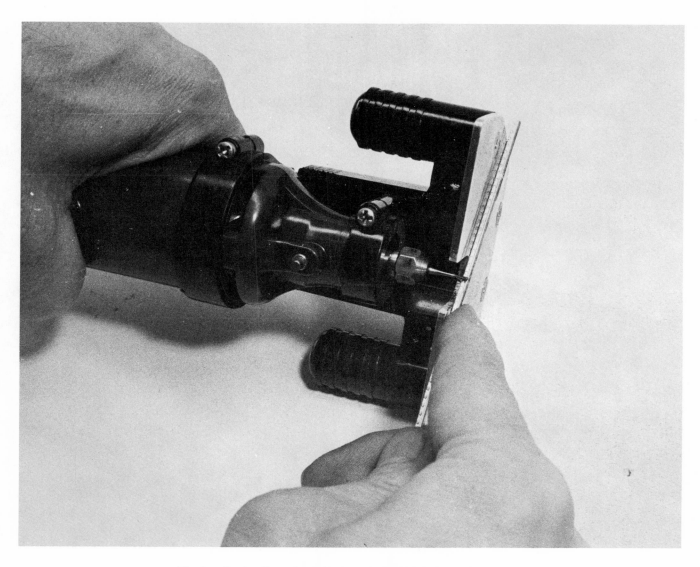

Fig. 80—Setting Dremel and burr to cut proper depth for tang of fret.

Chemical Company's Star Bright) and wax the surface of the fingerboard, not using so much wax as to get it in the old fret slots. Allow this to dry for a few minutes to a half hour and you are ready for the next step.

The next step is with the Dremel Moto-Tool and a #229 router attachment. For this job, I use only the base itself, without the edge guide. I have changed the base plate also, with the express idea of using it for fretting and closer work than the larger plate will allow me to do comfortably. Check the photographs and patterns for the making of this new base plate.

The fret wire must now be decided on. I use two sizes of wire, one being fairly small, designed for use in small guitars, banjos, etc., and the other is the standard size as used in the Martin guitars. I generally use the smaller wire on electric guitars also, as the small wire seems to note out just a little bit better.

When you decide on the wire, check the thickness of the tang, and using a small engraving cutter, clean the fret slot out to where the fret will press in with the fingers, instead of having to drive it in. Dremel makes a small engraving cutter (the # 111), but you can find an infinite supply of different sizes at a dental supply house. My dentist gave me a couple of pounds of used high-speed steel ones that were too dull to use on teeth anymore but were plenty sharp to work in wood.

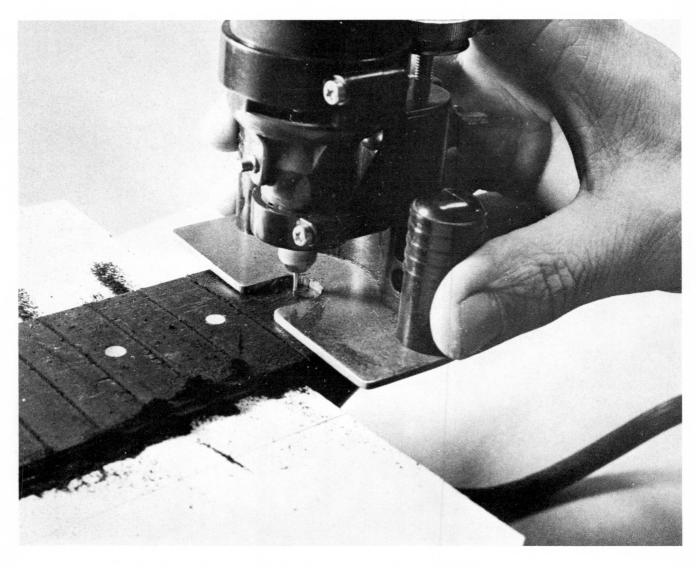

Fig. 81—*Cleaning out the fret slots with Dremel and small burr. Notice that the cardboard is still in place on the top.*

If you can acquire some of the new tungsten carbide dental cutters, you will have burrs that will last for many a fingerboard.

Set the depth of the cutter to where it will cut slightly deeper than the tang of the fret, and starting at one side, exert a steady and straight line pressure on the burr, and it will center itself right on the fret slot. Just looking at it, you wonder if that is so? Here is where you should have an old fingerboard to try the burr on first. You can get off if you are not careful, but it is surprisingly easy to keep the burr centered. After a burr has dulled a bit, you almost have to try on purpose to get the burr off

center. In other words, it works quite accurately and quite well.

On a bound fingerboard, the procedure is the same with slight differences. Insert your burr into the fret slot right at the edge where the binding joins the fingerboard and cut about ¼" towards the middle and stop. If the binding is pretty thick, I usually cut half of the diameter of the burr into the binding, and if it is thin, I cut close enough to see white at the end of the fret slot.

Do this at each end of all the fret slots, and only then do you finish cutting all the way across. The reason for this is that if you make a cut all the way across the finger-

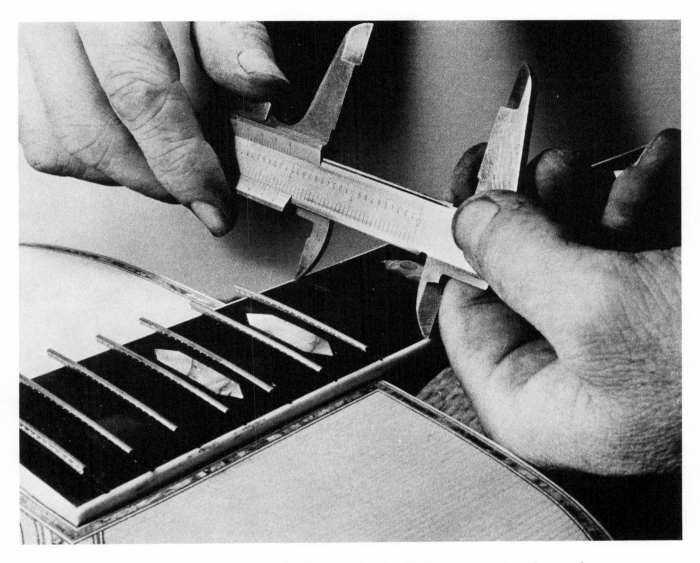

Fig. 82—*Measuring bound fingerboard for fret length with the vernier calipers. Reverse the calipers to the outside measurement jaws for unbound fingerboards.*

board, the burr will be so hot that it will instantly burn through the binding. In fact if the binding is celluloid, it can actually catch fire from a hot burr.

Clean all the dust and residue from the slots with a small scribe or screwdriver. Sometimes it is necessary to make a second pass with the burr to clean out the fret slots. Anyway, double-check the slots to make sure they are clean, so nothing will hinder the seating of the frets when they are installed.

Now, take your vernier calipers and start measuring and cutting your frets. If the fingerboard is bound, measure from edge to edge with the calipers' inside measuring points. If the board is unbound, use the outside measuring jaws. I measure each fret as close to the needed length as possible, and then with the fret wire in a small vise, I transfer the measurement to the wire and cut it off with either a razor saw or a jeweler's saw. As I cut each fret, I lay it in its particular slot so I will not duplicate the fret. After they are all cut, I set them into a board with holes drilled in it to keep them from getting mixed up.

I then take a standard pair of pliers with the end re-worked to grip a fret nicely (see drawing in specialty tool chapter) and curve the fret to fit the fingerboard. Skip this step, of course, if the fingerboard is flat. You may bend the fret to fit the fingerboard perfectly, or you may

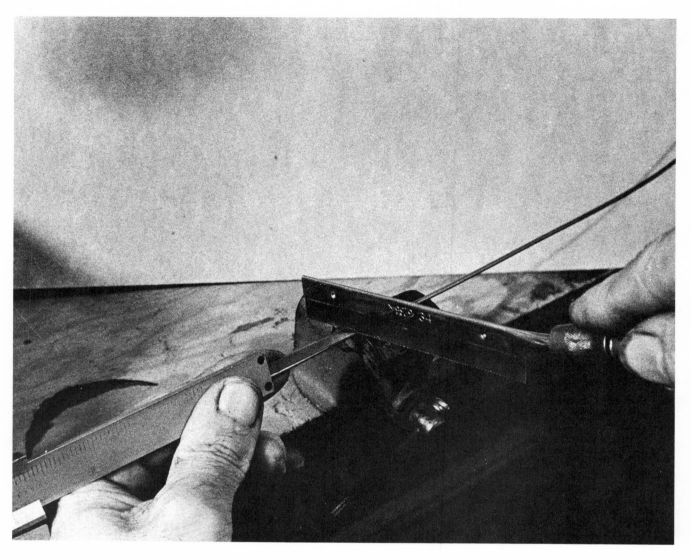

Fig. 83—Measuring and cutting fret wire for proper length using the depth measuring end of the calipers, razor saw, and hobbiest's vise to hold the wire.

leave a *very small* amount of spring in each end of the fret. When clamped, this small amount of spring will pull the fret down all the way across the board. If you leave too much spring, however, the frets will bow up in the middle when clamped.

A word of warning. On an old or rotten fingerboard, shape the contour of the fret to fit the shape of the board exactly. This is the only way I have found to keep a fret on some of these. The fact of the matter is, I developed this technique working on antique instruments and now use it for all my refret work.

For those of you who would like to take advantage of the Dremel to clean up your fretboards and still drive

your frets in, just use a small enough burr to leave around .003" to .005" interference fit, apply a little white glue or Titebond to the fret, and drive it in. To use my method, remember that the slot is cleaned out just wide enough so that the fret can be pressed in with the fingers.

The next step is to tape off the fingerboard slots to prevent glue from getting all over the board. If the board is unbound, run a piece of masking tape along the side of the board, with the top edge right at the bottom of the fret slots. This will prevent epoxy from getting all over the neck when the frets are pressed into place. This step is unnecessary with a bound board. After everything is taped, mix up some Elmer's epoxy and fill all the slots

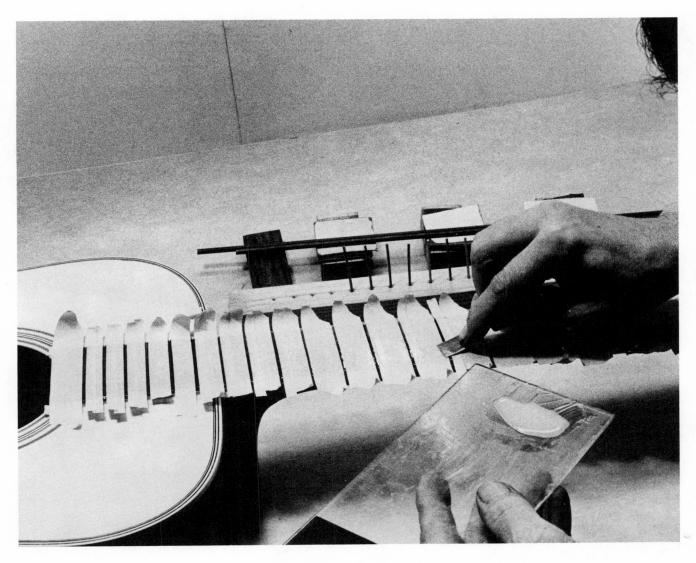

Fig. 84—*Fingerboard fret slots taped off during application of epoxy glue with glue spatula. Notice frets in drilled board in background to prevent mixups.*

with the glue. Be sure that you mix the glue with *exactly equal* amounts of the resin and hardener, and mix until the glue is *creamy in color*. The wrong mixture or haphazard mixing, and your fret job may be back for another go round.

After the slots are filled with glue, remove the tape from the fretboard surface and set the frets into their respective slots. On the unbound boards, be sure the frets do not protrude on one side and come out short on the other.

If you are working with a flat fingerboard, apply a strip of waxed paper over the frets and lay a wooden block as wide as the widest point on the board (and long enough to cover all the frets) on top of it. The block should preferably be made from ¾" plywood for strength.

If the fingerboard is ovaled or convex, lay a ³⁄₁₆" rod along each edge about ³⁄₁₆" from the ends of the frets and hold in position temporarily with masking tape. Lay a plywood block on top of these rods of the same dimensions as mentioned in the previous paragraph.

Get out the fitted neck clamping blocks, leather and cardboard pads, and four "C" clamps. You will also need a small block to place under the face of the guitar, under the fingerboard area.

If the guitar fingerboard was sanded out with a slight backward bow, as mentioned earlier in this chapter, lay

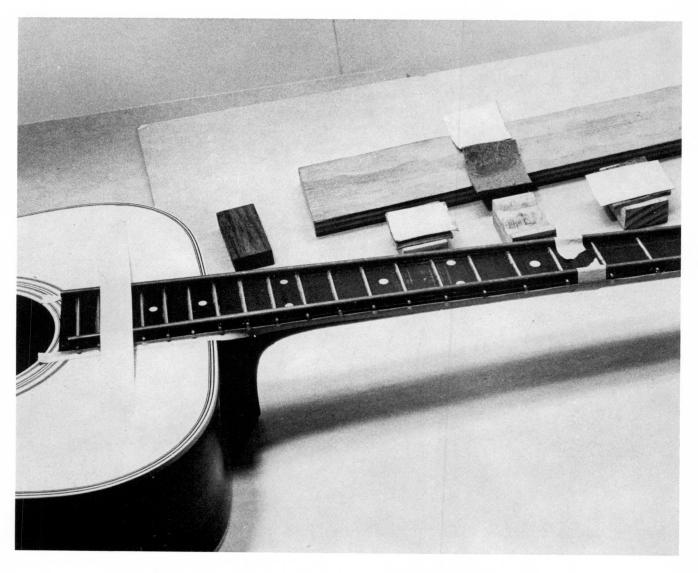

Fig. 85—*Frets set into board and rods taped into position on oval fingerboard in preparation for clamping.*

a piece of cardboard about .020" thick (common poster board) across the top of the two rods, above the first fret before you lay the wooden block on the rods.

Next, place a "C" clamp and clamping pad setup at the midpoint of the neck and tighten down snugly. Apply the clamp and small block through the sound hole and over the face end of the board. Now, apply the other two clamp and pad setups, one near the body and the other between the first and second fret positions.

Now comes a very important point to remember. Here is where people using this technique for the first time usually goof up. Tighten the clamps *only enough* to pull the frets down on the fingerboard flush. Over-tighten the clamps, and you press the frets into the wood under the clamps and rods and spring them up in the middle. When you remove the clamping setup, check the frets carefully at the point of contact with the pressure rods. If the clamps were too tight, there will be slight dents in the frets, immediately under the area of the "C" clamps.

After removing the clamps, rods, and masking tape along the side of the neck, take a sharp wood chisel (I use a ¼" chisel for this job) and peel the excess glue from either side of the frets. If you waxed the board as

Fig. 86—Clamping setup with board over rods and clamps, contoured clamping blocks, and protective pads in position to keep frets seated until epoxy dries.

directed, it should come right off. The glue will not stick to the wax or the smooth surface of the fret crown. The tang down in the slot has little beads that, when the glue is set, hold the fret in place. Note that should you get hold of some fret wire with a smooth tang without any beading, you must rough this up so the glue will have something to bond to. On some of the old Martins, a solid piece of silver wire was hot-rolled to a flat rectangular shape and set into the fingerboard. On re-doing some of these, I used the razor saw to scrape each side of the wire. The teeth scratched the soft silver nicely, and, to be on the safe side, I took a sharp cold chisel and

using it by hand, dinged the bottoms of all the frets. This expanded silver past the edges to provide a burr for gripping power. This same trick may be used on extruded fret wire with a smooth tang.

Also, if there were any small irregularities in the extruding of the fret along the bottom of the crown, or if there are small chips of wood missing from pulling the original frets, the glue will fill these in and seal the fret to the fingerboard. When you clean the excess glue off, you can look along the edge of the fret crown where it contacts the board surface, and you will not see any gaps.

The next step is to smooth off the ends of the frets. I

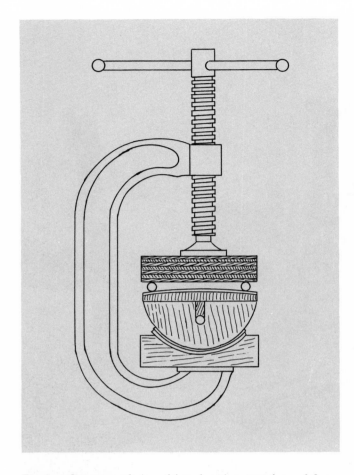

Fig. 87—*Cutaway end view of fret clamping setup for oval finger-board showing positioning of the 3/16" rods at ends of frets, top clamping block, cardboard and leather neck pads, contoured neck clamping block with C-clamp in position.*

do this with the special file block I have designed. I have included plans for making it in this book. The block holds the file at a 45° angle, and since it covers quite a bit of area at one time, you get a smooth, straight edge on the fingerboard. I file the frets with the block until I touch the edge of the wood of the fingerboard. If the board is sanded down quite a bit, there will be a sharp edge on the wood. File the frets and the board until the sharp edge is removed slightly. This leaves a rough 45° angle on the frets, and then I take a hand file and smooth off the rest by hand, rounding the ends of the frets and blending them into the edge of the fingerboard.

Next, we drag out the sandpaper file again. This time, a strip of 150-grit finishing paper is used. Hit the tops of the frets very lightly with the paper file, and look for any fret not touched by the paper. You can tell by the silver dust on either side of the frets and by the look of the top of the frets. If you are not touching all the frets, dress

them a little more or until you are touching all the frets.

This sandpaper file may be used also for dressing worn frets to a new surface quite successfully.

Should you flatten the top of the fret out more than one third of its total width, the crown should be rounded with the special fret file available from most guitar supply houses. The teeth on this file are on the edge and are cut in a concave channel, so that the rounding of a wide fret is made easier. The reshaping of frets usually needs to be done if you are reworking the old frets. If the new fret job was done properly, you should just have to touch the tops of the frets with the sandpaper file.

A bit earlier in this chapter, the old Martin "square" frets were mentioned. After clamping and gluing these in place, and cleaning off the excess glue, these have to be leveled, particularly if you have shimmed up the old fret for more height above the fingerboard.

I use a 10" or 12" mill bastard file, and I flat file all the fret tops until they are flat and level. Then the special fret file comes into use. Reshape the crowns on all the frets to remove the sharp edges, and then go over them lightly with the sandpaper file and the 150-grit finishing paper.

The next step is to go over the frets with 320 or 400 Wetordry sandpaper, wrapped around a couple of your fingers, using quite a bit of pressure to round off the frets and smooth down the edges of the fingerboard. Switch to 600 Wetordry and go over this again, using the heavy pressure. This will polish the frets nicely. Now, switch to a wad of #1 steel wool and buff the fingerboard and frets. This will clean up the surface of the board and, if you did not get all the frets down completely, will hang up under the ends of the frets where they contact the wood. Usually on the epoxied-in fret, this does not happen. If it does, take a safe-edge file (no teeth on the edges), lay the smooth edge against the board, and round the edge towards the middle of the fret. Do this from each side of the fret and each end. If you drove the frets in, you will, in all probability, have to do this anyway. That is just another reason why I like my system.

After all of this is done, and the steel-wooling is complete (if you are working on an electric guitar, tape off all pickups from steel wool shavings), take a rag with a small amount of lacquer, and wipe the edges of the board a few times, or, if you prefer, just hit it with a rag with a few drops of lemon oil on it. Use the lemon oil on the surface of the fingerboard also.

I have heard of people using regular motor oil, and I had one job that had actually had light machine oil used on it for several years. I replaced the fingerboard on this one. None of these oils will oxidize. They just soak in and build up in the wood. In the case of rosewood, with its porosity, the board can be ruined.

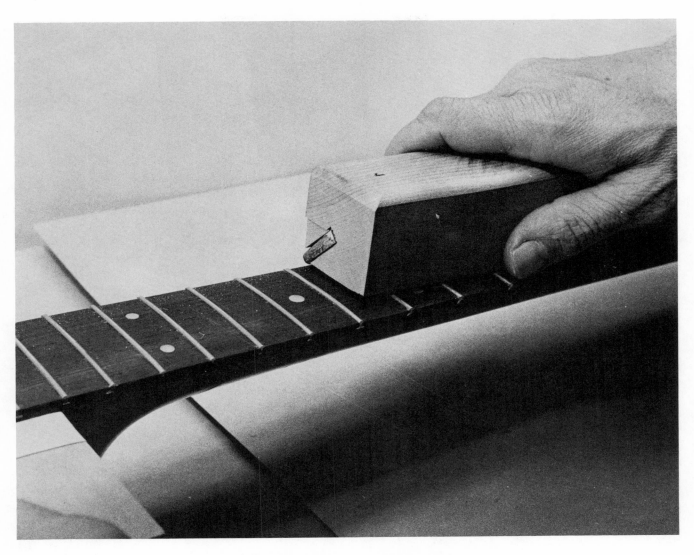

Fig. 88—Dressing ends of frets to 45° angle with file block.

I have also had problems caused by the excessive use of chemicals to make a neck faster, such as Finger Ease. When I removed the frets for refretting on several of these, I found that the Finger Ease had penetrated all the way to the bottom of the fret slots. There was actually some liquid in the bottoms of some of the slots. By the use of many washings of naptha, and the use of the air hose to blow things out, I was able to clean up things enough to do a fret job on them. The excessive use of these chemicals sure makes things hard on us repairmen when we have to work on the guitars.

The best bet is to use a little lemon oil once in a while, but just a few drops on a rag instead of soaking it in.

The guitar should now be ready to reassemble. You will find that if you removed much wood in cleaning up the fingerboard, on reassembly of the instrument the action will have to be readjusted. Chances are, you will at least have to rework the nut, and maybe even the bridge saddle. Refer to the chapter on setting tension rods and string actions for this.

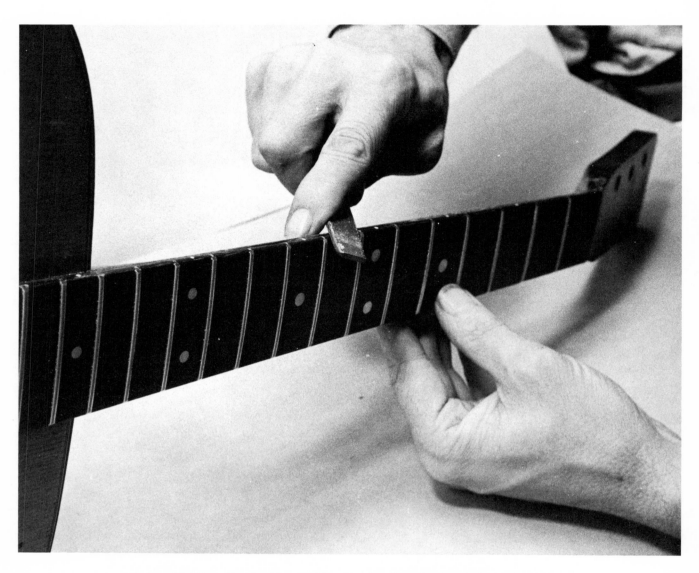

Fig. 89—*Finishing off ends of frets and blending into fingerboard with fine-mill bastard file.*

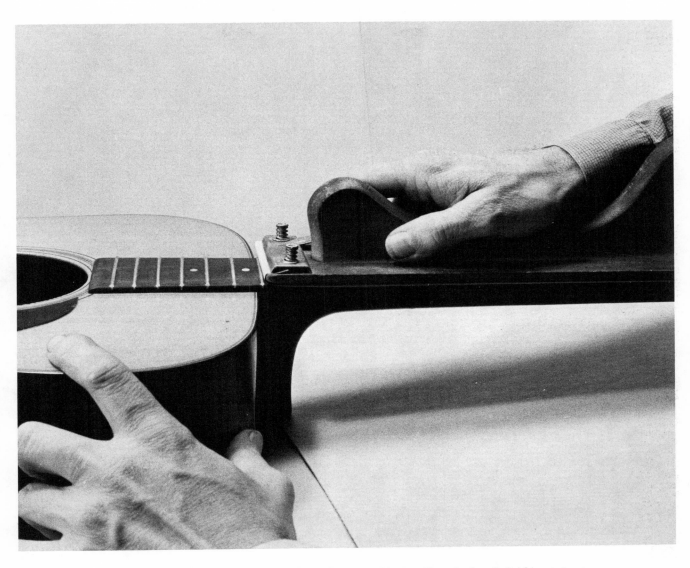

Fig. 90—Dressing the tops of the frets lightly with sandpaper file and 180-grit finishing paper to insure that all the frets are the same height.

Fig. 91—*Polishing the frets by hand with 600-grit Wetordry sandpaper without water.*

10.
Neck Reinforcements: Operation, Installation, and Repairs

Most guitars today, using steel strings, have a metal reinforcement of some type. Some of the nylon-string or classic models are reinforced also. Up until after the turn of the century and into the early teens even, most guitars were strung with "cat gut" strings. These were made usually from the intestines of sheep or goats, carefully cured and twisted to form strings. The methods for doing this were, compared to modern day methods, pretty slow. It was mostly hand work. They resulted in the best strings available then.

One of the main problems was to make a string uniform in diameter for the length required and also to make it resonate properly on the tuned frequency. If the strings varied in diameter much, the frequencies would break up into various harmonics resulting in a bad sound. On the heavier strings for the bass, they finally resorted to wrapping them with silk and finally with brass wire to make them resonate on the proper frequency and to give them enough power (from the weight of the brass windings) so they could be used singly instead of in pairs, as used on the ancestor of the Spanish guitars, the lute. Besides being irregular in diameter at times, they were very sensitive to humidity changes. Just playing on them for a while would cause changes in the tonal qualities of the string, resulting from the absorption of moisture from the hands. During rainy periods or other high atmospheric humidity conditions, they were extremely unstable and almost impossible to tune or keep in tune. This tuning problem with the many-stringed lute was one of the reasons for its loss of popularity. The guitar was simpler, with fewer strings, but the tuning problem was still there.

After the turn of the century, some of the luthiers began making guitars using piano wire for the strings instead of gut, and in the late teens and 1920s, most of the guitars made in the United States were being made with the steel strings.

Gut was still being used on classic and flamenco guitars until after World War II, when nylon strings came into prominence. They have almost completely domi-

nated the classic market since. A few brands of gut strings are still offered for guitars, however. The nylon strings are practically unaffected by humidity changes, and the main problem with them is getting the initial stretch from the nylon. After this is gone, the string gives very few problems with tuning.

Perhaps you are wondering what I am getting at with all this talk of strings. What I am leading up to is the problem of guitar neck warpage. The old gut strings put very little tension on guitar necks, and, as a result, a light, relatively thin neck could be made that would not bow up under normal conditions. Also, the neck was fairly wide, usually from $1\frac{7}{8}$" to $2\frac{1}{8}$", to give the strings room to vibrate without hitting the fingers fretting the string next to it. This same wide fingerboard and neck was, and is, being used on the nylon-string instruments of today for the same reason. Another important reason for the width was the style of playing. The bare fingers were used to pluck the strings. With the wide neck they could get deep enough between the strings, while plucking, to get a full resonant sound without interfering with adjacent strings.

This extra width meant extra wood in the neck, and even with the higher tension of the nylon strings, necks were usually strong enough to resist warping.

Now we come to the steel strings. These were played originally with the plectrum or "flat pick" by the majority of the people, and the wide fingerboard just didn't lend itself very well to this style of playing. They found that by moving the strings closer together on a narrow neck they could get a much better sound from the strings and that the narrower neck was easier to chord.

This narrowing of the neck removed a fairly large percentage of the wood from the neck, actually reducing the strength while adding more stress with the metal strings. Results? Problems with the necks bowing.

Also, many of the older guitars, designed for the gut strings, were being strung up with the new steel strings. This is the reason, I believe, that there are so few of the old guitars (those made from around 1920 and be-

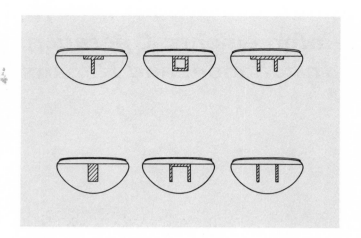

Fig. 92—Non-adjustable neck reinforcements. Top, left: Martin T-bar. Top, center: Martin square-steel tube. Top, right: Double "T" usually extruded aluminum. Bottom, left: Steel key stock. Bottom, center: Inverted steel "U" channel. Bottom, right: Flat steel, power hacksaw blade, etc.

fore) left in existence. They were literally pulled to pieces by strings much too strong for them. I get one of these old timers in my shop every once in a while, and in almost every case they are strung with steel strings of some sort. I have once even found heavy-gauge strings on an old Martin made back in the 1870s. I almost gave this one up as a lost cause, but I was able to save it by installing a concealed tension rod in the neck and re-strutting the top.

It was during the 1920s that various ideas started cropping up for strengthening the necks. Some people used ebony pieces laid under the fingerboard, and others started laminating hard maples and mahogany or laying maple pieces under the fingerboards with the grain, as in the ebony, running up and down at a 90° angle to the fingerboard surface. Some started using a steel rod, set under tension, to resist the pull of the strings. Gibson, I believe, was one of the first to use the adjustable tension rod in a production instrument.

In the mid-1940s, Martin started using a steel "T" bar in their necks as strings became even heavier. The T-shaped piece of steel resisted sideways movement of the neck as well as the pull of the strings as guitars grew larger and heavier. These larger guitars, when played with shoulder straps, had quite a bit of weight leaned on them by the arm while playing, as most of the straps were tied to the head of the guitar. Another method of helping this side stress is installing a strap peg screwed carefully into a *drilled* hole in the heel of the neck. This is becoming an accepted practice and is particularly help-

ful with the standard tension rod, as it does nothing to strengthen the side stress.

Martin, by the way, changed to a welded square-steel tubing in late 1967. This has, of course, two vertical and horizontal members in lieu of only one vertical and horizontal member in the T-bar.

Other instruments I have worked on have used solid-square bars of mild steel embedded in epoxy putty. I have found this on some of the Mexican twelve-string guitars and have found similar layouts in the Japanese cheapies marked "Steel Reinforced Neck." I have found "U"-shaped channel iron, extruded aluminum channel used in combination with an adjustable tension rod, and I even found one that had a pair of heavy industrial power-hacksaw blades set edgewise into the neck. The many types and combinations seem to be endless. The two most common types of reinforcements found are the T-bar and square tubing (non-adjustable) found in Martin guitars and the many variations of adjustable tension rods.

These non-adjustable reinforcements, when properly engineered, give very little trouble unless the instrument is mistreated. The solid setup used by Martin works very well, whereas a large percentage of cheap instruments using similar setups have been having a lot of bad warpage problems. Most of these, I believe, are caused by not careful enough selection of well-cured, top quality wood and/or too mild a steel used in the reinforcement.

Being authorized to do warranty work on Martin guitars, I get quite a few from about a five-state area to work on. I would say that about 90 per cent of the Martin necks I have to straighten were caused by carelessness. In fact, one of the first things I check when a Martin, or for that matter, any instrument, is brought to me with a badly bowed neck is the back of the bridge. If it is coming up, the guitar has, in a large percentage of cases, been hot. The dead giveaway is if, while running a thin blade under the loose bridge, you meet small obstructions which prove to be strings of glue between the bridge and the top. The guitar has been hot enough for the glue to melt and slip. On cooling off, it resets in its new position. The glue holding the fingerboard has slipped also, with the tension of the strings pulling the neck upward in a bow, and it resets there when cooled off.

The most common cause of the overheating of these instruments is to leave them locked up in a car, or even worse, the trunk of a car on a hot day. Actually, it doesn't have to be very hot if the sun is bright enough and the car is a dark one. On hot days, the temperature of the interior of a car can almost double that of the outside, and most of the glues used in guitar making soften at around 160°. If you must leave your guitar inside a car

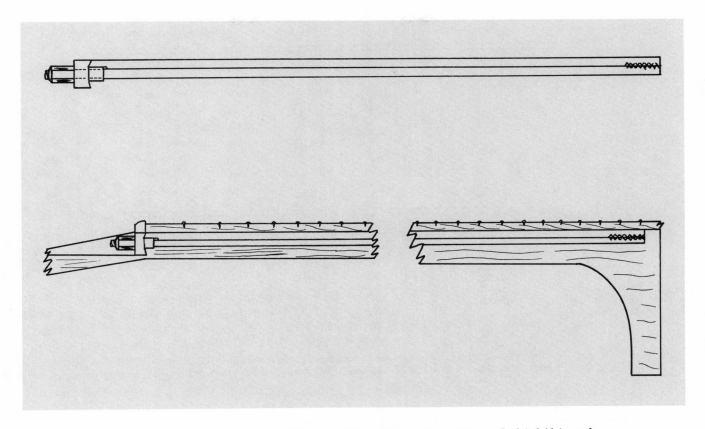

Fig. 93—*Top: Harmony patented "Torque-Lok" tension rod setup. Bottom: Rod is laid in neck directly under the fingerboard surface. May be removed if necessary without fingerboard removal in most cases.*

in these conditions, let *all* the tension off the strings and allow the instrument to cool thoroughly before tuning up again.

If the neck has bowed up slightly, it can be cured by planing the fingerboard true and refretting, or if it is in really bad condition it can sometimes be salvaged by the installation of a tension rod.

There are, as I mentioned before, many types of tension rods and several theories on which they operate. Some people advocate a straight rod laid into the neck. Others prefer to lay their rod in the neck with a graduated curve at one end and, in some instances, at both ends.

The Harmony people use a rod laid on top of a rod, welded together at one end. The lower rod is longer and is threaded for an inch or so. A machined sleeve slides on this lower rod, bearing against the upper rod, and a nut is installed, screwing up against this sleeve. When the nut is tightened, the lower rod is shortened, forcing the sleeve against the end of the upper rod, causing it to bow upward in the middle and straightening the neck.

These rods are made of mild steel and are rather easy to break if improperly adjusted (see string action chapter) and are also rather easy to replace when compared to other types of tension rods. They are laid in a groove routed immediately under the fingerboard and are not glued in place. Usually the nut (the ivory one, not the metal) can be removed and the end of the rod pulled out enough with needle-nose pliers to get a set of Vice-Grips on the rods. They can then be pulled right out of the slot by tapping on the jaws lightly with a plastic hammer. If you cannot get hold of the rods, the fingerboard may be loosened by the heating method for about 6" towards the body and the rods can then be pried up to where a grip can be had.

Buy a piece of ⅝₂" *drill rod* (the rod normally comes in 36" lengths), cut it to the proper lengths, using the old rods as a pattern, thread the end of the lower rod to a #6 x 32 thread, shape the upper rod end the same as the old one, stack the two rods together like the old ones, holding them with rubber bands, and have them either welded or brazed the same as the original rods. If you

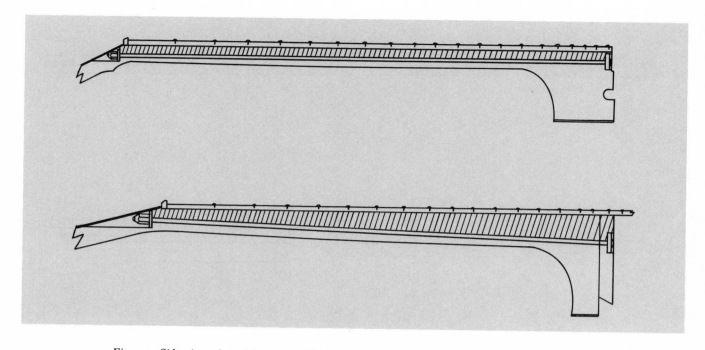

Fig. 94—Side view of straight-type rod laid in banjo and guitar neck. This rod must be laid as deep as possible to perform properly. Shaded area shows hardwood filler over rod.

braze them, make sure you get a good penetration with the brass so it will hold.

By using drill rod instead of the mild steel used originally, we have a much tougher set up. The drill rod is easily machined or threaded, but it will take much more tension because it is a high-carbon steel.

Slip the assembled rod assembly back into the neck, reglue the fingerboard (if partially removed), and adjust the rod to the proper tension.

The other main type of tension rod works by tightening the rod against the wood of the neck itself rather than another rod. There are two schools of thought here on how the rod should be laid in. Some say to lay it in straight, and others say to put a curve in the rod. I vote for the curve, myself.

The straight rod will work if it is properly laid in place. If the rod is laid deep enough so that approximately 90 per cent of the wood of the neck is between the top of the rod and the bottom of the strings, it will work. This rod operates just like the tension of the strings. The strings try to pull the neck upward by collapsing the wood slightly at the upper surface of the neck, and the straight tension rod works by trying to do the same to the wood at the back of the neck. In fact, the straight rod would work better if it were outside the back of the neck about the same distance as the strings are from the fingerboard. If the rod is not laid deep enough, all it does is to try to collapse the whole neck on itself. The older Goya steel-string models used the straight rod setup with a multi-piece laminated neck, and I had one in for repairs a few years back that had literally sprung apart, bulging the laminations outward on each side, from over-tightening the rod.

This type of rod is perhaps used most successfully on banjo necks, as they are usually of about the same depth the full length of the neck, and the rod can be laid in a groove routed to within about ⅛" of the back of the neck. The rod is waxed carefully to keep it free and is set in the groove with a hardwood filler glued over the top of the rod and trimmed flush with the fingerboard surface.

On the guitars, however, setting the rod to within an eighth of an inch of the back of the neck is a little more difficult, as a guitar neck is almost invariably thicker as it approaches the heel. The rod would have to be laid on a slant to keep the proper ratio of wood between the pull of the rod and that of the strings.

On the banjo, the strings are rather light and little tensioning of the rod is needed to keep the neck straight. On the guitar, however, this is a different matter. With

114

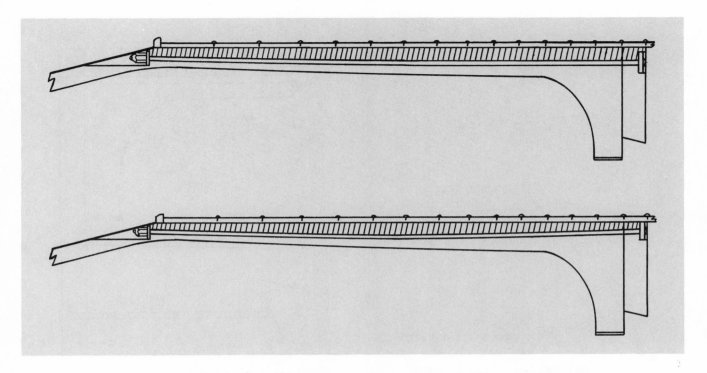

Fig. 95—*Top: This drawing shows rod curved up at the head end of the neck. This setup may be set up to adjust at either end. Bottom: This drawing shows rod curved up at both ends. Adjustment is at head on this one. This very sensitive setup is especially good for the long, slender necks, such as the extra-long-neck folk banjo or Greek Bouzouki.*

six or more heavier strings, it takes quite a hefty amount of tightening to counteract the pull of the strings.

I would rather take advantage of the curved rod setup, as it requires much less tension to operate and doesn't tend to crush the wood as the straight rod does. The principle this rod works on is very simple. The neck of the guitar, as mentioned earlier, gets thicker as it nears the body. Most, if not all, of the natural stress warpage occurs from near the midpoint of the neck out towards the head. Lay the tension rod fairly deep into the neck at the body, run it straight until near the midpoint of the neck, where a gradual upward curve is started, resulting with the rod being around $\frac{3}{16}$" shallower near the nut than at the midpoint of the neck. A hardwood filler is glued in over the well-waxed rod, as before with the straight rod.

Now, as for the operation, imagine that we can lay a straight line from the center of this rod at the butt end of the neck to the center of the rod at the nut end of the neck. There will be a curve hanging below the line. Since the rod is fixed at both ends and is solid in the neck with the filler glued above it, the line of stress would be in this imaginary line drawn from one end of

the rod to the other. If this were the straight rod, this would be so, but not with the curved rod. Instead of trying to compress the wood, the curved rod, when tightened, merely shortens the rod by pulling the curve out of the rod, forcing the belly or low point of the rod up and pulling the high point down. Since we actually have a high point at each end of the rod with the curve, it will affect the point of least resistance, or the weaker end where the bow normally occurs. We, in effect, get a much more sensitive adjustment with a very large reduction in the tension required to do the job.

On a very long, slender neck, such as an extra-long-necked five-string banjo, or in, as I had an opportunity to do a couple of times, renecking a Greek bouzouki, a variation of the bowed rod may be used. As these necks are very near the same depth below the fingerboard for the greater portion of the neck, the rod may be made a bit more sensitive by setting the rod high at both the butt end and the nut end of the neck with the rod dropping about $\frac{3}{16}$" lower in the middle of the neck.

I prefer, when installing a tension rod in a guitar not previously set up with an adjustable rod, to install the rod in such a way as to retain the original appearance. In

115

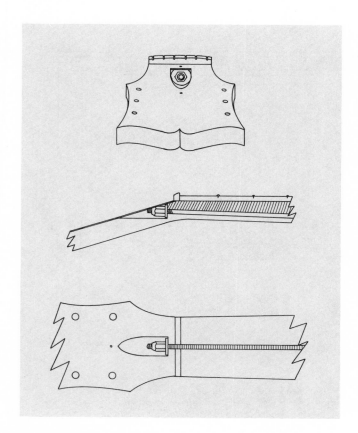

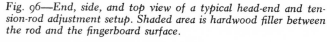

Fig. 96—End, side, and top view of a typical head-end and tension-rod adjustment setup. Shaded area is hardwood filler between the rod and the fingerboard surface.

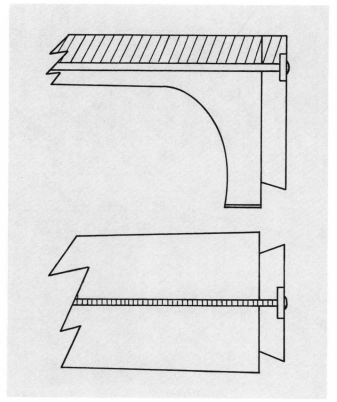

Fig. 97—Anchor set at butt end of neck for head adjustment setup. Anchor does not have to be set all the way to the butt of the neck. It may be set satisfactorily two or three inches up the neck in a slot similar to the hidden rod anchor setup.

other words, I bring the adjustable end of the rod out under the face of the instrument just far enough down to clear the struts to allow slipping a socket wrench on the nut. This setup is almost invisible, except to a mirror, and does not weaken the head by making a large cutout on an instrument that was not designed to have a cutout there.

On the guitars I make once in a great while, I am setting the adjustment into the butt of the neck far enough that I can slip the neck into the dovetail slot and it will clear the block. A measurement is made from the top surface of the neck (less fingerboard) to the center of the tension rod setup, and this measurement is transferred to the inside of the dovetail slot, measuring down from the face of the instrument and centering the measurement with the neck. If a ⁵⁄₁₆" O.D. nut is used (normal outside measurement for #10 x 32 thread brass adjustment nuts), a ½" hole is drilled through the neck block, centered on this measurement. If a different O.D. nut is used, the hole must be drilled to the proper size to

admit the socket used to adjust the nut. This setup may be used if you have the neck out of the guitar you are working on, but it is easier to run the rod on through the neck block if the neck is not to be removed. The hole should be drilled on a slight angle downward through the block so a wrench may be slipped over the nut.

The drawings will give you a better picture of the various setups and how they are laid into the necks.

If you are rodding a neck that has a solid or non-adjustable type reinforcement, the first task after removing the fingerboard is to get the reinforcement out. Most of these are bedded in glue or epoxies of some sort. The easy way to remove these is to lay some square-steel key stock (available at your local hardware store) on top of the reinforcement and set your electric iron on top of the key stock. The heat will usually soften things up enough so that the reinforcement may be removed by prying around on it with a couple of screwdrivers. The key stock transfers the heat to the metal reinforcement without heating the wood surrounding it too much, as

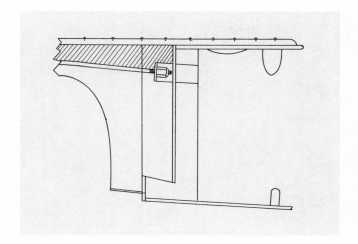

Fig. 98—*Hidden adjustment setup installed while neck is removed. Nut is sunk into dovetail of neck and neck block is drilled to receive wrench. Notice that rod curves down slightly starting at curvature of heel. This is to allow adjustment wrench to clear struts. See tension rod chapter. Shaded area is hardwood filler over rod.*

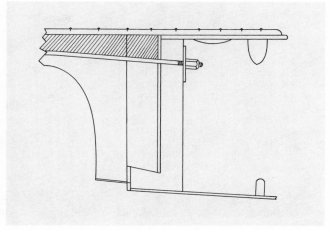

Fig. 99—*Easiest way to install hidden rod setup with neck in body is to run the rod on through neck block and heavy metal plate. Adjusts like other setup but requires a shorter extension for wrench. Shaded area is filler over rod.*

would be the case if the iron were set directly on the wood.

Of course, if you are removing a broken tension rod, you will have to chisel out the wooden filler above the old rod. Work carefully here, trying not to remove any wood on either side of the filler, but only the filler itself.

In the case of the broken standard tension rod, we need merely replace the rod using the existing slot and installing a new filler over the new rod.

In the case of the solid-type reinforcement, after removing it, we have to glue in a piece of hardwood to replace it and then rout out the proper width and depth slot for the new rod setup.

A special guide jig may be made (see special tool chapter) to allow the use of a common router not only to cut the proper width slot, but also to cut the proper contoured depth. The only thing that has to be done is to clean out the end of the slot for the anchor on the end of the rod. This anchor should be at least ½" square and ³⁄₁₆" thick so the end of the rod may be threaded into the anchor and bradded on the end to prevent its screwing back out. I drill a .150" diameter hole in the anchor and tap to a #10 x 32 thread. I then chase a #10 x 32 thread die down the anchor end of the rod slightly over ³⁄₁₆" so that when the anchor is screwed on the rod, the rod protrudes about ¹⁄₃₂". Using a ball-peen hammer, I peen the end of the rod so it is locked solid to the anchor. It can be brazed or welded if you like.

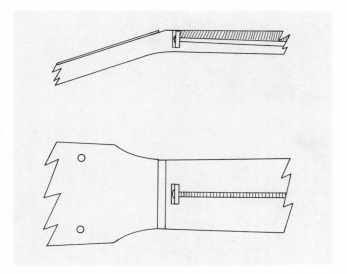

Fig. 100—*Side and top view of anchor for the hidden-rod setup. Shaded area is hardwood filler over rod.*

The other end of the rod should be threaded for around one inch with a #10 x 32 die. The rod I use is a ³⁄₁₆" diameter drill rod. Again I mention the fact that using drill rod gives a much stronger setup than the cold rolled steel rod and is available in 36" lengths at almost any industrial supply company. It is also relatively inexpensive.

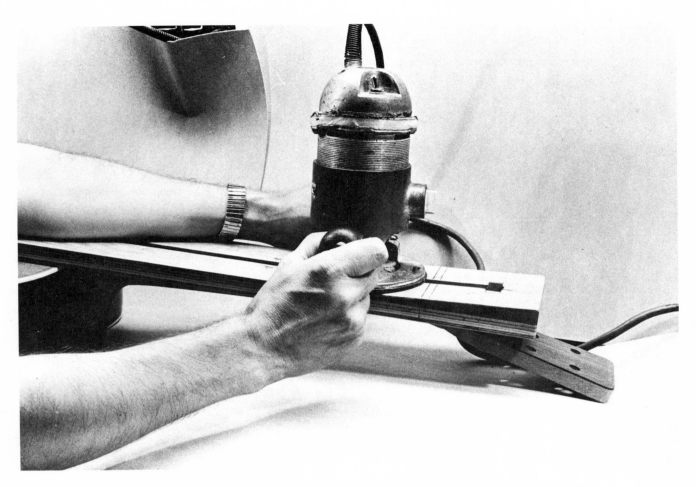

Fig. 101—Routing out the tension-rod slot with router and contoured slot jig screwed to the neck.

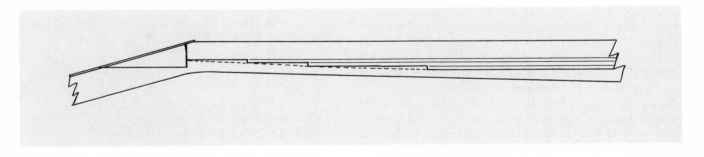

Fig. 102—A simpler version of the tension-rod jig can be made without the contoured bottom provision. The contour can be obtained by step cutting the neck at different depth settings and area designated by the dotted line cut out with a wood chisel to provide the proper slot bottom curvature.

As for finding the nuts, lots of luck. I was lucky, as one of my customers had access to a single-spindle screw machine (automatic lathe) and made me a double handful of the nuts. They can be made of $\frac{5}{16}$" brass hexagon stock, drilled and tapped for a #10 x 32 thread. It is preferable to make the nuts of brass since it is a different metal than the rod. By using dissimilar metals for the nut and rod, we practically eliminate any problems of the two rusting or corroding together, making adjustments difficult or impossible.

The job of installing a tension rod is not for a rank amateur, but with proper care, it can be done. I would suggest trying your first installation on a cheapie, so if you do mess it up you aren't in bad trouble.

I have designed the hidden rod setups for a couple of different guitar companies, one of which is using the design and the other is currently market-testing the idea.

One more thing about the installation of the rod. The wooden filler should be made of a good hardwood, such as maple, walnut, or other wood of comparable density. I also shape the bottom of the filler close to the required contact edge of the filler. This makes for a good fit and when the rod is waxed and the filler and rod are set in the neck with epoxy, the only movement of the rod will be the small amount of shortening done in pulling the curve out with the tightening of the nut.

After the setup is glued in and the fingerboard reglued, there is another step I feel should be done before re-fretting the instrument. The initial adjustment of the rod can sometimes be a little erratic, so I adjust a small amount of pre-tensioning into the rod, giving the neck a slight backward bow. I then true and refret the board with my usual technique. The adjustment of the rod from then on is done the normal way.

These two subjects are very closely related. The setting of the intonation, or the ability of a guitar to note out properly, is a process of elimination. One of the very first things to check when a customer brings you a guitar that will not play in tune is the strings. Strings start aging the minute they are put under tension. They will vibrate only so long before metal fatigue starts developing, actually changing the molecular structure of the metal. With this change in structure and the acidity of the sweat of the human body affecting the string from the outside also, they lose their ability to perform properly. The harmonics change and corrosion and rust build up in the windings and make it impossible to tune properly or to play in pitch. This is why you have so much trouble tuning when you install one new string with a set of old strings. It is better in the long run to change the whole set if they have quite a bit of playing on them.

The lighter the gauge of the string, the quicker it wears out also. Some of the extra light rock and roll strings (.008" first string) are good for only a few hours playing before needing replacement. I have seen the first strings of these sets go dead with six to eight hours playing on them. One quick way to check for this is to fret the string at the twelfth fret and then hit the harmonic over the twelfth fret. If it is quite a bit flatter when fretted, the string is gone. I have seen the lighter gauge strings almost a half tone flat at the twelfth fret. Look at it this way. If you were that skinny and were shaken and twisted around that much, you would get tired too.

If the frets are in good condition, the neck is properly adjusted, the strings are new, the action is correct, and the guitar still does not note out properly, the one thing left to check out is the bridging.

Fret the first string at the twelfth fret and then check the harmonic over the twelfth. They should be almost exactly the same. When fretted, it should sound just the smallest bit sharper than the harmonic. Check the sixth string this way also. I may get some argument about this

slight sharpness, but in checking with the Conn Strobotuner, this is the best compromise I have come up with.

If, when checking at the twelfth fret, the strings are sharp, the scale is short and the distance between the nut and bridge should be lengthened. If flat at the twelfth fret, the distance should be shortened.

A certain amount of correction can be made by shaping the bridge saddle differently. In other words, leading the string off the back edge of the bridge saddle or vice versa. If this doesn't do the trick, the bridge must be reworked or replaced with one that has a properly located saddle.

Perhaps I better stop here and explain some of the whys and wherefores of bridge saddle configurations. You may have noticed that on most nylon-string guitars, that the bridge saddle sets at a 90° angle to the strings, whereas most steel-string guitars have the saddle slanted, with the bass strings being longer than the treble. Some models have individually adjustable saddle pieces for each string, as do most electric guitars. The whole idea is compromise. No fixed tuning instrument can be set to where it will note out perfectly. The only so-called perfect instruments are your non-fretted instruments such as those of the violin family. The frets, not being movable, force us to compromise. An instrument may be set up to where it notes out mathematically perfect, but this sounds unpleasant to the human ear. To sound right, the notes are very slightly sharper as we go up the scale and flatter as we go down the scale. Piano tuners run into this when working with the octave range of the piano. Mathematically perfect tuning makes a terrible sounding piano. if you have ever watched a piano tuner at work, you may have noticed that he tunes certain strings with a tuning fork and starts playing chords, tuning the other strings of the chord to where they sound right to the ear.

What we do with a guitar is to try to get the string to play a note on pitch when played open and on the same note when fretted at the first octave or twelfth fret. If you have ever measured the distance from the nut to

Fig. 103—The Conn Strobotuner. Electronic strobe used for tuning and custom bridge work, etc.

the twelfth fret and the distance from the twelfth fret to the bridge, you will notice that the latter distance is longer. Theoretically, the twelfth fret, or octave fret, should be exactly half way between the nut and bridge saddle, but in actual practice is not. We have to make the distance from the twelfth fret longer to allow for the amount the string is sharped when it is pushed down to the fret during playing.

On nylon strings, the treble and bass strings sharp out pretty much the same, hence the straight saddle usually found on these.

On steel strings, the bass strings sharp out considerably more than the treble strings, hence the slanted saddle. This slanted bridge saddle is, at best, a compromise also. When the first string is set right on and the bass E, or sixth string, is right on, the second string will be sharp slightly, the third string will be slightly flat, the fourth string will be close, and the fifth string will be very close.

By the way, on the rock and roll sets, the third, or G-string, is usually unwound and will be sharp like the second, or B-string, instead of flat like the wound G-string. The only way around this, other than compromise tuning, would be to set each string individually. On the bridges with an adjustment for each string we can do this easily, but on the fixed bridges there are problems.

Even different gauges and different brands of strings change the requirements needed to make the guitar note out properly. The same gauge string in a different brand may be different, owing to the different metallurgical composition of the different brands of wire used. Confusing? Sure is.

As a result, in making production-model guitars, a compromise has to be reached, as the factories cannot possibly bridge for every combination of strings and actions desired. If a closer setting is required for an individual, it is up to him to have this done on his own.

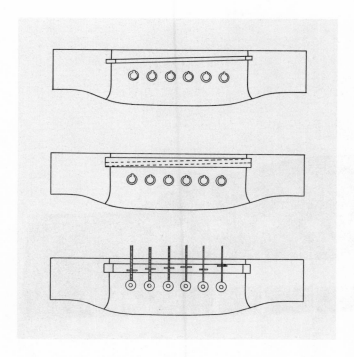

Fig. 104—Top: Top view of Martin style bridge with compromise slanted saddle. Center: Same type of bridge cut with wide saddle slot to set up fully compensated saddle. Dotted line shows the original location of the original saddle slot. Bottom: Bridge with temporary wooden saddle in place and movable pieces under each string to determine proper location. Actual location will probably resemble this drawing.

I have found an invaluable tool for setting individually adjustable bridge saddles and custom bridging of any type of instruments. I find it extremely useful in stringing twelve-string guitars, actually cutting the time involved by a good half. This tool is made by the Conn Organ Company and is called a "Strobotuner." It is an electronic strobe, set up to measure the frequencies of all twelve notes in the musical scale just by changing a twelve-position switch. It can be used with either a microphone, which is included with the instrument, or by using a patch cord, may be plugged directly into the pickup system of an electric guitar. It has a gain control, so when it is plugged into the pickup system, you can cut the value down to prevent overdriving the strobe. I just adjust the gain to get a good black reading on the strobe dial. The tone control on electric guitars should be set in the middle range, usually the number five marking on the control pot. My Strobotuner paid for itself in three months time just setting electric guitar bridges.

The procedure for setting the individually adjustable bridge is relatively simple. The strings should be in good condition, the action right, and the guitar fairly close in tune. I start with the first and sixth string and set the "C" marker on the note selecter switch (the guitar is considered a C-range instrument except in the case of the twelve-string tuned down two frets, when it becomes a B-flat instrument) on the "E" position. I adjust the string until the strobe stands still. I then fret it at the twelfth fret and adjust the bridge piece until the strobe stands still there. If the strobe is spinning towards the sharp side when fretted at the twelfth fret, I lengthen the string slightly, and if it is spinning towards the flat side, I shorten the string slightly. Adjust until the strobe stands still when the string is played both open and when fretted at the octave. Do this on all the strings, switching the dial to the proper note for each string.

Another thing the strobe will do is pinpoint a string that is going bad or one that has gone. You will notice that the dial has several bands denoting seven different octaves marked on it. You will get several readings on different bands as the strobe picks up harmonics and overtones. The reading you use is the dark one nearest the center of the dial. The other readings will be moving slightly at times when the main one is still. When you get the main band standing still and one of the other bands spinning sharp and maybe a third band spinning flat, shut her down and put on new strings. This little trick helps stop arguments with customers as to whether they need new strings or not. You can set them down and show them.

You won't find any of this information on guitars with the instruction booklet that comes with the Strobotuner, but I have learned it by experience. With practice, the Strobotuner is invaluable as a tool and is also very impressive to your customers.

I use the Strobotuner in making custom non-adjustable bridges for flat-top guitars. With the proper care, a compensated saddle can be made that will cause each string to note out very closely all the way up the neck. Before you start the new bridge, the string action and the brand and gauge of string to be used has to be set up to satisfy the customer. Impress on him that changing the gauge or brand of string may throw the compensation off. After he has decided that the action is satisfactory and has selected the flavor of strings, we can go ahead with the custom bridge.

In setting up a custom bridge, compensated for all the strings on a standard type bridge, I make a new bridge from scratch. We will use the predetermined height of action decided on as the basis for the height for the new bridge.

The first thing to do now is to locate the saddle position of the first and sixth strings. The best way of doing this, I have found, is to install a temporary tailpiece, clamping it on the butt of the guitar with a cam clamp

Fig. 105—Closeup of a completed compensated bridge saddle.

and padding things carefully so you don't damage the finish. Run masking tape along the line where the front edge of the bridge should be. Cut a block of wood the thickness of the bridge to be, less the diameter of a nail that we will cut into short pieces to simulate the bridge saddles. Set the block into position with the front edge located along the edge of the masking tape marking the front edge location of the new bridge and tape it into position with a couple of strips of tape across each end. Install the first and sixth string and tune up to pitch. Set a couple of the cut off pieces of nail on the bridge, one under each string, and roll them back and forth under the string until the string notes out on the Strobo-tuner when played in the open position and when fretted at the octave or twelfth fret. This will give the location of the saddles for two strings which will be enough to

lay out the new bridge. Measure carefully from the front edge of the bridge to the center of the nails with the vernier calipers and transfer this measurement to the new bridge blank.

I design the new bridge for a saddle slot of around ¾₁₆" to ¼" wide. I cut this slot so that the first string location is ¹⁄₃₂" from the front edge of the wide saddle and the sixth string is ¹⁄₃₂" from the back edge of the new saddle. Cut the saddle slot and finish out the bridge and glue it on. We are now ready for the next step.

Make a temporary saddle of hardwood, preferably of ebony, about .018" lower than the height needed. Cut short pieces of an .018" (this diameter is unimportant so long as the total height of the temporary saddle and string are right) unwound string such as a heavy-gauge B-string, install a new set of strings, and tune up to pitch

Fig. 106—Drilling the bridge pin holes in the new bridge blank using the old bridge as a pattern to insure the proper hole spacing.

with the short pieces of string under each string. Using the Strobotuner again, move the short pieces of wire back and forth under the string just like you were doing with the individually adjustable bridge pieces. When you get each piece properly located under its respective string, make a measurement with the vernier calipers from the front edge of the saddle to the center of each piece of wire and write the measurement down.

If you can find ivory or bone wide enough to make a one-piece saddle, consider yourself lucky. Otherwise, sandwich two or three saddles together with epoxy to make the new saddle. Trim to the proper height and

top configuration and lay out your measurements on the new saddle. Using a small vise and files, slant the ivory away from the markings in front and behind for each string. The result will be a somewhat staggered top on the saddle and, by your working carefully and blending the edges, it can be made to look very neat. The main thing is that the intonation will be great.

I have made quite a few of these bridges and the results have been highly satisfactory. Perhaps the most spectacular improvements can be had with the twelve-string guitar. Talk about a job, though!

On the average twelve-string guitar with the standard

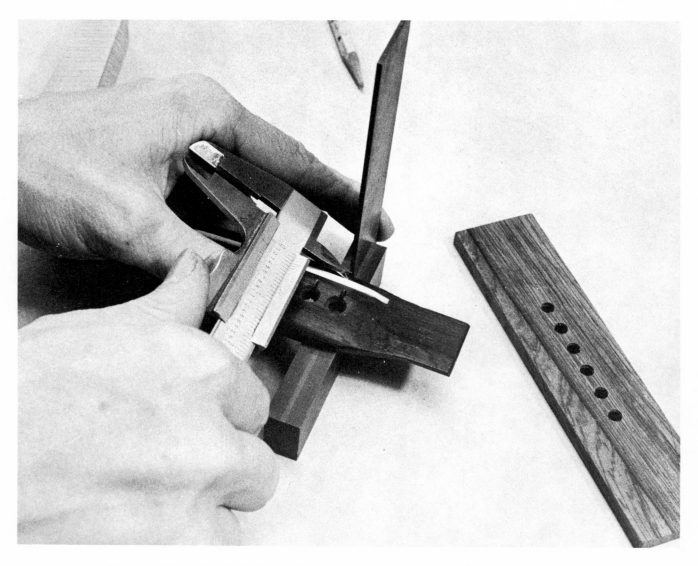

Fig. 107—*Measuring the bridge saddle location from the front edge of the bridge using the calipers and master square.*

slanted saddle, you have inherent problems. The bridge is slanted to favor the heavier strings, and the octave strings, being half the diameter, need to be shorter to note out properly. As you go up the neck, the octave strings start going flat and are consequently out of tune. With a fully compensated bridge in proper tune, the result is a harpsichord-like sound all the way up the neck. This is particularly great for recording purposes, as it seems to project much better and records exceptionally well.

I am not going to get into the making of bridges of all kinds too far, as anyone getting into this business seriously should be able to figure out some things for themselves. The available books on guitar making show very well how to make the classic or nylon-string, tie-type bridge. Most of these can be made with simple saws and hand tools and a drill for the string holes.

Making a bridge for a steel-string instrument is a little more involved. We have a slanted saddle to contend with and usually a curvature to match the curvature of the fingerboard also. On the Martin and Gibson as well as some of the other guitars, we have a curved back or front configuration also.

When replacing a bridge, I try to determine the

Fig. 108—*Transferring the saddle measurements to the new bridge blank using the depth measuring end of the calipers and steel rule.*

proper height beforehand so I have something to work with. Use the old bridge as a pattern if possible, as this simplifies the spacing of the pin holes and the shape of the bridge. The new bridge blank should be cut to such a thickness that the saddle will protrude at least ⅛" and not more than ³⁄₁₆" above the wood of the bridge top. You can settle for less if absolutely necessary, but higher than ³⁄₁₆" puts undue stress on the wood and can even warp the ivory saddle.

After cutting the wooden blank to thickness, clamp the old bridge to the blank with a couple of small spring clamps and, using a ¹³⁄₆₄" drill bit, drill the new holes

using the original holes for the spacing pattern.

The next step is laying out and cutting the saddle slot. I set a square under the old bridge and butt the edge of the square against the front of the bridge to measure from. Take a measurement at the first and sixth string location, measuring from the edge of the square to the edge of the old bridge saddle (see photo) and lay this measurement off on the new bridge blank.

I then set the blank down on the edge of my workbench and slant the blank so that I get the same distance from the edge of the slot layout to the edge of the workbench. I then set up my Dremel with the #199

Fig. 109—*Using the Dremel with router base and saw blade to cut the new saddle slot with the blank clamped to the workbench and guiding from the edge of the workbench so that the proper angle on saddle slot is obtained.*

saw blade and the router base. The blank is held to the bench by a couple of spring clamps and, using the bench edge as a guide for the router base, I saw the first cut along the laid out line on the bridge blank. I then re-adjust the Dremel to make another cut behind the first one to make the slot wide enough to accept the piece of ivory I am using for the saddle. After the slot is cleaned out and wide enough for a thumb-press fit with the saddle, you are ready for the next step.

Using the old bridge again as a pattern, mark the out-line of the back or front curvature and bandsaw off the excess.

The next step is to thin down the ends and radius

from the thin part up to the thicker center section. On some bridges, this is a square corner, but on most of the steel-strings, though, it is a radius. I have made an attachment that makes a small thickness sander out of my belt sander. I have an adjustable and removable table that sets under the end of the sander. The table adjusts (see special tool chapter) up under the end roller of the belt so I can thin the end of the bridge down to the proper thickness. The round roller leaves a nice radius, matching that of the Martin bridge nicely.

The rest of the shaping may be done by hand-holding the bridge blank and using the belt and disc sander, keeping the old bridge handy for comparison purposes.

Fig. 110—*Trimming contoured edge on the bridge blank with the band saw.*

With a little practice, you will be able to duplicate just about any type of bridge.

In case you have trouble locating rosewood or ebony to make bridges, Vitali Import Company sells extra-thick ebony fingerboards (rough, unfinished) that can be used, each board making several bridges. I recommend using only ebony or rosewood or members of the rosewood family for bridges, as they are very strong and resonant woods and can handle the stress requirements needed.

When we have the new bridge made and ready to install, the next step is to decide on the clamping setup to use. There are several setups and jigs in use, but I

have had some problems with some of them. I will cover the system that I use for regluing bridges that have come off as well as gluing on new bridges, as I use the same system for both.

On regluing old bridges, the first step is removing the old glue and, the one thing that almost all old bridges need, flattening the bottom or contact surface. This is best done with a medium or coarse-grit belt on the belt sander, but can be done by hand scraping or sanding. Clean off any glue left on the top of the guitar also.

One of the difficult steps of gluing on a bridge is to prevent it from moving around while clamping. I have several sizes of polished brass pins that I simply insert

Fig. 111—Using the belt sander to finish cleaning the contoured edge on the bridge blank.

in the first and sixth pin holes of the bridge until I find two snug pins, which, when inserted after the glue application, will keep the bridge from shifting. I next place the bridge in position, without glue, and set the two alignment pins in place. I then tape around the bridge with masking tape. On the curved Martin types, I run two strips of tape, one close to the curve and another under the curved area, overlapping the first strip slightly. I then take the X-acto knife with the polished rounded point mentioned earlier and trim the tape, leaving a few thousandths of an inch clearance for the glue to squeeze out. If you get the tape too close, the glue can squeeze

out under the tape, defeating the purpose of the tape.

For clamping the bridge, I use three of the wooden cam clamps. For the X-strutted tops, the center clamp should have a block about ¾" thick taped on the bottom contact point so the clamp will clear the struts. The two outside clamps will ride with their cork tips on the struts themselves and need no blocking. On the classic or ladder-strutted models, all three of the clamps need the clearance blocks.

On the top of the bridge under the center clamp, I set a block with a slightly rounded top, since the top of the bridge isn't usually flat and this allows the clamp

Fig. 112—Using the belt sander with thickness sander attachment to radius thin part of the bridge into the thicker center of the bridge. See special tool chapter.

to select a spot on the curvature where it wants to set when tight. On each end of the bridge, I set a block about ¾" square. These blocks spread the clamping stress evenly over the thin area of the bridge. They also give you some clearance to get your glue spatula in to clean the squeeze-out off onto the tape. If you wax the non-contact surfaces of the bridge, the cleanup of any glue left there is simplified.

After the clamps are in place and tightened, be sure to pull your alignment pins out. This isn't too critical with metal pins, but if you used wooden pins, you will have to drill them out.

By using the three clamps for holding the bridge down, you are assured of getting a good solid contact for the whole area of the bridge, and the bridge stays flat with the top.

What kind of glue to use? If I have a good flat contacting surface, I use Titebond, but if things are pretty rough, with splinters and chips missing from the spruce top, I use epoxy. This will fill up any missing chips or splinters and insure a full contact between the bridge and top for better sound conduction.

By the way, I discussed the use of alignment pins for a pin-type bridge, but the classic or tie-type bridge has

Fig. 113—*New Bridge is held in position with pins while taping off. Run tape under contoured part and trim with X-acto knife so tape under bridge may be removed.*

no pins. Now what? Remember the trick with the hay wire to align fingerboards? Well, just remove the bridge saddle, drill a ⅟₁₆" hole in the bottom of the saddle slot near each end and insert waxed pins cut from the hay wire. This stops all sliding around while clamping, and when you are finished, the saddle will hide the tiny holes from view.

After the glue has cured, remove the clamps and the masking tape. You should have a small line of glue to clean up with a sharp chisel around the bridge. Any glue up on the edge of the bridge itself should clean right up if you waxed the bridge before gluing. Take a small

artist's brush and some clear lacquer and run a fine line of lacquer around the bridge to seal off the glue line. If you got a really clean job, the last step isn't really necessary, particularly if you used epoxy, since it is unaffected by humidity and needs no sealing.

If the bridge was a classic bridge, pull the aligning pins, set in the saddle and string it up. If it is a pin type bridge, there is more work to be done. Take the ¹³⁄₆₄" drill bit and drill the excess glue out of the pin holes. Take the #3 taper pin reamer and ream the holes out to where the head of the bridge pins will seat down to where the bottom shoulder of the head is level with the

Fig. 114—*Clamping setup for the bridge with three cam clamps and blocks. Notice that pins are removed after the clamps are in place and excess glue is cleaned out on the tape.*

top of the bridge. Take your countersink and chamfer the top of the pin holes slightly. This makes a neat looking job.

Take a fairly large straight-sided dental burr and the Dremel without the router base and clean out the string slots. The next step I consider pretty important. On most factory guitars, the string slot is cut straight up and down. The string makes an abrupt bend as it comes out of the string slot and angles towards the bridge saddle. This almost square bend can cause string breakage at times, and it also tends to concentrate the pull of the strings in one area across the bridge. This can cause the

bridge to split between the string holes and, if the bridge saddle is very low, can result in a shallow angle of attack where the strings meet the bridge saddle. This can lead to a low tension over the saddle and to wear from string movement and sometimes a mushy kind of sound. I have found a noticeable improvement in tonal qualities if the strings meet the saddle at about a 30° to 45° angle of attack.

Take the Dremel and burr and work the top of the string slot in a smooth radius towards the bridge saddle. The string, when coming over the smooth radius rather than the abrupt corner, spreads its stress over more wood,

133

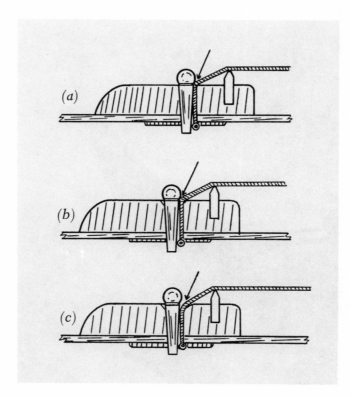

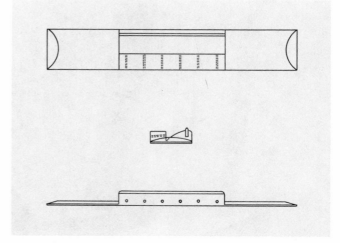

Fig. 116—*Top, end, and back view of typical classic or flamenco-type bridge. Sizes and minor changes in shape and any fancy work depend on the particular application. You will find this type bridge on most Mexican steel-string guitars also.*

Fig. 115—*(a): Typical bridge with no chamfer at top of pin hole. Arrow shows point of potential string breakage because of sharp bend. (b): Bridge with chamfered pin hole. Arrow shows string slot still has sharp edge. (c): Bridge with chambered pin hole. Arrow shows top of string slot radiused with Dremel and large dental burr or with needle file to spread stress over larger area.*

reducing the tendency to split through the pin holes and, when slanted towards the saddle, gives a better angle of attack with more stress concentrated on the saddle itself. It makes sense to me.

Also, on some of the pin-type bridges, the saddles have been cut down very low, and so has the wood sometimes, to lower the string action enough to allow playing. This radius trick will help the tension problem usually run into here by increasing the angle of attack.

On these very low bridges, and particularly with some brands of strings, the windings used to lock the ball-end to the string will pull up too far and end up on top of the bridge saddle. This can cause a bad string action, string breakage from trying to bend the heavy winding, and saddle chipping from the heavy winding catching on the ivory while installing or tuning the string. I cut the ball off an old string and thread the new string through the hole in the old ball and down on top of the winding. When pulled up to the bridge pin for locking purposes, it will lock farther down, preventing the winding from pulling up so far.

On some models of steel-string guitars, particularly the old Kay line, some models of Harmony, and a few others, a pull-through type of bridge is used instead of the pin-type. In cutting some of these down for a proper action, the saddle is cut so low that the angle of string attack is practically non-existent. Most of these, with the exception of the Spanish or Mexican guitars, are ladder-strutted. Remove the bridge, install a bridge plate under the top if it doesn't have one, and make a pin type bridge for it. The change in sound is amazing. You will get a fuller, richer, and much better quality sound in most cases with the change to the pin bridge, and you will have some string tension over the bridge saddle.

Don't try this with the Mexican guitars. In drilling through the top, the chances are you will go up through one of the fan struts, weakening the top. About the only way to help these is to remove the bridge and make a new one with the string holes drilled farther down towards the face of the guitar. I have plugged the string holes with wooden pins and, using a long aircraft drill, re-drilled the string holes without removing the bridge. This is touchy business though, so go easy if you try it.

I have learned a little trick on the Mexican twelve-string guitars, which use the classic-type pull-through bridge, that I think is worthy of passing along. Twelve strings put quite a lot of strain on a fan-strutted top, even with light gauge silk and steel strings tuned down two frets to D-tuning. I install a short six-string tailpiece and run the six octave strings off of the tail piece through the holes in the back of the bridge. I run the standard strings from the bridge normally. This six and six arrangement relieves the rotational stress and the combination gives the guitar the sweetest harpsichord-like sound. I have done this on quite a few Mexican twelve-string guitars, and the results have been excellent in almost every case. The little trick sure did make some happy customers.

For more information on formulae for determining saddle height, etc., see the chapter on string actions.

RATTLES, BUZZES, THEIR CAUSES AND REPAIRS

There are several areas where funny sounding rattles or buzzes may occur. The most common area is in the string action department. If the action is checked and found to be correct with no irregularities in either the frets or neck condition, the next thing to check out would be the bridge area.

Sometimes, during string installation, the string does not pull up all the way and the long end hanging under the face can vibrate against the lower end of the bridge pin. In this case, loosen the string, pull the bridge pin about halfway out, pull the string up until the ball end contacts the taper of the pin, and push it back in. Sometimes the wrappings on the ball end of the string keep the pin from seating properly and the string slot in the bridge may have to be enlarged to correct this. You can check for an improperly seated string by simply slipping a mirror in the sound hole and looking at the bridge plate. The ball end of the string should be pulled up against the bridge plate from underneath. If not, correct it.

Some guitars are made with small bolts with nuts and washers holding the bridge down as well as the glue. These may come loose, causing a rattle that sounds somewhat like a string rattle. If they are very loose, they may be spotted with a mirror, but the best way to check these is to remove the strings and feel for looseness. If they are loose, put a wrench on them.

If the rattle still persists, take your knuckle and thump around lightly over the entire face and back area of the guitar. If you get the rattle in one spot but not in others, check the strutting located under that area. You will probably find either a loose or split strut. If the strut is very loose, you will usually spot a distorted area in the back or top in the area of the split strut.

To glue loose or split struts can be relatively easy if they are not loose all the way. One that has fallen completely off is very difficult to relocate in its proper place and to glue it properly without removing the top or back unless it is close to the sound hole. If it is one of those located towards the butt end of the guitar, I won't even try to do it through the sound hole. You usually end up with a mess and have to pull the back anyway.

On those that are loose just a short distance, I use the hypodermic needle to apply the glue. The spaghetti slipped over the needle insures getting the glue in the proper location under the strut, and using the cam clamps (or a combination of my strut jack and cam clamps in the event the cam clamp alone won't do the job) makes this a relatively minor repair job.

Another cause of vibration can be a top or back crack. Also, check the struts under the cracks, because they often will vibrate loose after the crack has been there for a while without being repaired.

An excellent tool for checking for loose struts may be made from a used X-acto razor saw blade. Cut the blade down to about ⅜" in width by about 3½" long. Wrap tape around one end and grind the other end off to a rounded shape. Either hone on a stone or hit with a cloth buffing wheel and jeweler's rouge to smooth up the edges. The method for using the tool is to slip your hand through the sound hole and attempt to slide the tool under the suspected strut. If it slides under, the strut is loose, and you can move the tool back and forth to determine the amount of looseness. This tool is useful also in spreading the glue injected under loose struts with the hypodermic needle.

Another fairly rare cause for rattles may be a loose pickguard. This sounds like a loose strut while the guitar is being played, but it can be spotted quickly if you tap on the guard with your knuckle. If it is loose, remove and reglue. I prefer a good contact cement such as Weldwood for this job.

A very rare cause can be a loose tension rod, which may be cured by tightening the nut slightly. I also have had one solid-type neck reinforcement vibrate badly. To cure this, I removed a couple of the pearl position markers, one on each end of the neck, drilled down to the

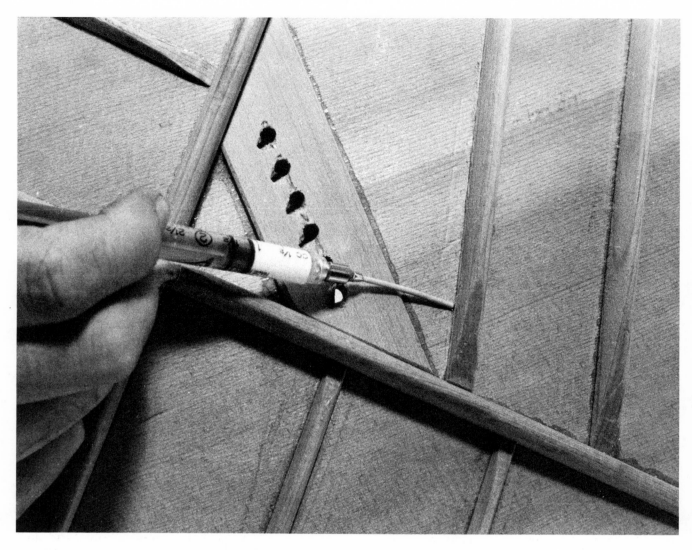

Fig. 117—*Using the sleeved hypodermic needle and syringe to apply the glue under loose or split strut.*

reinforcing bar and injected glue with a needle. No more rattles.

Another rare rattle, but one I am running into more often, is the separation of plies in a plywood top. I have seen this on a couple of new imports and in several cases after impact damage.

Sometimes, these loose plies may be repaired by taking a very sharp, slender-pointed knife and starting a splinter in the affected area. This should go through the first ply, which is usually the loose one. Take a hypodermic syringe filled with Titebond and slip the needle under the first ply and inject as much of the glue as possible under the area. Hold your finger over the entry hole and, using the other hand, work the glue out under

the ply by massaging away from the entry hole. Apply a piece of waxed paper over the entry hole and, using a block and cam clamps, apply pressure to the area. If you are lucky, no more rattles. Just use a damp rag to remove excess glue and touch up.

If one of these plywood tops has been impacted hard enough to knock a hole through it, it is usually better to replace the top or the whole guitar. This type of damage usually starts plies separating in all directions and is very difficult to repair satisfactorily.

CRACKED AND BROKEN PEG HEADS

Most cases of broken or cracked peg heads are caused

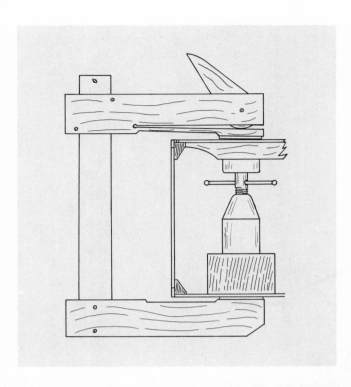

Fig. 118—*Strut jack and block in position inside of guitar with external pressure from cam clamp to pull loose or split strut back into position after injecting glue with hypodermic syringe and needle.*

by impact damage to the head itself. The strings put quite a lot of tension on the area where the head slants away from the fingerboard and the wood grain direction here does nothing to help the strength. The cut for the slant of the head runs angling across the grain in most cases and the result is one of the weak points of the neck. In fact, I have seen guitar heads break off from the shock of slamming them around in a hard-shell case. This is why you should always relax the string tension when shipping a guitar anywhere. I use crushed newspaper to prevent any movement in the case.

A cracked head may be repaired if it is a clean and long crack with plenty of contact area for gluing. If the crack is tight and difficult to expand for applying glue, I go back to the hypodermic syringe and the longest needle I can get. I use my pinvise and a .030" drill bit and drill several holes in the crack, following the direction of the grain as much as possible. The bit will follow the crack pretty well, as it usually is the path of least resistance. The .030" hole is usually a good tight fit for a 21-gauge needle, and you can put quite a bit of pressure down deep in the crack. I inject Titebond until it works out through all areas of the crack and clamp for eight hours, clean up, and touch up.

If the head is broken off completely, a different technique must be used. Usually, there are several small pieces that break off of the area along with the head. These should be saved if possible, because if there is any wood missing, it must be replaced.

Investigate the break carefully. If the contact area is short or the head is broken off square, the success of the repair could be in doubt. In the case of a square break, the end grain usually has a shattered, splintery appearance. Looking at the side of the break will usually show many small cracks in the finish and extending away from the break. In this case, it is almost impossible to do a successful repair. You cannot possibly get glue into every hairline stress crack in the grain, and these are potential weaknesses for it to break again. A re-neck job is in order here.

If it is a clean break with no stress cracks showing, the chances for repairing are fairly good. If on a slant with the grain, the chances of repair are good to excellent.

To repair these jobs, I use epoxy glue dyed to as close a shade as possible to the wood in the area. Use plenty of clamps to get as close and tight a fit as possible.

These breaks slip around quite a bit during gluing and care has to be used to maintain proper alignment until the glue has set.

If the break has split through the flat portion of the head surface, as it usually does, you have the flat surface of the head for alignment purposes. I clamp a flat board with waxed paper over it to one piece (usually the neck side of the break) and apply glue and clamp the other piece on. Sometimes I will use a half-dozen spring clamps and a couple of cam clamps for one of these setups to prevent slippage and to get a close, tight fit. Sometimes I may use a couple of metal pins through the break to keep the alignment until the glue dries. Waxing the pins makes them removable after the glue dries, and you can fill the holes with pegs if necessary.

As each break is usually different to a degree, owing to the difference in the grain pattern and density of the wood used for the necks, I shall have to leave these clamping jigs and setups to your imagination and ingenuity.

After the glue has cured about eight hours, remove the clamps and start the cleanup. If you were successful in lining everything up properly, you can use files to dress the hardened epoxy down to the level of the finish, leaving only a thin line of glue showing.

Next, I either rout or chisel a slot ³⁄₁₆" wide and extending about 1½" on either side of the break. I chisel two of these slots, one·on either side of the tension rod or other reinforcement. I try to make them at least ¼" deep at the shallowest point. I glue a piece of very hard

Fig. 119—*Using a thin spatula (made from used X-acto razor saw blade) to spread glue or also to check for loose struts.*

wood, usually maple, into the slots with epoxy. This gives extra added strength to the joint. Actually, if the glue area is large enough, you can skip the keying of the break. If in doubt, key it.

To hide the keys is the next problem. I usually shade the area in with a little dark finish as mentioned in the finishing chapter. The use of the air brush with a little dark lacquer of the proper shade can do wonders towards hiding one of these breaks.

On the short breaks and shattered necks that people insist on having me repair, I make no guarantees and make sure that they understand that they are having the work done at their own risk. If it breaks again, that is just too bad. I just don't like to do work that I can't put some sort of a guarantee on. Standing behind as much of your work as possible means a lot to your reputation and gives your customer confidence in you.

CRACKS IN FINGERBOARDS

These cracks are usually caused by too much drying out, such as in a low humidity situation. You will also find these cracks on older and antique instruments. Along with the fingerboard cracks, you will usually find the frets protruding on either edge of the fingerboard, owing to shrinkage of the wood through the years. On

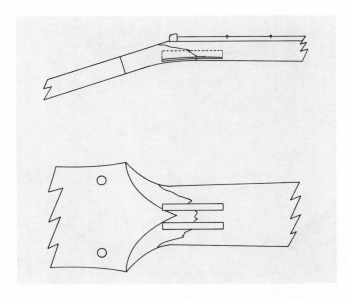

Fig. 120—*Top: Bottom view of repaired broken off head with hardwood reinforcing keys. Bottom: Side view of same. The full lines show top of key shaped to neck contour while shaded area shows key extending through the break on either side for reinforcing strength.*

these jobs, if the frets are in reasonably good condition, they may be dressed off as per instructions in the refretting chapter.

The cracks in the fingerboard may be filled with a glue and sanding dust mixture. I keep small flat tobacco tins full of rosewood, ebony, and several other kinds of sanding dust. This is mixed with epoxy glue and forced into the fingerboard cracks with a small spatula. After it is cured, it can be leveled off with the fingerboard, sanded with the grain, and waxed or oiled. In the event the board was made of ebony, you might not even see the repair after it is handled for awhile.

There is little chance of a fingerboard splitting very far because the tangs on the frets help hold things together and, if further drying out is prevented, the repair should be permanent.

Flattening a Badly Bellied Top

Sometimes, owing to mistreatment usually, the top of a guitar will pull up very badly behind the bridge and cave in between the bridge and sound hole. This is what is called "rotation." In other words, the strings are trying to pull the bridge over towards the sound hole of the guitar, or the bridge is trying to rotate, pulling the top with it.

A certain amount of this rotation is normal. If the top is perfectly flat, it shows that the top is built heavier than may have been necessary or that a heavier gauge string might result in an increase in sound.

This type of top warpage is usually found on the fan-strutted or classic-type guitars and also on the ladder-strutted tops. By ladder strutting, I mean those with the top struts all crossing from edge to edge like the back struts or, in other words, like the rungs of a ladder.

On the badly rotated fan-strutted top, not much can be done except for going to lighter strings or removing the back and adding a couple of more fans to the strutting layout. Or the old fans could be removed and heavier ones could be substituted. This is a major job, though.

On the ladder-strutted tops, a larger bridge plate with the special clamping described later in this chapter can help.

On the X-strutted tops, a different kind of pulling occurs. The whole top bellies up. These tops are built almost perfectly flat but are designed in such a way that quite a bit of this pulling up is normal. In fact, I don't worry much about them unless they are pulled up to about ¾₁₆" above the level of the sides. This usually occurs in older instruments that have been used with too heavy a string or those that have been exposed to too much heat and humidity or a combination of these factors.

I have learned a technique used by one of the factory repair shops for flattening these with the use of a larger bridge plate and a special clamping setup combination. A word of caution here. This technique is pretty touchy and I would not recommend it for the beginner until he understands the guitar a little better. You remember the warning in the disassembly chapter about the grain changing its direction as you cross the center line of the top? Well, this is doubly important here. The bridge has to be removed so the direction of the grain can be determined for sure. This grain direction will be *reversed* when working from the inside of the guitar. A special tool is required to remove the old bridge plate when working through the sound hole.

I heated a fairly thin wood chisel (⁵⁄₃₂" x ¾" thick and wide) to a cherry red, bent it into a hook, and re-sharpened it after re-tempering. A full detailed description will be found in the special tool chapter on making this bridge-plate puller. This puller is inserted into the sound hole along with your hand, remembering the direction of the grain from side to side, and hooked under the original bridge plate. Pry the plate down, working across the plate a small amount at a time. Go back again and hook it under farther. When you get to the center seam of the face, work from the front edge of the plate the same way. Chances are, you will get the plate out in pieces. Be very careful not to hook the tool under a strut,

Fig. 121—*Pulling old bridge plate with specially reworked chisel. Many thanks to the Martin factory repair shop for the idea on this tool and technique.*

as it will pull the strut loose also. If you are afraid to tackle the job blind, you can remove the back for the job. In fact, when using the hook for the first time, it might be a good idea to use it on one you have the back off of, just to get the feel of the tool. I repeat again, it is very easy to tear things up here if you get careless.

The next step after the plate is removed is to check the area with a mirror to make sure you haven't left any of the old plate stuck to the top. Using coarse sandpaper, remove all the old glue so that you have a nice flat area to work with.

The next step is making the new bridge plate. I use a good hard resonant wood for this, rosewood if I can get it, or maybe maple or walnut. The plate should be about $\frac{3}{32}$" to $\frac{1}{8}$" thick and should extend about 2" from the center line of the bridge pin holes towards the butt of the guitar, and about 1" from the center line towards the sound hole. This plate will be rectangular in shape for the ladder-strutted guitars and should be slightly longer than the bridge under where it sits. In some really bad cases, it wouldn't hurt to extend the plate an inch or two longer than the bridge for extra reinforcement.

The larger plate will be five-sided for the X-strutted instrument. It has to be tapered off on each end to clear the legs of the "X" and also cut at the back to clear the tone bar slanted across the belly of the instrument. A

Fig. 122—Reverse clamping the top to flatten out the belly in preparation for installing the larger bridge plate.

relatively easy way to get the fit for the "X" plate is to use a piece of cardboard, trimming a little at a time, until you have a good fit. Transfer the cardboard pattern to the wood to make the plate.

Another real sneaky method to get the angle measurements is to make a small angle square. A couple of pieces of metal or hardboard ⅜" wide and 3" long are used. Drill a hole near the end of the two pieces and rivet the two pieces together tightly enough to make it hard to adjust the two pieces. The ends should be rounded where they are riveted also. To use this gauge, set it up against the struts under the face of the guitar and open or close

the legs of the gauge until they fit the angle wanted. Transfer this onto a piece of cardboard and check the fit until the cardboard fits where the plate will fit and then use the template to make the actual plate. This little angle square saves quite a bit of time in fitting the plates, and if you are used to things, you can lay out the plate without having to make the template. If you goof, though, you have ruined a good piece of wood.

A word on the wood to make the plate. Make sure the grain runs across the grain of the top, or, in other words, the same direction as the wood in the bridge. Also, the grain should be quarter sawn on the wood selected for

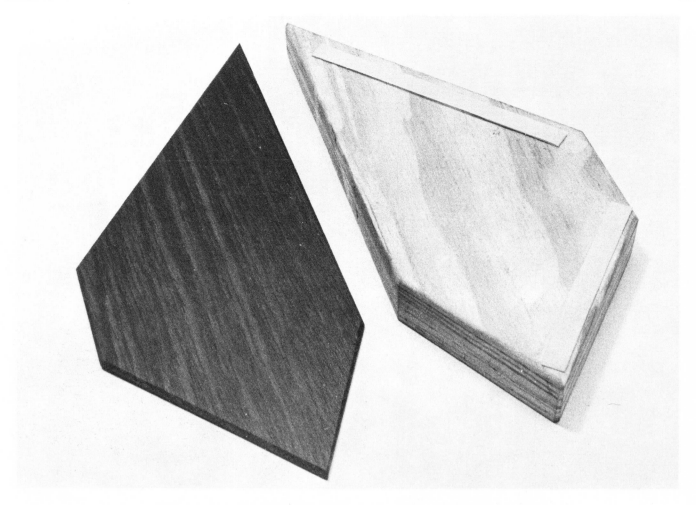

Fig. 123—*New larger bridge plate and clamping block. Notice the tape on the block. This can be double-stick tape or tape folded back on itself.*

Fig. 124—*New bridge plate stuck to the clamping block with the tape.*

Fig. 125—Inside view of the larger plate clamping setup using three cam clamps for maximum contact.

the plate, or, in other words, running up and down at a 90° angle to the top. This is for maximum strength and a cleaner resonance.

Now, we will get into the clamping setup. I have a 1" thick walnut board 20" long and 6" wide. This board has a $\frac{3}{32}$" warp or bow in it. This is placed across the face of the guitar with the bowed side down and clamped at each edge of the guitar with a cam clamp. A piece of waxed paper is used over the pin holes at the bridge area to prevent gluing the board to the top. When the plate is clamped into place, glue will be forced through the bridge pin holes, so be sure and *do not* forget to use the

waxed paper or a piece of thin plastic under the board. The curve of the board forces the face of the guitar into a reversed or concave condition instead of the convex or pulled up condition. A clamping block slightly smaller than the new bridge plate is made and concave curvature, matching that of the curvature in the top board, is sanded into the surface to contact the bridge plate. This clamping block should be at least $\frac{3}{4}$" thick, preferably of plywood, and heavily waxed so any excess glue dripping down on it will not glue it to the plate or nearby struts.

Apply a couple of strips of double-stick masking tape

Fig. 126—*Outside view of the same plate clamping setup. Notice the reverse clamping board in place to flatten the top until the glue dries.*

or fold a couple of pieces of ¼" regular masking tape back on itself and stick the bridge plate to the clamping pad. Insert a cam clamp through the sound hole, apply glue to the contact surface of the new bridge plate, insert through the sound hole into position, and hold it there with one hand. Lift the cam clamp into contact with the other hand and snug it down. Remove your hand from inside the guitar and check the positioning with a mirror. If the plate is in proper positioning, apply the other two clamps as in the photo. Either Titebond or epoxy glue may be used to hold the plate. If you did a

pretty rough job of removing the plate and tore up some wood, or have some splinters missing, it might be a good idea to use epoxy. Otherwise, Titebond will do fine.

Allow this setup to cure for at least eight hours and remove the clamps, clamping pad, and reverse clamping setup. The top should be quite flat. When the bridge is reglued and the string tension is back on the guitar, it should pull up about half of what it was. The larger plate doesn't seem to hurt the sound a bit either.

See the chapter on bridging for bridge gluing techniques.

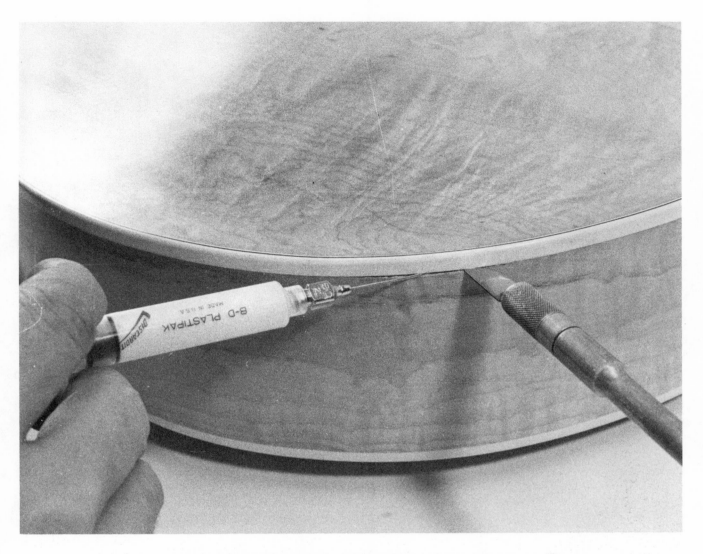

Fig. 127—*Using the hypodermic syringe to inject the glue under the loose edge of the guitar.*

Loose Areas on Backs or Tops

Impact damage to a corner of a guitar may jar an area of a back or top loose from a couple of inches to quite a few inches from the sides. Sometimes, this may be repaired by slipping an X-acto knife or other thin blade under the area and lifting it to where a hypodermic needle can be inserted, injecting glue in the affected area, then clamping back into position. In some cases the binding will have to be removed to get the area opened up to where it may be worked on and then glued afterwards. If it is close to a joint, start there and remove (see chapter on disassembly). If it is quite a ways from a joint, you may want to cut the binding near the place to be glued. When regluing the binding, you will usually be a little short from the shrinkage of the binding. I keep all scraps of binding material I can lay my hands on and can usually find a piece that will match the old binding. Cut and repair with a small piece of this.

Loose Binding Repairs

On some older instruments, or on instruments that have been stripped for finishing carelessly, the binding may be loose at the waist. This can be caused by normal shrinkage of the celluloid through the years or, on strip-

Fig. 128—Using a long bar clamp to pull side into proper position and a spool clamp to insure good bond between side and back.

ping a guitar, allowing the stripper to contact the binding, with the resultant shrinking as the binding dries. Also, extreme heat will sometimes cause the binding to shrink and pull away at any place where there is a concave curve, the waist, a cutaway, etc. Sometimes this can be repaired by strapping the binding with a heavy strap and stretching it back into position while gluing. I haven't had very satisfactory results with this method, though, because in about 50 per cent of the cases, it pulled loose again. I find that it works better to cut the binding, pull it back into position, and insert a scrap of matching binding in the gap. This method removes the stress that caused it to pull away in the first place and is permanent. This gives an extra joint in the binding, but

you don't have to worry about it coming loose again. You can use Titebond, epoxy, or one of the plastic glues such as Duco cement for this job. I generally use Titebond because it is easily cleaned up. Touch up with white India ink and seal over with clear lacquer. You may use white lacquer for hiding also if you like, but they both work well.

CRACKING BETWEEN MACHINE HEAD HOLES

This problem usually occurs on the slot-head models and is rarely found on flat-head models. It is found mostly on the classic guitars with the large-diameter string rollers. The larger diameter holes drilled in the

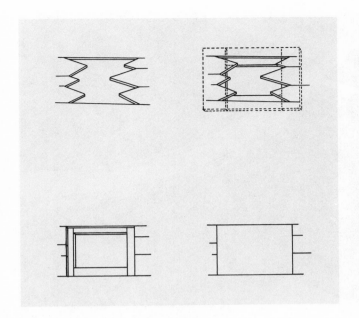

Fig. 129—Top: Left drawing shows impact damage with hole and missing wood. Right shows reinforcements (dotted lines) to prevent further cracking and give backing to patch. Small hole may be backed with solid piece if you want. Bottom: Left drawing shows hole trimmed for patch. Note backup pieces all the way around hole. Right shows patch glued in ready for finishing.

thin sides of the slot heads weaken the wood, and sometimes the screws used to hold the machine heads in place will be a little too tight and start the crack. The best way to cure this is to remove the machine heads, force glue into the cracks, and clamp. After the glue is dry, cut a square hole into the side of the head across the crack. Do this carefully so that the machine head plate will cover the repair. Cut this hole about ⅛" deep and cut a patch to fit with the grain running across the grain of the head. Apply glue and insert the patch and clamp. Apply one of these hidden patches at each area of the crack where an attaching screw for the machine head plate is located. After the glue has dried, trim flush, seal with lacquer, and reinstall the machine heads.

GRAFTING TO FILL DAMAGED AREAS

When getting into guitar repair, you should start a collection of wood scraps of all kinds used in the making of guitars. I have boxes of various kinds of scraps that I have been saving for years. I can usually find a scrap that will match just about any kind of wood I am likely to come into contact with. I also try to lay my hands on badly broken instruments for scraps also. These scraps are useful in grafting impact damage or holes of just about any kind.

Most of the holes to be repaired are from impact dam-

age. I glue cross-patches inside the guitar across the grain at the end of each repair to be done and overlap these into the area to be patched to provide a backup for the new wood to be grafted in. I select a scrap of wood with the color, density, and grain as close to the surrounding wood as possible. I even try to find a patch where the grain ends will match the grain ends of the mating wood. Lay the patch in position and cut around it with a sharp-pointed knife to provide the border for the cut-out. I then set the Dremel depth, using a dental burr and router base, to the thickness of the patch and cut out the wood. Finish trim and fit the patch by hand, using knives or chisels until the patch is a perfect fit all the way around. Dye a small amount of epoxy the color of the surrounding wood (actually a bit lighter as it dries darker), apply the glue to the contacting surfaces, and set into place. Trim the patch flush if necessary, fill, stain, and touch up with air brush or refinish the whole area if necessary. Sometimes, refinishing the whole area is better if the patch is very large, because hiding even small repairs in wood is pretty difficult and big ones can be nasty.

When grafting a curved area of a side, you may have to fire up the bending iron to bend a patch to fit. I try to lay my hands on old wrecked guitars, as mentioned before, to have pre-curved sections of wood for repairing these. If you have to, though, find a piece of wood that matches the section to be replaced, cut it to the proper width, cut it a couple of inches too long to give something to handle it by, soak in water for an hour and bend carefully over a hot bending iron. After it is dry, cut to size and fit as before.

Grafting of tops is the hardest job, because not only do you have to match the grain widths, the slant of the grain lengthwise must be running the same direction as the grain in the top. The spruce is translucent, and if you get the grain running opposite from the top in the patch, the refraction of light from the patch will be different from the surrounding wood, and even if you have matched the grain width and color to a gnat's whisker, when the light hits the patch from the right direction, it will stick out like a sore thumb. I also recommend completely refinishing the top, as this will help in the hiding of the repairs. If the top is broken up very badly, it is better to go ahead and replace it completely.

I will not go into making a new top other than stating that it should be made as close to the original as possible unless a custom job is in the offing. The old top makes a nice pattern if you can get it off intact, and if the old original strutting is in good condition, try to remove it and use it. Study the books on guitar making for making complete tops, backs, etc. These will give you valuable information on selecting woods, edge gluing, etc.

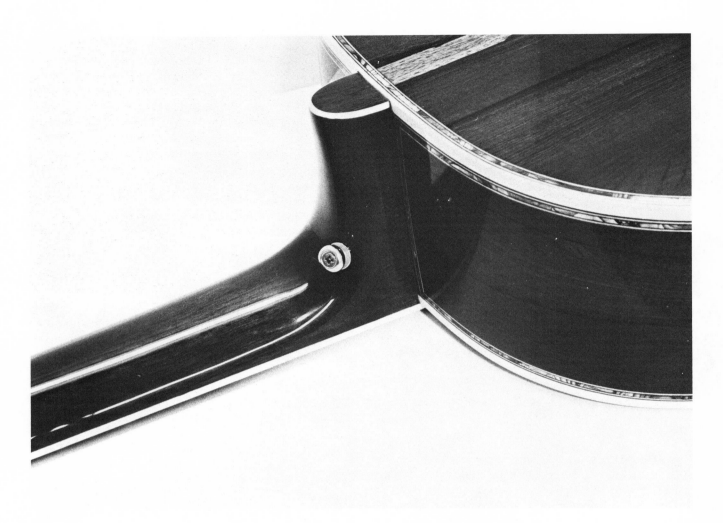

Fig. 130—*Location of strap peg on heel of a guitar. It should be angled slightly towards the treble side of the instrument. Author's personal instrument.*

Strap Pegs

Strap pegs often become loose in their holes, pulling out at the most inopportune times, sometimes with damage to the guitar from bouncing off of things such as the floor, etc. If things are very loose, an oversized peg may be used by reaming the hole larger. A tapered reamer such as the #6 taper-pin reamer can be used for this purpose. A quick and dirty method is a thin piece of paper wrapped around the tapered part of the peg. Another is to scrape around the contact area of the peg with a saw to rough up the surface, apply a few drops of white glue, and insert the peg in the hole to dry. The glue will stick to the wood and dry into the grooves scraped on the plastic surface, holding the peg in place.

On the larger, heavy-bodied guitars, I recommend a strap peg be screwed into the heel of the neck to remove the sideways strain from the neck. I am getting an increasing number of these larger guitars with more bow on one side of the neck than on the other. I have been asking questions and have found out that in around 90 per cent of the cases, a shoulder strap was used that was fastened to the head on one end. This long strap seems to be the logical culprit to blame for this.

In installing a peg in the heel of the neck, a hole should be drilled for the screw angling slightly towards the bottom or treble side of the instrument. The angle is for a reason. When the guitar is played, the neck end of the guitar is higher and if the strap peg is angled down slightly, the strap will have a tendency to pull tighter on the peg rather than slipping off.

The hole should be drilled to reduce the stress in the area where it is applied. I had to repair a cracked neck one time when a guy used an ice pick to start a hole,

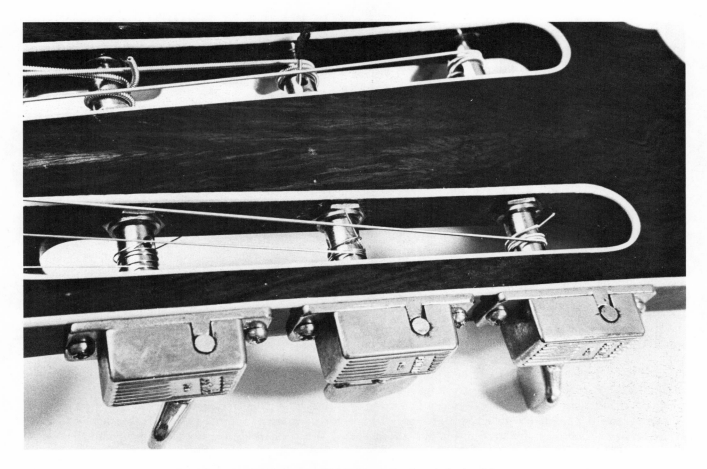

Fig. 131—*Closeup of metal bushings installed inside of the slot of slot head instrument to support the inside end of the machine head shaft. Author's personal instrument.*

then screwed a large screw into the heel, splitting the heel clear through. Check the screw you are going to use to fasten the peg on, and use a drill that is the same diameter as the solid center section of the screw less the threads. When the peg is properly installed, there should be no problems.

Machine Heads

Machine heads are one of the most commonly neglected parts of a guitar. All but the most expensive ones usually have exposed gears where dust can collect. They are seldom, if ever, lubricated and people wonder why they wear out so fast. Also, a large portion of the cheaper guitars, particularly the imports, use such inferior machines that after installing a dozen sets or so of strings, they are virtually useless.

All exposed gear machine should be lubricated about every other set of strings or if new strings are being in-

stalled every couple of weeks or sooner, once a month. If you are using a rapid wind crank in stringing up the guitar, lubricate lightly for every set on the exposed machines. I use a hypodermic needle for this, applying a very small drop of light machine oil such as 3-in-1 or other various brands to each end of the worm at the bearing points and a couple of drops where the worm meets the shaft gear.

Some closed machines such as the Kluson Deluxe, have a small oil hole on the outside cover. These have grease applied at assembly and can use a drop of oil every six months or so. Most of the other closed gear machine heads, such as the Grover Rotomatics or Slimline models and their German competitors, the Schaller line, are sealed in grease for life. I install quite a large number of machine heads, particularly the Grover Rotomatics. I keep the old machines and have acquired quite a large box of used parts. Sometimes, just replacing a missing screw or gear will fix a set of machines, and the junk box is invaluable for this.

Always check the customer's guitar for loose screws and gears on the machine heads. The screw that holds the gear on the string shaft also has the job of maintaining the proper friction to keep the string from going out of tune. If you get the screw too tight, you will ruin the worm and gear and if it is too loose, it will not stay in tune. I tighten the screw tight, loosen it off, and then snug it back down. The knob should turn freely with a small amount of drag. If it is difficult to turn, you either have it too tight or the machine is worn out and binding. You can usually tell if it is binding or galling by looking for small metal flakes coming off the gears. Once this starts, it is time to install a new set of machines.

Installing new machines can be a simple and difficult job at the same time. There are many types of machine heads. Some need larger holes. Others have different pin spacings and having all the machines on one plate would require plugging the holes and redrilling to install. I usually stock a couple of different plates with different pin spacings, one with an American spacing and one with foreign spacings. Again, there are several variations between different brands of machine heads. The simple method is to stock a couple of sets of individual-type machines. On the individual machines, you may have to plug and redrill some of the retaining screw holes, but you don't have the problem with spacing as in the plate types. Some of these will also need drilling or reaming of the pin holes to fit a larger size or a different type of head.

The Grover Slimline model for twelve-string guitar needs very accurate drilling for a proper fit. I had a drilling jig made at a machine shop (see specialty tools) strictly for the purpose of fitting these machine heads. The holes are drilled large enough that when aligned on one of the holes near the center, the larger holes overlap enough to drill out the smaller holes. Grover has allowed enough of this overlap so that few twelve-string holes will have to be plugged. Once in a while you will run into a model that will require plugging of a couple of holes on each side. I run the drill bit on through the side and into the center section deep enough to install a metal bushing in it. This way the machine head is working against metal all the way and receives very little wear and is extremely sensitive for ease of tuning.

This jig may be clamped to the side of a six-string slot-head model and centered on each hole individually to drill for the individual Slimline heads.

For installing the Grover Rotomatics or Schaller machine heads, I use a pair of tapered reamers instead of drilling. I start with the #6 taper-pin reamer and finish with the #7 taper-pin reamer to ream the hole to the proper size. I start the smaller reamer from the face of the head and the larger reamer from the back of the head. The reamers, being tapered, tend to center themselves on the existing holes with a little care. The reamers may be used by hand with a "T" handle or as I prefer, a variable-speed electric drill. You can control the reamers with ease at a slow speed and get a better job than by hand. I then use the countersink bit to knock off the sharp edges of the reamed holes to prevent chipping and to clean up any burrs left by the reaming. I usually take the old machine heads for the price of installing the new ones, thus increasing my supply of used heads. As the old screws and bushings aren't needed for the new heads in some cases, I have a stock of bushings and screws on hand also.

FIGURING FRET SPACING FOR ANY GIVEN SCALE

Eventually you will have to make a fingerboard from scratch. The problem here is getting the accuracy needed to make the instrument note out properly. In laying it out for the frets you have a couple of choices for figuring the proper spacing. You decide on the scale length required and lay the fingerboard out using an existing fingerboard in that scale as a pattern. The other alternative is figuring the scale from scratch. Sometimes this is necessary if a fingerboard of the right scale isn't available for a pattern or you have an oddball scale of some sort.

When figuring from another fingerboard, the proper way to determine the scale length is to measure from the inside of the nut to the center of the twelfth fret and double this measurement. Never judge the scale by the total string length, as a certain amount was added to the scale to allow for stretching the strings when fretted. If you cannot find a fingerboard in your scale requirements, figure it from scratch.

To figure the fretting, the scale length has to be decided on. Once you have determined the scale to be used, this has to be broken up into the correct spacing for each fret. This fret spacing is very critical because any mistakes made are accumulative and will throw the whole fingerboard off, particularly if they are made in the first few frets.

The formula I use for figuring the spacing is the number 17.8170. By figuring to four decimal places, you will only be off a plus or minus .002" at the twelfth fret and you can't work any closer than that when dealing with wood.

I use an office calculator for this job and double check everything to prevent mistakes. Divide 17.8170 into the total scale length. The answer is your first fret. Subtract that answer from the total scale length. The answer will be divided by 17.8170 to determine the second fret. Subtract that and divide again, etc. Each time you are dividing you are in effect working with a new scale length as you shorten the original scale the distance of each fret as it is figured. Since you are shortening the scale with each fret, the next fret will be closer together, and so on down to the last fret, which will be the shortest. Using the 17.8170 formula, you can figure any scale you might need, regardless of the shortness or length. I use a calculator for this job, as mentioned before. In figuring long division, it is very easy to make at least one mistake and on a twenty-fret fingerboard you will have a minimum of forty problems of division and subtraction. The calculator will prevent mistakes.

I have a little trick on laying out the frets on the fingerboard after the figuring is done. Vernier calipers should be used for this job as they are accurate to .001". A 6" caliper will measure just over 5" maximum. We add together however many frets, starting at the first fret, that will total up to around 5". Let's use the 25⅛" scale as a "for instance." The first four frets total up to 5.182". If we add the next five frets, we come out at 5.001". The

frets are getting smaller, and more will fit in the 5" limitation of the calipers.

What we are doing here is sectionalizing the frets into several sections. Lay out the sectional spacing on the fingerboard with the calipers. Then start with the first section and lay out the frets in between the section layouts. You should come out right on the line. If you don't come out exactly on the line, go back and find where you goofed. Only when you have the first section figured do you go on to the next section, and so on. This sectionalizing of the layout procedure insures complete accuracy by giving you a double-check system.

Some guitar makers of the old school recommend shortening the first fret around ³⁄₃₂" to allow for sharping the strings while fretting. This, to me, seems like defeating the purpose of accurate figuring. With nylon or gut strings, the intonation may not be far off, but with steel strings, forget it. Add length to the bridge end of the scale instead.

Quite often on some of the older instruments, the inlaid mother-of-pearl or abalone-pearl fret position markers will be partly or wholly missing. Also, on some of the older instruments, the name is painted on and will be destroyed or badly damaged during refinishing. In these cases, the name may be cut from pearl and inlaid to preserve a near-original appearance.

Some older instruments had elaborately inlaid head and fingerboard patterns. These included the Washburn "Tree of Life" series, the many Gibson Mastertone banjo patterns, and the slightly simpler Martin "45" series. Many times certain pieces of the pearl will be badly chipped, worn, or missing and so need replacing.

The first problem is getting the patterns to cut the new pieces. One way is to use onionskin paper and try to trace the pattern by placing it over the inlay. Sometimes you can put a piece of paper over an inlay and, using a soft lead pencil at a flat angle, rub across the inlay. On older instruments, this may work because the wood has worn away slightly from the harder pearl. Another method is photographing the patterns, but the problem arises here in making the enlargements the same size as the original patterns. Some people "eyeball" the patterns, drawing them freehand.

The sneakiest and best method I have discovered for exactly duplicating patterns is Xeroxing them. I have found that the Xerox machines found in most public libraries will copy the fingerboard and head inlays to a gnat's whisker. Just remove the strings and machine heads and place the neck and/or head down on the machine, lay the flap over as much as possible and insert your dime. You may have to make two or more passes on a long neck. The patterns may be somewhat faint, but they will be clear enough so that you may go over them with a *black* ball point pen or with India ink. Now you may run off as many copies as you want of a particular pattern. The particular library I use has a very co-operative librarian and will set the machine at maximum contrast for better copies. You may get a few funny looks doing this in a public library, but that's all in the game.

Be sure to keep a master copy of all your patterns on file because you might need them another time.

Now that we have our pattern problem whipped, the next thing to do is to cut the pearl from the pattern.

There are several kinds of mother-of-pearl used, and it is also available in a couple of different thicknesses. The most commonly used thickness is around .060" and is commonly called "two ligne." It can be purchased in 1½-ligne thickness or around .035" thick, but the thinner material is pretty well limited to flat fingerboards or flat peghead inlays.

On ovaled fingerboards, it is imperative that the thicker material be used so it may be dressed off to the contour of the fingerboard surface. I highly recommend the two-ligne pearl, especially in abalone, as it is less prone to breakage during cutting. 'Nuff said?

There are several kinds of pearl available, as previously mentioned. First, there is the white pearl most commonly found in fingerboards of the more expensive instruments. The cheaper instruments usually use "Pearloid," or a fake pearl made of plastic and pearl dust. You can usually tell the difference by looking or by sticking the sharp point of a knife into the inlay. The point will penetrate the plastic rather easily and you will only scratch the pearl.

There is an off-color pearl called "golden pearl" that is available from some suppliers. This has a light yellowish or gold cast to it.

Next we have abalone pearl. This varies from dark greens and purples through the spectrum of reds and blues to plain white. The most colorful portion of the shell is the "green heart." This is the portion of the shell where the muscle is attached and is a very small portion of the shell. Since not much can be cut from each shell, this is the most expensive pearl. The rest of the shell is cut up and sold as "red abalone."

Abalone pearl is much more fragile to work with than the white pearl. Often, while cutting an intricate pattern of the *very* fragile green heart, I have glued a thin hardwood backing to the shell. This may be glued with a water-soluble glue and soaked off later or, if you are

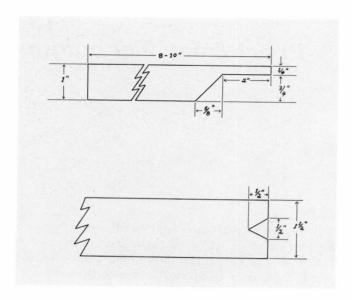

Fig. 132—Top: Edge view of workbench block used for cutting mother-of-pearl. Bottom: Top view of workbench block showing "V" notch in working end.

working with 1½-ligne shell, left on and inlaid in with the pearl.

Cut out the Xeroxed patterns and, having selected the pearl you plan to use, glue the pattern directly to the surface of the shell. This paper is left on the inlay until after it is set into the work piece. This is so you may number the pieces in the proper order and mark them in the direction they go. The paper is sanded off when the pearl is dressed down flush with the work surface.

Now comes the hard part, cutting the inlays. The first thing required is a jeweler's saw, which resembles a small adjustable coping saw. Get a dozen or so blades in two or three sizes, such as 0, 1/0, 2/0, and 3/0. These are inexpensive and, until you get the feel of things, you will break a mess of blades. The blades should be set in the frame with teeth pointing down towards the handle, since we will be making a pulling cut rather than pushing. The blade should have enough tension on it so when plucked with the nail, it will give a "ting" sound. A loose blade will break almost immediately, because they are highly tempered steel. In fact, if you take it easy, you can cut most of the softer metals with it. I have even cut mild steel with them.

The next step is to take a piece of 1½" wide by 1" thick hardwood, 8" or 10" long. Thin this down to ¼" for about 2" at one end with your bandsaw. Cut a "V" notch ½" wide and ½" deep into the thinned-down end. Clamp this to your workbench with the "V" end of the

block extending approximately 4" or 5" out from the bench for working room.

Buy a small metal spring clamp such as the #1 Hargrave and glue a thin piece of leather to one of the jaws at the contact point. This padded jaw contacts the pearl and reduces the chances of breakage during cutting.

The pearl to be cut is placed in position over the "V" notch and clamped at one side with the padded spring clamp. To make the cut, hold the saw at a 90° position to the pearl with the handle down under the workpiece. Place the thumb and forefinger on the pearl, gripping snugly. This step is *very* important. The thumb and finger, being soft, act as a shock absorber to kill the vibrations caused by the saw teeth passing through the pearl. This eliminates most breakage unless you get careless and bind the blade by changing the angle of the cut.

Cut into the pearl, using full strokes, about one a second or slower to prevent overheating the blade. Cutting too fast will cause the fine blade to heat up and lose its temper, with the result being blade breakage. Stop whenever necessary to shift the pearl, always keeping the working area over the "V" notch, until you have the piece sawn out. Stay as close to the line as possible or, as I do on some of my patterns, cut out the line.

If you have any rough or irregular places on the cut out piece, use the X-acto needle files to shape and smooth things out. Sound tedious? Believe me, it is! After a while your eyeballs get to jumping up and down with the rhythm of the saw. If you are a real nervous type, take a tranquilizer or forget the whole mess.

On simple inlay pieces such as rectangles, squares, or hexagon-shaped pieces, just rough them out with the jeweler's saw and use a disc sander to shape them. Use a dust mask to filter out the sanding dust. Dust from the abalone shell is very toxic. I was sick for two days one time after trying to rough out a shell. Play it safe and use the dust mask.

The next step is inlaying the pieces. In the case of having to remove broken pieces, heat up your soldering iron and apply directly to the broken piece. After a minute or so the broken piece may be carefully pried out with a knife point or scribe. In the case of plastic (Pearloid) pieces, drill a few holes in them and cut them up with a sharp knife and they will usually come right out. Sometimes they may be pried out intact with a sharp knife if you will cut around the outside edge. Using heat on these will often result in a small fire, as this material is usually very flammable and can cause burn scars on the surrounding wood.

Inlaying simple dots may be done by drilling the proper sized hole, squirting a few drops of Titebond into the hole, and pressing the dots into place. Let dry and

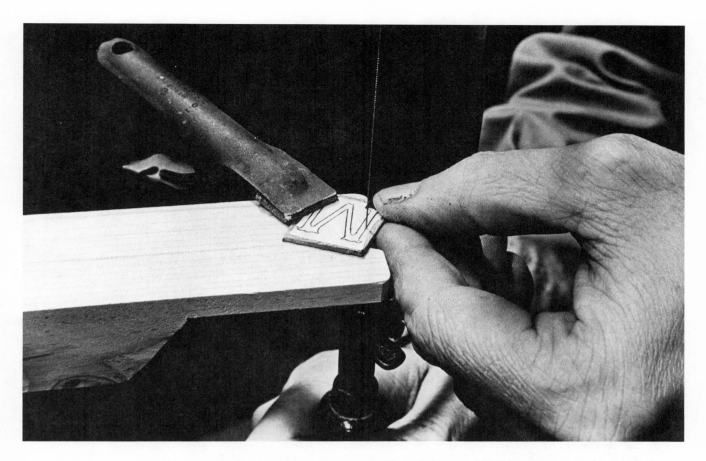

Fig. 133—Cutting out the pearl inlay piece with the jeweler's saw and "V" block setup.

dress off with a fine mill bastard file and sand with the grain to eliminate cross grain scratches.

Inlaying elaborate pieces is much more complicated. The material you are working with has a lot to do with how elaborate an inlay pattern that can be satisfactorily inlaid. In rosewood for instance, if you lose a chip, it is almost impossible to hide, so stick with simple patterns till you get the hang of things. Inlaying in ebony is much easier because you can pretty well hide your mistakes because of the near absence of a grain pattern. In rosewood, if you lose a chip, you have to dye your filler as near the dominant background color as possible and then, using a fine artist brush and graining liquid dyed to the dark grain, draw in the grain to imitate the missing chip. This technique cannot be used too satisfactorily unless the area is to be finished over, because the graining liquid is not very durable.

On pegheads such as Gibsons, if you make a few mistakes, don't worry too much, because the surface is usually painted black. After inlaying the name and dressing it down flat, apply clear Scotch tape over the name, trim around the outline of the name with a sharp knife, peel off all the tape except that covering the pearl, spray with black lacquer, let dry, peel off the rest of the tape and presto, no mistakes showing. Shoot on a few coats of clear over the black and pearl, polish down and you are home free. Sneaky, huh?

If you are replacing a missing or broken piece, the next step is to clean out the area where the piece was. This can be done with a small chisel or as I do, set up the Dremel Moto-Tool with the router base and insert a small dental cutter. If you have not removed the frets, set the depth of the cutter to the thickness of the inlay plus the height of the frets and clean out the old glue and filler. Actually, it is best to leave a small amount of the pearl protruding above the surface of the work piece so that it can be dressed off level with the surface. It is a good idea to keep air flowing on the burr at all times

Fig. 134—Pearl temporarily glued to the head and marking the location with a sharp scribe.

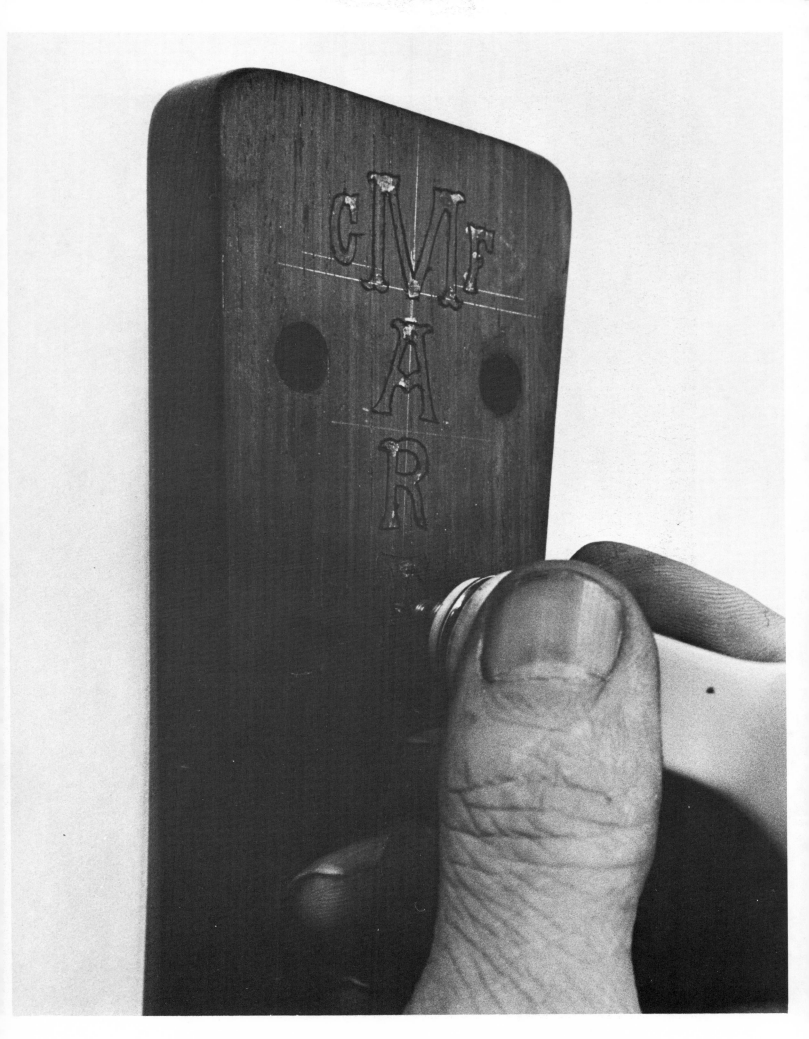

Fig. 135—*Deepening the scribe line with vibrating engraver and chisel bit. This can be done with a sharp pointed knife also.*

Fig. 136—Routing out the scribed area for inlay piece with the Dremel Moto-Tool and burr.

and to keep the dust blown out of the way, because the burrs can get pretty hot and start something. To clean out the square or sharp corners, I use the small X-acto knife handle with the #4B blade. Clean things out until the new inlay piece will drop in snugly. Do not force things, or you may be cutting a new piece. They break rather easily.

After it is fitted, I mix up Elmer's epoxy glue and sanding dust, rosewood dust for a rosewood board and ebony for an ebony board. Another tip. When mixing with rosewood dust, mix only enough to color the glue about half as dark as the board since it dries much darker. If you like, you may use alcohol-soluble dye powder to color your glue, or a mixture of dust and dye. Mix the glue thoroughly *before* adding the dust and only then mix in the dust or dye. Fill the hole with the mixture, lay the inlay into position, and press into place very carefully with a small screwdriver or other blunt object, allowing the glue to squeeze out slowly. If you try to

force it, you can break the inlay. Do not clean off the residue yet. It will settle around the inlay piece, filling the discrepancies. After it has hardened, dress the glue and pearl flush with a smooth mill bastard file if you didn't remove the frets, and sand with fine sandpaper with the grain. If you have removed the frets, the long sandpaper file can be used, working with the grain all the way.

So what if you are doing an inlay job from scratch and not just replacing missing or damaged pieces? This is where the fun begins. If the job is very extensive, the frets should be removed so you can have maximum control of the cutter. You will find another reason in the next paragraph.

The first thing to do after cutting your inlays and removing the frets is to dress off the fingerboard with the sandpaper file to clean the board down to new wood. This is to remove any wax, oil, and other crud from the surface. If the surface is still a little oily, clean it up with

Fig. 137—Finished "D-45" Martin-type peg-head inlay. Head is bound and purfled to resemble original D-45.

alcohol, being very careful to keep the alcohol off of any finished portion of the instrument. This is to clean the wood up to where glue will stick to the board surface.

Next step. Lay out your inlay pieces on the fingerboard surface and get them lined up properly and in the order that they are to be inlaid. Using a hypodermic syringe, sharpened match stick, or what-have-you, apply a drop of glue about the size of a pinhead to the bottom of the smaller pieces. On the larger pieces a couple of drops spaced out will hold them. Press them down on the fingerboard, making certain they are in proper alignment. Do this with all the pieces and allow them to dry for a couple of hours or longer. As to the type of glue, any white glue (polyvinyl resin) or Titebond will do the job.

After the glue has set, take a fine, very sharp scribe and scratch a mark all the way around each piece. It would be a good idea to go around them a couple of times to make sure you get a good mark in the wood.

I next mark each piece with a felt-tip pin, pointing to the head of the guitar so it will be easy to set the pieces back exactly as laid out. I next lay out a piece of double-stick tape or a piece of masking tape folded back on itself on a small board. As each piece is removed from the fingerboard, I stick it to the tape in the order of removal. This effectively prevents mixing up the pieces. This is particularly important if there are duplicate pieces in the pattern. Very seldom can you cut each piece exactly the same, so things have to be kept straight.

To remove the glued on pieces, I break a double-edged razor blade in half (I want to remove the inlays, not my fingers) and carefully slide a piece of the blade under the inlay, separating the inlay from the board.

The scribe marks should be nicely visible in an oblique light. The next step in very important. You can either use the tip of a very sharp knife blade or, as I do, use a Dremel vibrating engraving tool with a small chisel bit I made from a drill bit, and cut through the fingerboard surface several thousandths of an inch deep following the scribe lines as nearly perfectly as possible. The reason for this is that in using the Dremel and cutter to rout out the unwanted wood, a burr is formed at the edge of the cut. This makes it almost impossible to see the scribe line, but when the line is cut into the wood, as you come up to the scribe line with the cutter, it will chip out clean with no burr. This lets you know that you are exactly where you want to be.

After deepening the scribe lines with the knife or chisel, sand the fingerboard lightly to remove any excess glue left after removing the inlays, and this will also show up the lines a little better.

Set the cutter depth to where you want it and have at it. I mention again that it is a good idea to have some sort of air flow blowing on the cutter to keep the chips blown out and to keep the cutter from overheating. Rough out everything you can with the round cutter and finish the job with the earlier mentioned X-acto blade or a small chisel.

Check and fit each individual piece as mentioned earlier and set in glue and wood dust, allow to dry, and dress down flush with the wood. If you are inlaying a peg head, you are ready for the finish work. If you are inlaying a fingerboard, dress down flush with the sandpaper file, wax with a good non-silicone wax, and do the fret job.

I must say before closing this chapter that inlay work is one of the most tedious, nerve-wracking, and ego-satisfying jobs (that is, if everything turned out as planned) in the business.

Probably one of the most difficult areas of instrument repair is the finishing or refinishing. The main secrets are in the preparation, the materials used, and the use of proper equipment.

You should have a good external-mix spray gun of the non-bleeder type. The external-mix spray gun may be used with various varnishes and enamels as well as lacquers of all types. The internal-mix gun cannot be used with lacquer finishes because the spray head will stop up constantly. It is excellent, however, for varnishes or any slow-drying finishes.

Your compressor should be large enough to maintain a constant air-flow at a given pressure, or it should have a large enough storage tank to provide a constant pressure for at least ten or fifteen minutes at a time. The amount of air pressure required will depend on your particular equipment.

I use a Model 69 Binks syphon-feed spray gun with the S99 nozzle and a working pressure at the tank of 45 to 50 psi. On the smaller rigs, around 30 psi is a good working pressure. Most guns, especially the pressure-feed ones, are limited to 50 psi. The finishing materials may be thinned accordingly.

All compressor setups should have a water-trap system or, better yet, a dehydrator system such as the Series A, Model 4001-2 Wilkerson Corporation dehydrator. The air is filtered through a couple of pounds of desiccant (silica gel) before it enters the air lines and filters *all* the moisture out. This desiccant may be used over several times by simply heating it in an oven at around 300° until it changes back to a bright purple and then storing it in an air-tight container until needed to recharge the dehydrator. The dehydrator really helps when the humidity is around 50 per cent or better, as the water buildup is very rapid and will get into the air lines. In fact, I will not do any finishing work unless the humidity is at 50 per cent or less. Even though the pressurized air is filtered, the expansion of the air leaving the gun condenses moisture between the gun and object being sprayed and can cause blushing of the finish. This

"blushing" can be identified as a milky or hazy look, particularly around corners and holes, such as where the neck meets the body of the guitar or where the machine heads have been removed. This haze consists of many very fine bubbles. During sanding or polishing, the tops are removed from these bubbles and if more coats are to be sprayed, they will pinhole very badly. If they are removed during the polishing, they will collect polish and grime and you end up with a bad case of freckles. The thing to do is to start over and try again. The best solution to the problem is not to do any finish work during these humid conditions.

FINISH REMOVAL

There are several methods of removing old finish. Sanding is one method, and, when you are working with some of the older varnishes, is probably the best. Also, a good sharp cabinet scraper works well and, depending on the finish, it may work better than hand sanding. Power sanders are not practical for removing old finish on musical instruments, as the heat generated will melt the finish and gum up the sandpaper. This can also melt the finish deeper into the wood or cause deep scratches. With some of the new polyester finishes, about the only way to remove them is by sanding or scraping. Even the modern paint strippers won't penetrate them enough for removal.

Lacquer is by far the most commonly used finish and has been used on most of the better made instruments in the United States for the last fifteen or twenty years. It is probably the most versatile finish and is easily removed with one of the semi-paste, self-neutralizing paint strippers. These strippers will remove most varnishes and enamels also. I use Zip Strip myself, but any of the others such as Strip Eze, Clean Strip, Star Wax Free Remover, etc., are good. Use only the *semi-paste* form of any of these. The stripper must cling to the irregular surfaces of the instruments without running off. A word of warning about these strippers. Not only will they remove

Fig. 138—*Air compressor for spraying, blowgun, etc. Notice the water trap and silica-gel dehydrator to filter out condensed moisture from the air line.*

finishes, they also have a tendency to remove the skin and hair from your body. Rubber gloves may be used, but they are a little clumsy, so I just keep some water handy and should any of the stripper contact the skin, I quickly wash it off. Problem cured.

Before using any of the strippers, you *must tape off all plastic or celluloid* bindings and purflings with masking tape. I tape at least ¼" extra to either side of the bindings and purflings. The reason for doing this is that the stripper will destroy the bindings, or at least soften them, and on drying out, they will shrink, often badly enough to have to be replaced. I have had to rebind several instruments that other people tried to work on themselves and thoroughly messed up.

Follow the instructions on the can and apply the stripper to a small area at a time, such as half a top, back, or maybe a side. When you are used to the product, you may try a larger area such as a whole back, etc. After it bubbles and wrinkles good, remove as much as possible with a small *dull* putty knife, then use #2 or #3 steel wool to remove the residue. Remove the masking tape from this area and scrape the finish off the binding. The stripper penetrates under the tape slightly, and a cabinet scraper will remove most of the finish left. Part of the time I will scrape and tape the binding before I strip the rest of the guitar. You still must tape at least ¼" extra on either side of the binding for safety. Continue this process until the whole instrument is free

Fig. 139—*Using* semi-paste *stripper to remove the old finish.* Important. *Notice the tape on the binding to prevent contact between the stripper and the binding.*

from finish, with the exception of the peg head. If the name on the head is a decal or painted on, it would be better to leave the finish alone unless you have access to new decals or plan to inlay the name in the head. The old finish on the head may be washed with VM & P naptha and alcohol to remove old waxes and polishes. It can then be sanded lightly and when the finish coats are applied to the rest of the instrument, shoot a couple of light coats on the head facing.

After the stripping process, the instrument should hang in a well ventilated place for a minimum of six hours or preferably overnight to allow thorough evaporation of the stripping chemicals before sanding. This will allow any bindings to dry that may have been softened by accidental contact with the stripper.

The sanding should be done very carefully, removing no more wood than is absolutely necessary to prevent weakening of the thin wood. Many of the later instruments, especially the imported ones, are constructed of plywood, and vigorous sanding will go right through into the second ply, leaving you no alternative but to finish it with a very dark or solid color finish to hide the mistake. Start with no coarser than #100-grit production paper for roughing, then to about #150 finishing paper, and then to #220 finishing paper. This should give a very smooth surface.

An in-line motion power sander may be used, working with the grain, for roughing out larger areas such as the

Fig. 140—*Using a dull edged putty knife and scoop to remove the stripper-softened finish.*

Fig. 141—*Steel wool immediately to remove any residue left on the wood by the putty knife.*

Fig. 142—*Scraping the finish from the binding in preparation for stripping finish from instrument. This step may be done before or after the stripping. A cabinet scraper is the tool being used.*

back, etc. Also there is a very high speed, small-base orbital sander, that can be used to rough out almost the entire guitar. The orbit is so small with this sander that with the proper stepping of sandpaper from coarse to fine, you can almost finish sand with it. Only a small amount of hand sanding is necessary to clean up after it. The sander is the Rockwell Model 330-A. I have used mine now for seven or eight years and would not part with it except for another just like it. By the way, the C. F. Martin Organisation has twenty or thirty of these sanders at work in their factory.

During and after finish sanding, the bare wood should not be handled with the bare hands as the oils and acids in human sweat can cause problems in adhesion of the fillers and finishes. Use clean dry rags or cotton gloves to handle the bare wood.

After the sanding is complete, the wood, with the exception of the spruce tops, should be brushed with the grain with a moderately stiff brush. A common vegetable brush will work fine for this. The brushing loosens any sanding dust clinging to the fibers of the wood. Now take your air hose and blow out the dust from four different directions. It is necessary for a good fill job to have the pores of the wood perfectly clean. On the spruce top, do not use the brush, as the bristles will scratch the soft wood. Blowing off with the air hose is sufficient. We

Fig. 143—*Soaking the decal in water in preparation to applying to* partially finished or sealed head. *Do not apply decals over bare wood.*

Fig. 144—*Apply the decal to the head and locate properly with tweezers.*

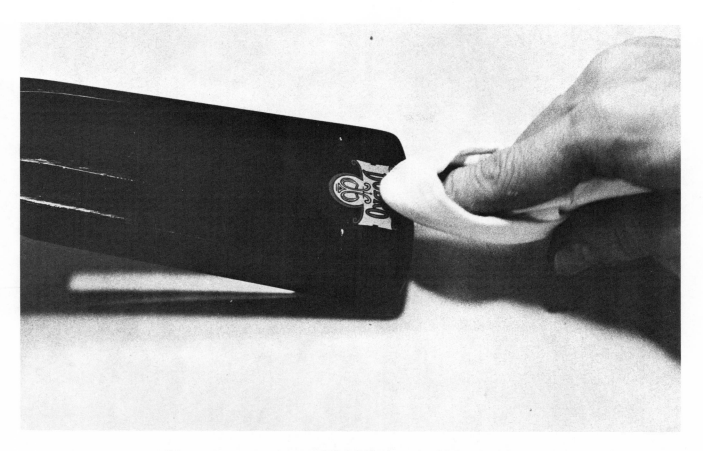

Fig. 145—Remove the excess moisture and air bubbles from the decal with clean rag and with a rolling motion of the finger. Do not blot but use a rolling motion.

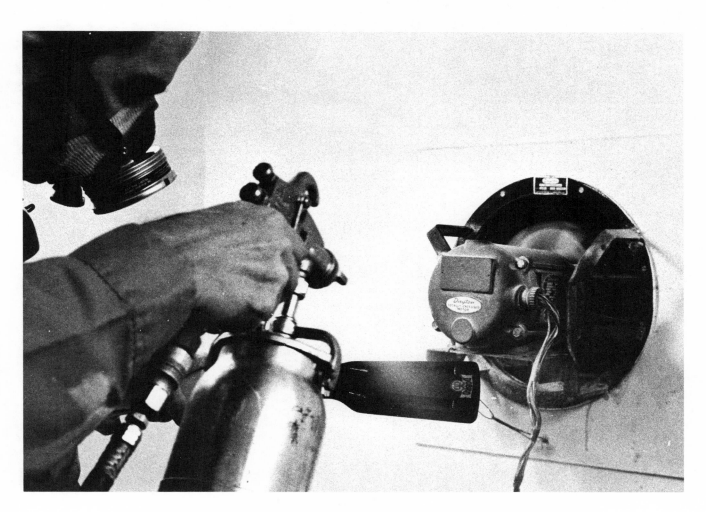

Fig. 146—Sealing the decal down with finish lacquer. Notice the exhaust fan in the background and chemical respirator to prevent breathing of the lacquer fumes.

Fig. 147—*Sanding the bare wood with the high speed Rockwell sander. Sand only enough to clean up the wood.*

have now completed one of the most difficult parts of wood refinishing, the preparation.

STAINING, WASH COATING, AND PREPARATION FOR FILLING

The spruce top should now be sealed so that during the staining and filling of the back, sides, and neck, any stain or filler accidentally contacting the top will not penetrate and can be easily removed.

There are several ways of doing this. If the guitar is to be finished in lacquer, a lacquer-based sanding sealer may be applied, or if it is to be finished in varnish, use a varnish-based sanding sealer. The sealer *must be com-*

patible with the finishing product you are planning to use.

A friend of mine, Gary Price, learned a trick from a repairman back east on using epoxy glue to seal a spruce top. Tom Morgan, according to Gary, used the glue over the complete top, spreading it out with a wooden squeegee. I did some experimenting with the Elmer's epoxy. I found that after mixing thoroughly, the mixture could be thinned readily with alcohol, and the setting of the glue was not inhibited in any way. I used a 50-50 mixture of alcohol and epoxy applied with a small, clean, soft rag wadded up into a ball. I swabbed the spruce with this and then went over it again a sec-

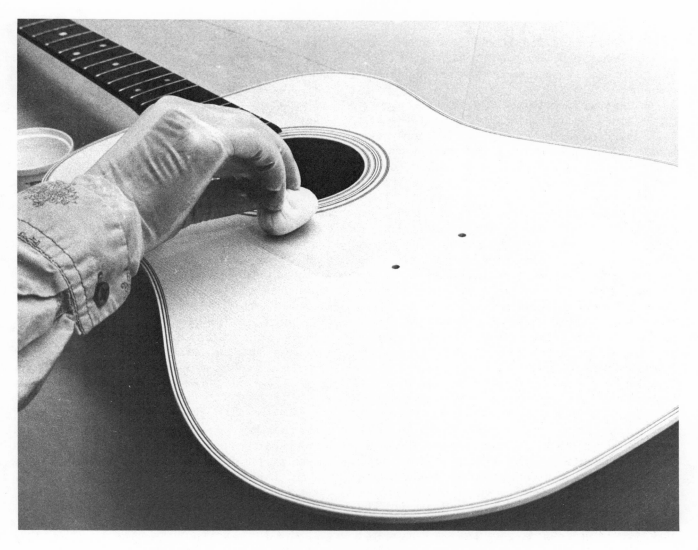

Fig. 148—*Sealing the spruce top with epoxy-alcohol mixture and cloth pad. Notice the Tru-Touch examination glove to prevent contact of glue mixture with skin.*

ond time as soon as I finished covering it the first time. Then I went over it with pure alcohol to finish flowing out any streaks. The alcohol evaporates almost immediately, leaving a very thin layer of glue that has penetrated only a few thousandths of an inch. This thin layer of epoxy is very flexible and, when scuffed up with #0 steel wool, will accept either the lacquer- or varnish-based sanding sealer.

I will mention here again that you should prevent contact between the skin and fresh epoxy. Some people are allergic to the driers used to catalyze the glue. I find that the best method is to buy the "True Touch" plastic gloves used by doctors. I also find them very helpful

when staining or removing wood filler. Do not use them with paint stripper, because they will dissolve. If you must use gloves with the stripper, use rubber ones.

'Nuff said about the gloves. Back to the top. The epoxy method of sealing works especially well on aged tops. I have had to spray antique spruce with four or five coats of sealer at times before I start getting a surface build. This extra finish adds weight and stiffens the top, thereby reducing the sound and tonal qualities. With the very thin epoxy seal, a couple of coats of sealer, even on old wood tops, will give plenty of build to sand on.

Now the decision has to be made on the rest of the

instrument. What kind of woods are involved? What kind of porosity is involved? Should you stain or leave it natural? What color wood filler? What kind of finish? What about the compatibility of a given finish to a given type of wood?

The most common types of woods found in guitar making are Honduras mahogany, maples of various kinds, birch, various fruit woods, and the more exotic hardwoods, such as Brazilian and East Indian rosewoods. There are others used also, such as pecan, etc. You will find pecan used in most of the inexpensive Mexican guitars.

All of these woods will accept a lacquer-type finish or a shellac-type finish, such as the Frenching finishes. Some of them, primarily the rosewoods, can be very difficult when using the modern synthetics. East Indian rosewood is the worst offender. I finished an East Indian rosewood guitar with one of the new satin synthetic alkyds and it took six weeks for it to dry out enough so that it wouldn't stick to everything it touched. Should you decide on one of the synthetics, a scrap of comparable wood should be finished first to check for compatibility, drying time, adhesion, etc.

Before filling of rosewood and other high resin content hardwoods of the rosewood family, special steps should be followed. I've learned these the hard way, and they will save you time and not a little grief if you follow them. If the wood is East Indian rosewood, I wash the wood thoroughly with three different solvents. I use a clean rag with each of the solvents and throw it away after each washing. I wash first with V M & P naphtha, then with lacquer thinner, and last with alcohol. This removes the surface acids and resins and actually leaves the wood sort of muddy looking. The color comes back with the finishing process. On Brazilian rosewood, a simple washing with lacquer thinner is enough to clean it.

The next step is to wash-coat the rosewood. The wash-coat is simply sanding sealer mixed one part sealer with five parts thinner and applied liberally with a brush. This seals the pores of the rosewood close to the surface of the wood. The pores in rosewood will sometimes run for several inches and will not fill properly if not wash-coated. Go over the wood with fine sandpaper, baring the wood again after the wash-coating.

Another point to remember. To tell East Indian from Brazilian rosewood, remember that the Indian will almost invariably be a light to medium purple in color and have an acrid stench when sanding. The grain will also have very little figuring in most cases. Brazilian rosewood, on the other hand, varies from a light yellow, through the browns, brick reds, on to the purple blacks. The color will seldom be uniform, with at least two or three different colors and various figuring, from simple dark streaks, to spectacular bands and streaks. Another thing to remember about rosewoods. Do not attempt to stain them. The density and resin content of the woods prevent satisfactory results. The rosewood is now ready to fill after completing these steps.

Now we return to the other types of woods. If there is any staining to be done, now is the time to do it. There are quite a few different types of stains available, such as oil mix, water mix, lacquer mix, alcohol, and various types of wiping stains. I have used quite a few different types myself and have settled on the alcohol-soluble, analine dye stains. I use mostly three colors of stains, Star Chemical's #103 American black walnut, the #107 black, and the #113 dark red mahogany. I also use a combination of these three mixed together, giving an appearance of rosewood when applied to woods with figuring in them. There is some difficulty in applying alcohol stains without streaking. I mix the stain fairly weakly and apply many saturation coats to bring out the shade I want. If you get it too dark, you can remove some of the stain by wiping with an alcohol-soaked rag. After the stain is dry, steel-wool lightly with #0 or #00 wool, brush again, and blow off carefully as before. The wood is now ready for filling.

FILLING TECHNIQUE

If a guitar has light-colored wood binding or purfling, it should be taped off with masking tape and sealed with a small amount of lacquer *before* any staining or filling is done. This will prevent it from being discolored by the stain in the wood filler.

Most woods need proper filling with paste wood filler before the sanding sealer can be applied. There are exceptions, of course. Maples, birch, or cherry need little or no filling unless the wood is very old. In this case, it is sometimes necessary to fill to close up the pores. The darker woods should be filled with a dark wood filler. I use the Star Chemical #T403 dark walnut filler in almost all cases. To get the color used by Martin on their mahogany instruments, I stain to a light tobacco brown with the American black walnut stain and fill with the #T403 filler and have always been within the proper color shades. The color shades are within tolerances on the rosewoods also with this filler. If you are unable to purchase the wood filler in colors, you may purchase the natural and color it with artist's oil colors. To get the brown shade, mix Van Dyke brown, black, and a small amount of Rose Lake, to enough filler to cover the job at hand. You must add five or six drops of paint shop dryer to the mixture to make it dry properly. Don't go overboard on the dryer, though, because too much can make a gummy mess.

The wood filler should be thinned down to a semi-

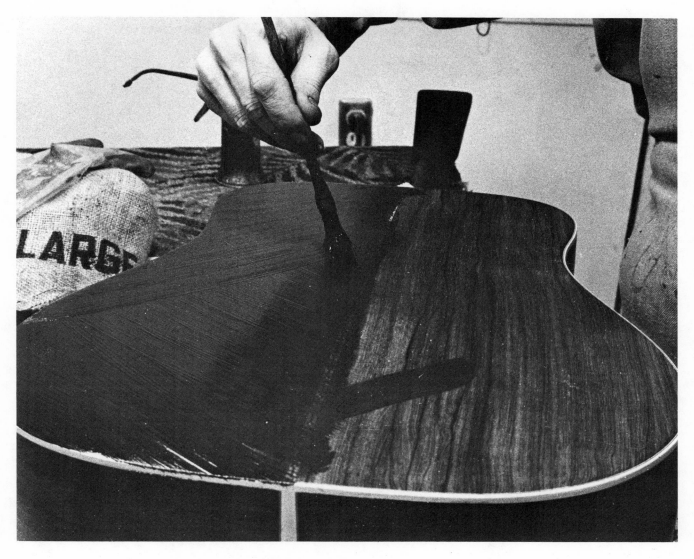

Fig. 149—*Applying the paste wood filler with stiff brush working in several directions to force the filler into the grain.*

paste form with V M & P naphtha. You can use other solvents such as lacquer thinner, benzine, or turpentine, but I seem to get the best results with the naphtha. It is fast evaporating, but not so fast as to make it hard to work with.

The wood filler should be applied with a stiff brush, working with the grain, across the grain, and back with the grain again. Work with one area at a time, such as a side, etc. Trying to work too large an area at a time can sure make a mess. It is rather difficult to remove the filler if it sets too long before removing.

The filler should be allowed to dry until it flashes or turns dull, usually from fifteen to twenty minutes. You can also check by rubbing a finger lightly across the filler. It should crumble slightly.

The filler should now be removed by rubbing across the grain with a coarse cloth such as burlap, packing the filler into the pores. I buy feed sacks at the local seed store and cut these up for use. One of these burlap bags, cut up, will clean several guitars.

After wiping across the grain, there will be a small amount of filler left, usually small streaks across the grain and in corners, etc. This residue should be wiped off with a soft cloth and light pressure working *with* the

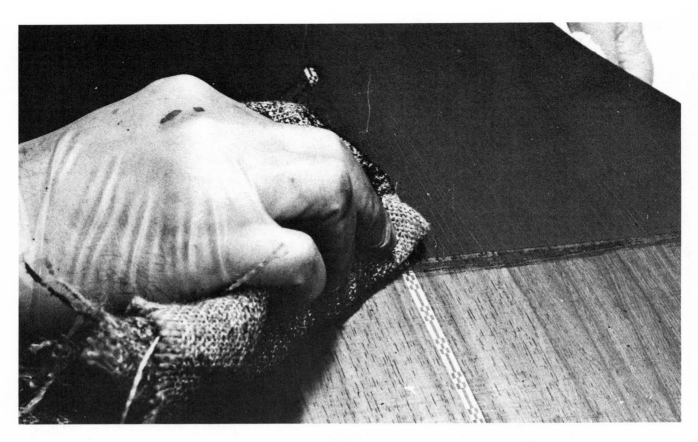

Fig. 150—*Wiping off the filler across the grain with burlap. Notice the examination glove to prevent staining your hand with filler. Use glove for staining wood also.*

Fig. 151—*Scraping stain and filler from white binding with wood chisel. Again, thanks to the Martin factory for this technique.*

Fig. 152—*Tape off bridge area and fingerboard in preparation for spraying the guitar.*

Fig. 153—*C-clamp applied through the sound hole for handle while spraying. Notice crushed newspaper in the sound hole.*

Fig. 154—*An important tool is the humidity indicator, or hygrometer, located on the right end of the weather station pictured here.*

grain. The guitar should now be hung out of the way and allowed to dry for a *minimum* of eight hours. Allowing twenty-four to thirty-six hours will let it dry thoroughly.

Some instruments use white bindings and trim and these should now be cleaned off. This can be done by careful scraping with a sharp knife or chisel. I use a ¾" wide chisel held between the thumb and forefinger. The thumb lays behind the chisel on the edge of the guitar as you are scraping the binding. It is a good idea to use a cotton glove or rag in handling the chisel and guitar. Sweat and body oils don't do anything for the finish, and neither does blood, if you carve up a finger scraping the binding.

After cleaning the binding, the guitar is almost ready for the sanding sealer. You may be wondering why I've mentioned nothing about sanding the paste wood filler. You should have removed all the excess filler with the soft rag earlier. To sand or steel-wool the filler after it dries can dislodge the filler from small or shallow pores and, when the instrument is sprayed leave you with a mess of pin holes.

Sealing and Finish Coats

Before spraying the sealer coats, the fingerboard should be carefully taped off with masking tape. I also tape the area of the top covered by the bridge. Some shops prefer to go ahead and finish this area and clean the finish off with a sharp chisel after the top is polished out. Lay a 1" wide by ¼" thick or better piece of wood over the fingerboard where it covers the face of the guitar. Place a steel "C" clamp through the sound hole and under the fingerboard with a small block between the bottom of the clamp and the top of the guitar. Tighten the clamp down on the two blocks and you have a handle to hang on to while spraying and also to hang it up by. Stuff crushed newspaper in the sound hole and around the clamp until the hole is full. This prevents spraying finish inside the instrument and blowing dust from inside the guitar all over the newly sprayed finish.

The instrument is now ready for the sanding sealer. There are quite a few good brands of lacquer sanding sealers on the market. I have used Cooks, Sherwin-Williams, Pittsburgh, Sedlitz, and Star brands. There are many others also. I happen to prefer the Star Chemical Company brand because the salesman spent quite a lot of time with me some time back when I ran into a problem. I use the #405 lacquer sanding sealer made by Star and their W–35 solvent for thinning it. The thinning of the sealer will, of course, depend a lot on your equipment. It should be thin enough to spray well, but thick enough to get a good build. The sanding sealer acts as a primer coat to fill the remainder of the grain not filled by the paste wood filler and to smooth out any sanding scratches left from the finish sanding. I thin around two and one-half parts sealer to one part lacquer thinner. You may want to use a faster drying solvent, such as the W–27 Star or 3608–S DuPont, if the humidity is below 30 per cent. If the humidity is *above 50 per cent*, it is *not advisable to spray* because of the blushing problem mentioned earlier.

For the first sealing coat, I shoot a fairly thin coat of sealer over the whole works and let it dry for about an hour. This seals the filler and reduces the tendency for the lacquer to lift out the filler. Next, I shoot two double coats about thirty minutes apart. A double coat means two coats sprayed one immediately after the other, one across the grain and the other with the grain. This seems to assist in flowing out the finish better for smoother results and at times will even flow out small pin holes. I then apply one or two more double coats on the back, sides, and neck only, again allowing about thirty minutes between each double coat.

The porosity of the wood determines the number of sealer coats to be used. You may not need more than a couple of double coats on wood such as maple. Two double coats are plenty for the spruce top, particularly if you have epoxy-sealed it. On some of the old spruce tops, without the epoxy seal, the first three or four coats may soak in before you start getting a build. You will have to use your own judgment on these jobs.

The instrument should now be hung out of the way and allowed to dry for at least a couple of days and longer if you aren't in a rush for the job. This will give plenty of time for maximum shrinkage of the sealer.

Next the instrument is thoroughly sanded, removing as much of the sealer as possible without sanding into the wood itself. If you applied the proper amount of sealer, you should end up with a perfectly smooth surface, very thin, and with few shiny or unsanded spots left. A few small spots will not matter if they aren't deep. In doing the above sanding, I use #280 or #320 Wet-ordry sandpaper, without water, for roughing the sealer down and #400 for the finish sanding of the sealer. Then I go over it with #00 steel wool to remove any further shiny spots left from the sanding, and to also break down any sharp corners left. The finish will flow out better if there are no sharp corners.

If you happened to sand through the sealer on any stained portions and have a light spot, now is the time to correct this. An artist's brush dipped in the proper stain and brushed on the light spot and quickly blended out with a rag will take care of this. You may have to apply the stain several times to get the color right. Remember, though, you must check the color while the stain is wet, as it will dry lighter. When the finish lacquer is applied, it will bring the color back out and should blend in perfectly.

I now re-install my clamp handle in the sound hole (having removed it and the newspaper for sanding), fill the sound hole with fresh clean newspapers, and carefully wipe and blow off any remaining dust, and the guitar is ready for the finish coats.

For the finish lacquer, I use the #600 Star clear gloss finishing lacquer. I have used some of the water white lacquers, but they are very hard and chip rather easily on flexible surfaces such as guitar bodies. This #600 lacquer is a 27 per cent solids material and, unless you are spraying at very high pressures with a pressure feed gun, will need thinning down. I usually thin it two and one-half parts lacquer, one part #W–40 Star thinner and, if the humidity is near the 50 per cent mark, I will add one-half part of blush retarder. You cannot use much blush retarder on filled wood, though. The retarder is a very slow dry thinner and can penetrate all the way to the wood through the previous coats and lift the wood filler. Also because of the penetration, the drying time is lengthened considerably.

It is very important to add a silicone leveling fluid to the finish lacquer. Most companies put out a brand of this fluid. I use the Star Sil Flo myself. This fluid is added to prevent the "fish eyes" or cratering of the finish by silicone. Most older instruments, and not a few of the newer ones, have had a silicone-type polish applied at one time or another. This will penetrate all the way to the wood and is not removed by sanding, stripping, or washing. I have even had to add Sil Flo to my sanding sealer once or twice to get it to flow out. The best thing to do is to assume that the instrument has been treated with silicone and add the Sil Flo fluid to the finish lacquer on any job you do.

I spray only three coats on the top of the instrument, because the more finish you apply, the less sound you get. I spray four to six coats on the back and sides, depending on the grain. The neck gets at least six coats of finish because of the extra wear from the hand movement in playing.

There are many techniques in applying these finish coats. Some people sand lightly between every coat, others sand between every two coats, and some apply three or four coats and let cure for twenty-four to thirty-six hours. They then sand smooth and apply a couple of more coats. I have used all three of the above methods with excellent results. The method I use now is slightly different, but I am getting excellent results with less sanding. I apply the finish coats one at a time, allowing about an hour's drying time or longer between the coats. I seem to get a very smooth finish with very little grain lifting. I then allow the guitar to hang for a *minimum* of three days' curing time. At this point the finish is hard enough to sand and polish well without excessive scratching. You can allow a longer curing time if you like, but as the finish continues to cure, it becomes harder and requires a lot more polishing to get a good surface.

The instrument is now ready for wet sanding and polishing. I use #500 Wetordry sandpaper with soapy water to rough sand and finish up with #600 Wetordry. You can do the whole job with the #600 if you like, but it takes a little longer. As to the above-mentioned soapy water, any good wetting agent will do. I use common dishwashing detergent such as Joy. The old-time piano refinishers used flax soap for this purpose, but it is pretty hard to find. The soap breaks up the surface tension of the water, making it flow out better. This prevents the sanding residue from clogging the sandpaper grain and gives a much smoother surface than sanding with plain water. Work the finish down until all the shiny areas are eliminated.

The next step is polishing the finish. There are many polishing compounds used for this step. Some swear by the old pumice stone and rottenstone method. You can get just as good a result by using one of the many prepared commercial compounds. I use the DuPont #7 rubbing compound with a 1000 rpm power polisher for the initial polishing. If you use a power buffer of any kind, be sure it is a slow-speed one, not over *1500 rpm maximum*. See the chapter on tools for further explanation on the buffer. Of course, you can do the job by hand and eliminiate the heat buildup problem, except in your muscles. After the red compound, you can use the finer grit DuPont white polishing compound to finish the job. This is a fine compound, designed for hand use, for polishing *cured* enamels and acrylic lacquers. If you want to be traditional, instead of the white polishing compound, mix up a thin paste of rottenstone and water for the hand polishing. This will put a shine on the instrument that you can shave in. For this final polishing, be sure to rub with the grain of the wood and use long strokes.

Using these techniques, I have been getting a factory quality finish consistently. I hope you will too, but you may have to do several jobs to really get the hang of it. Just remember, even we experienced craftsmen still have problems at times, so don't get discouraged if you have some failures. When I first started, I had one job, an East Indian rosewood guitar, that I finished *seven times* before getting an acceptable finish. It takes practice.

Oh, yes, before we get into other types of finishes, I should mention another way to finish out the job instead of polishing. To get an antique satin-type finish or to dull down the face of an instrument being used under spotlights, Star makes an excellent product called Wol-Wax concentrate. Using this product, water, and #0000 steel wool to finish out the job gives an excellent high-sheen satin finish. After it is handled and polished a few times, it actually looks like an original old-timey finish.

OTHER TYPES OF FINISHES

Should you decide to use a varnish finish, the procedure is somewhat different. The instrument is prepared as in the lacquer procedure up to and including the filling with the paste wood filler. Instead of using the lacquer sanding sealer, you should use a sealer designed for use under the varnish finish. It is possible to use the lacquer sealer under a varnish finish, but it must be cured *thoroughly*. Under no circumstances use a varnish type sealer under a lacquer finish.

The varnish sanding sealer may be applied by hand with a good soft varnish brush or may be sprayed. It must be thinned to the proper consistency for spraying, using the recommended solvent for the particular brand of sealer used. This is usually V M & P naphtha. Use the naphtha to clean up your brushes, guns, and other equipment. The varnish sealers and finishes should be applied in a dust-free atmosphere, as they usually take at least thirty minutes or more to dry dust free, compared to two or three minutes for lacquer. In spraying the varnish sealer, spray a very fine mist coat over the complete area and let set for at least fifteen minutes or until it is "tacky." Now you can lay on a heavier coat over this. The tack coat will help hold the heavier coat and prevent running of the finish. Allow to dry as per instructions for your particular band, sand with #280 Wetordry, and apply a second coat of sealer. Allow this second coat of sealer to dry and sand again with #280 Wetordry. If the surface is smooth and free from graininess, you are ready for the finish varnish. I will mention here the importance of not sanding too smooth. The #280 Wetordry will leave a nicely scratched up surface for the following coat to bond to. Unlike lacquer, varnish does not melt into the preceding coat of finish and must have something to bond to or it will simply peel off the first chance it gets.

The finish varnish is applied just like the varnish sealer, except that you usually do not have to thin it. You use the tack coat and the heavier following coat. Allow to dry according to the instructions on the can, scuff well, apply a second coat, and that should be it. You can polish some varnish finishes after they cure for two or three months, but it is better to try to get a smooth enough finish without polishing. Also try not to get any runs if possible, because they are hard to work out. If you are brushing the finish varnish, you must be especially careful to brush out uniformly and watch the edges, as this is where most of your runs will occur.

Another good finish I have experimented with is called "Deft." It is a special lacquer-type finish that can be brushed or sprayed and is also available in spray cans. It is a one-product-type finish and should not be used over paste wood fillers or oil-type stains. Deft may be used over old finishes in some instances. They should be cleaned carefully of old wax, etc. Test a small area of the old finish to see if the Deft can be applied without the finish lifting. Only then do you go ahead and spray the rest of the old finish. It is better if you start from scratch on bare clean wood, though.

Deft has its own stains, and I have also used alcohol-soluble analine dye stains satisfactorily. There is some bleeding through the finish with red mahogany stains, but with care, this doesn't cause too much trouble.

Deft is a satin-finish, alcohol-resistant, bartop-type finish. It is relatively soft and is an excellent acoustical finish, especially for guitar tops. Although it is a satin finish, it can be polished to a low gloss. I have used Deft over an epoxy-sealed spruce top with excellent results.

The same preparation in the beginning of this chapter up to and including the staining of the wood is used. The application of the Deft depends on which type you use. The drying time of the Deft in the regular can and that in the spray can is different. You may either brush or use a spray gun to apply the regular Deft. Use it as it comes from the can with no thinning. You use regular lacquer thinner for cleaning the equipment. Apply a fairly thin coat, let dry for ten minutes, and apply a little heavier coat. Let dry for two hours, sand lightly to remove dust pimples, steel-wool with #o wool, and recoat. Apply as many coats as necessary to get the desired finish. On the final coat you can use the Star Wol-Wax and #oooo steel wool with water to put a high sheen to the finish. The same process is followed using the spray can, except it can be sanded and recoated in about thirty to forty-five minutes. When using the spray can of Deft, you must be working in a well-ventilated room. The solvents are extremely volatile and explosive. Also, you should be using a chemical respirator of the type using activated charcoal to breathe through. This kind of a respirator should be used anyway with any kind of spray work to prevent damage to the lungs. Also, some of these chemicals can cause brain and liver damage when inhaled. *Be safe. Use a respirator at all times.*

There are quite a few other types of finishes on the market, such as the polyesters and other plastic-type finishes. I have been experimenting with some of these, but, with certain exceptions and special applications, the lacquer finish is probably the most satisfactory finish for all the different types of woods you will run into.

One of the exceptions I mentioned above is the humidity-catalyzed plastic finish sold under the brand name Phelan's Lox Supreme. It is used primarily on hardwood gym and bowling alley floors and is one of the toughest and most flexible finishes I have ever worked with. I use it primarily to finish the maple fingerboard surfaces used on some models of Fender guitars. It has to be used over a perfectly clean, oil-free, bare-wood surface. It also has the disadvantage of having to be used up within a week or so after opening the can or it starts setting up to a jelly in the can. You can pour it off in small jars, filling them to the top to eliminate any air, and seal them. I have kept it for several months that way.

Colored Finishes

Some instruments are finished with semi-transparent colored finishes. These are usually some shade of red or brown, darker around the edges on the face of the instrument in what is called a "sunburst" finish. Some are the same shade all over. They are extremely difficult to match in shade when you are trying to refinish the same color, because the original color fades with age. The reds are particularly bad about this.

I usually try to discourage these jobs with the colored finish because, aside from the above-mentioned reasons, you have to lay on too much finish to get the proper shades, and the thick finish is highly susceptible to checking and chipping.

If you want to experiment with these clear colors, one source that you may use is your local auto paint supply house. If you can talk them into it, try mixing small amounts of maroon, red, and gold toners with the proper clear lacquers until you get the shades you want. This particular combination will give you close to the clear reds used on the Gibson, Guild, and several other brands of guitars. I use this mixture in various strengths for touching up nicks and repair jobs. You can make this into a dark wine shade by adding a small amount of black to the mixture. This must be done carefully, as adding too much will cause a muddy look. On the brown finish, mix brown toner, gold toner, and enough black to give the desired shade. You can mix a small amount of gold toner with clear and end up with the antique orange that you find on the tops of a lot of the old-time guitars and on the fronts of some of the modern guitars, such as the Pimentel and some models of the Guild.

A word of caution, though. *These toners cannot be used by themselves.* They are designed to mix with clear lacquers and other tinting colors, and they do not have the body to use by themselves. After you mix the toners, clear heavy-bodied lacquer with the proper binders included are added to complete the formula. Also, be sure that you use the regular lacquer toners instead of the

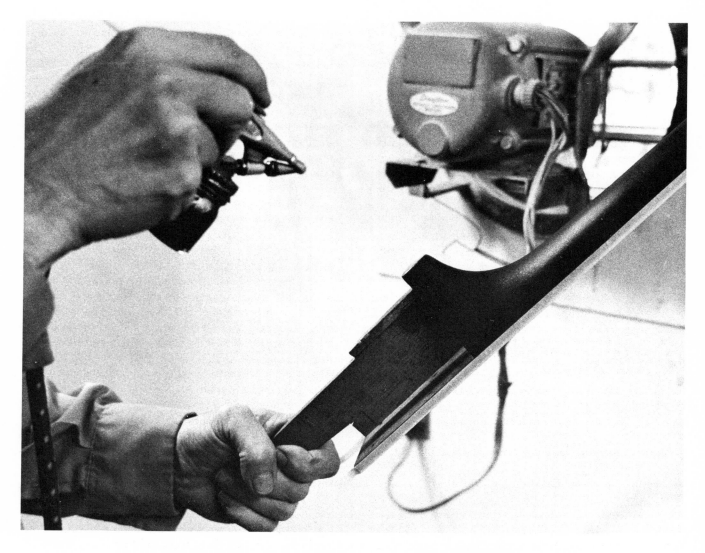

Fig. 155—Shading or "sunbursting" a damaged area with the Binks "Wren Model B" airbrush to hide the repair work on heel of a damaged Dobro neck.

acrylic- or plastic-based lacquer. You can use the acrylics if you know what you are doing, but unless you have quite a lot of experience, you can really get yourself into a mess. The thinning and spraying of acrylic lacquers is a pretty touchy business.

As to solid colors, I use the regular automotive-type lacquers in whatever shade I plan to use. As these usually chip rather easily when applied to wood, I usually apply just enough of the color to cover the wood completely, usually two or three coats depending on the color used, and then apply enough regular clear lacquer to get the proper build for the finish sanding and polishing. This seems to make a very durable finish and also gives some depth to the finish.

If you want to try the sunburst type front finish, all I have to say is, "Lots of luck." After all the steps are completed, up to and including the sealing of the top with sanding sealer, shoot the top with a coat or two of clear lacquer mixed with a small amount of yellow toner to give a base coat. Then you start spraying around the edge of the top with whatever color you have decided on, red, brown, etc. A very small spray gun such as the Binks Wren air brush with the "B" nozzle, which is designed for spraying paints, is an excellent choice for something like this. If you want to try shading with stain instead of colored finishes, the Wren with the "A" nozzle designed for dyes will fill the bill. After building to the shades you want around the edges, you start working towards the middle of the instrument with the color, always remembering to start shooting from the outside edge so that it will be darker at the edge and lighter towards the center. After you get the effect you want, you have to shoot a couple of coats of clear lacquer over the whole top. This is to give you something to sand and polish without spoiling the effect by sanding off some of the shading. I just don't like to do sunburst finishes because they are very difficult to make look right and because you have to use so much finish that it is hard to care for. A rapid temperature change from cold to hot or vice versa will cause checking, and extreme cold alone will do the same thing. The top is particularly prone to the checking, as the spruce has a larger coefficient of expansion between the finish than most other types of wood.

I hope I have given you enough of my knowledge and experience to help out. Again, I wish to state that my ways are not the only ways to do the finishing work, but they have worked well for me and with care they will work for you.

Touch-up Finishing

Touch-up work on crack repairs and other damage is difficult to do without the repair showing. In a lot of cases, it is impossible to do, as the repair will show through the finish. This is particularly so in light woods like spruce or maple with natural finishes. In the stained or colored finishes, the job is somewhat easier. You can use a combination of stains or colored lacquers to hide the repairs. On some of the larger repairs, it is better to refinish a whole panel rather than to try a spot job. Star Chemical Company sells a very good Service Man's Kit for touch-up work on furniture that has a lot of goodies that can be used in guitar repair. The number of this kit is 119 and it has twenty-four different colors of powdered stains, Frenching polish, patching sticks with patching knives and heater, instructions, and many other goodies. I have one of these and it has saved my life more than once. I have been using it for several years and still have many years of use left on most of the supplies. I particularly like the dye powders. More than once, I have used them to dye epoxy for repairing a crack with a small sliver of wood missing or to mix with a small amount of alcohol or graining liquid in concealing a repair.

Another way of hiding something like a repaired break on a head or heel of a neck is to shade it in slightly darker than the original finish, or even darken it to the point that no grain shows through, shading it lighter towards the middle of the neck. This is done on some of the sunburst finished guitars anyway. The thing to do is to try to do the repair neatly enough so that you have only a minimum of finishing to do. If you have a thin line crack, you can build the finish back up to slightly higher than the existing finish with an artist's brush, allowing time to dry for an hour or so between coats, and after it is built up and dry, wet-sand it with #600 Wetordry sandpaper and go over it with some fine rubbing compound to bring back the shine. Sounds easy, huh? Well, it's not. You just have to work at it, and the technique will come to you. Keep four or five sizes of small artist's brushes handy, several colors of lacquers, a couple of dozen colors of Star's stain powders, mix thoroughly with a large measure of patience, and eventually the knack will come to you. Even then, you will get jobs that will not co-operate. Just do the best you can. We can't be miracle workers all the time, even though some people think we should be.

Care and Feeding of the Guitar

I guess I could not put a more fitting end to this book than a chapter on properly caring for the guitar.

So many people have the idea that a guitar is indestructible from the way they take care of them. This couldn't be further from the truth. A lot of this misconception has come, I believe, from watching various groups and individuals slam their instruments around on television. They sling them across their backs in carrying them around and wonder why the strap slips off of the butt peg and the guitar goes crunch on the floor. A trick like this can be done if the butt peg is glued in and the strap is tied to the peg, but the average person doesn't realize this. Also, the instruments that some of the groups throw around are stage props and it doesn't matter if they get trashed because they aren't played.

A lot of the information found in this chapter will be found scattered through the book, but I believe a summation is in order, so here goes.

An acoustic instrument of the flat-top design, or for that matter, any instrument, is a very fragile thing. It is, with the exception of some of the solid body electrics, made of various types of thin wood with different coefficients of expansion all held together with thin and sometimes rather narrow glue lines. It is very highly stressed from the tension of the strings, and this stress is spread throughout the body of the instrument at every glue joint. Each part adds or helps to add strength to other portions of the instrument. To damage or weaken one part of the instrument can result in damage to some other part. In other words, a guitar is a highly engineered piece of work and should be treated accordingly.

I won't mention any names, but to show you what will happen when one piece of this highly engineered marvel is changed without proper thought, one of the guitar companies several years ago designed and put into production an injection-molded nylon bridge held on by four sheet-metal screws from underneath the front.

Now, the bridge is an important part of the top bracing, as are the struts underneath. A glued bridge adds important strength to the central area of the top where the strings are attached, and it conducts the sound much better. These bridges, fastened with the sheet metal screws, started pulling up and splitting the tops where the screws came through. There was also a noticeable loss of sound when compared to a glued wooden bridge. I replaced a couple of hundred of these in my area in a two- or three-year period. Needless to say, the company ceased production of this particular bridge.

A periodic check should be made over the whole guitar for cracks, neck warpage, and other signs of wear and tear. Wearing of the finish to a certain degree is normal, and it does not really need refinishing unless it gets really bad. However, small cracks should be checked out by a competent repair shop, as minor cracks in certain locations can, with the stress and vibration of the strings, become very serious cracks if left unrepaired.

Next are a few of the no-nos in handling of musical instruments.

Do not leave the guitar leaning against a wall where it can get knocked over or bumped into. If you must leave the guitar out of its case, lean it in a corner with its *face* to the wall. Leaning it with the back to the wall adds the weight of the instrument to the stress of the strings and can cause neck warpage.

If you must leave it out of the case, the best thing is to hang it on the wall suspended by the head. Do not hang it on an uninsulated outer wall, as the wall may be colder or hotter than the rest of the room. In the winter, these uninsulated walls will sweat and can damage the finish. Use one of the interior walls instead. Music stores, please take note of this. I have seen guitars hanging in music stores against painted cinder block walls, and I have repaired a few instruments damaged that way.

Do not lay the instrument on floors or on the edges of beds where they may get stepped on or knocked off or even sat on.

Do not lay the guitar on Naugahyde or plastic-covered furniture. There is some sort of chemical reaction that takes place between the lacquer and plastic that can and will either leave part of the finish on the furniture or vice versa. I have refinished several instruments because of the incompatibility factor. One guitar strap manufacturer used Naugahyde ends on a series of fancy straps for a very short period of time and messed up quite a few guitars. I finished the butts of several in this area. Most of these straps are made with leather ends now.

Do not leave an instrument in the trunk of a car or, for that matter, in a car, period, when the weather is very warm or extremely cold. If you must do this, *please* remove *all* the tension from the strings and allow things to cool off or warm up thoroughly before pulling up to pitch again.

The heat can soften glue joints, allowing things to slip around and reset at very upsetting angles as the strings try to pull the guitar apart. Sometimes they succeed in doing just this. The extreme cold by itself will crack even the best finish causing it to shrink up more than the wood it covers.

This difference in the coefficient of expansion of the wood and finish is another problem point. If the guitar is cold and you expose it to a rapid warm up, the finish will surely crack or check. The same holds true with a hot to cold change. Leave the guitar in the case and let it warm up or cool off gradually before removing it.

Another very troublesome problem has to do with humidity changes. When traveling from an area of high humidity to a low humidity climate, the rapid drying of the wood can cause bad cracks in the wood. The various woods used in guitar construction have different rates at which they absorb or lose moisture, and the stress created can really crack things up.

The same holds true in areas of the country with high humidity in the summer and cold temperatures in the winter. The heating systems, especially the central units, really dry things out, causing furniture joints to become loose, chapping the skin, cracking guitars, etc.

The humidity content of the air is also relative to the temperature. Cold air will hold much less moisture than warm air. Suppose the relative humidity was 80 per cent at 40° temperature. If you warm this up to 80°, you will have only 40 per cent humidity. Remember, you can dissolve more sugar in warm water than in cold. Same difference with humidity.

The solution here is to use a humidifier such as the Goya #355 guitar humidifier during these dry periods. This is a small absorbent piece of ceramic enclosed in a perforated plastic shell that soaks up moisture and releases it in your case to moisten things up. Sure does stop a lot of cracks.

Of course, we have exactly the opposite problem in other areas of the country. Some of the low-lying coastal regions run around 100 per cent relative humidity during hot weather. Too much of this can cause swelling and consequent warpage of the wood or softening of the glue joints. Sometimes, if things get too humid, mildew or mold will actually destroy the glue right in the joint. In these cases a dessicant of some sort, such as silica gel, may be used to absorb the excess moisture in the case. The silica gel will turn white when it has absorbed all the moisture it will hold. Simply put it in an oven and bake it until it turns purple and you can use it time and again.

An excellent and somewhat expensive solution (although not so expensive if you have to have the guitar rebuilt) is the highly insulated, watertight and airtight fiberglass case made by a factory in Vienna, Virginia. It actually has a hygrometer (humidity indicator) built right into the inside of the case so you can keep a constant check on the moisture condition. The case is very rigid and heavy and provides maximum protection against the elements and rough handling. The company address is as follows; Mark L. Leaf, Casemaker, 1844 Beulah Road, Vienna, Virginia 22180.

It would be nice if we could control the climate the way some of the guitar factories do. The C. F. Martin Organisation keeps its humidity at around 40 per cent, removing moisture in the summer and adding it in the winter as needed. I try to keep my shop around the same.

Music stores in the colder climates would do well to add humidifiers to their heating systems in the winter to prevent cracking of guitars, piano sound boards, etc.

A good rule of thumb to follow in caring for your instrument is to remember that when you are uncomfortable, so is your guitar. That pretty well sums up the no-nos.

The next item is the cosmetic care of the instrument. An instrument should be polished periodically with a good grade of instrument polish or furniture polish containing a small amount of non-silicone wax and maybe a little lemon oil. Lemon oil is fine for the older guitars with a varnish finish. Once in a while, a cleaner such as Freemans Furniture Cream or comparable product should be used to remove wax buildup. In between polishings, a soft damp cloth may be used to remove crud and finger marks, followed by a light buffing with a soft dry cloth.

The fingerboard on most guitars is not finished, and to prevent this drying out and cracking, a small amount of lemon oil on a rag applied to the wood will keep it in shape. If crud builds up on the board, remove all the strings and steel-wool it with #00 grade wool, using only as much pressure as needed to remove the crud. A word of caution here. If you are doing this to an electric guitar, be sure to tape off the pickups to keep the steel wool from getting into the electronics and shorting things out. While the strings are off, rub in a good quality non-silicone paste wax and lemon oil lightly.

Now, after playing the instrument, be sure to wipe the strings with a soft cloth to remove sweat and body oils before putting it away. This will help preserve the life of the strings, as some people's sweat (including mine) is very acid and can rust strings in a hurry. In fact, it wouldn't hurt to lemon oil the unwound strings lightly to prevent this.

Speaking of strings, they should be replaced periodically as they lose their brilliance. How often you change the strings is pretty much dependent on the type of strings, whether nylon or metal, the gauge or diameter of the string, the style it is played, the amount it is played, the acidity of the person's sweat (affects the steel strings most) and the climatic conditions. Some strings, such as the .008 first strings used by some rock guitarists, last only a few hours. You will just have to use your ears, and when the strings start making a thud when plucked, instead of a clear brilliant ring, change them. Also when they start giving trouble in tuning, this can be an indication that they need changing.

In changing strings, it is best to remove only one at a time and replace it before going on to the next one. This keeps the tension on the instrument, and you will have far less trouble getting it in tune because the guitar does not have to settle down again as it would if you removed all of them.

Treat your guitar like a baby. Clean it up and give her a coat of polish once in a while, give her a drop of oil on her tuning pegs (open gear type) every other string change, give her a new set of strings when the old ones start complaining, give her lots of playing, and you and your guitar should get along well for many years.

A few words on the storing of guitars. If the guitar is to be stored for a short length of time such as three or four months, it is not necessary to detune the strings more than a couple of frets' worth if at all. Place it in the case and store it where it will not get overly hot or cold and where it won't get bumped around. A good place is lying flat on an interior closet floor or lean the case in a corner of the closet with the top towards a corner.

In storing for long periods of time, use the same tech-nique as above, but let most of the tension off the strings. Leave some because if you don't, the stress will have to settle in all over again and may take a while for the full sound to come back. In both instances, the guitar should be cleaned and polished and the fingerboard lemon oiled before storing. When you take her out again, slip on a new set of strings and she's ready to go.

Now, a few words on shipping a guitar. Things get handled pretty roughly nowadays and certain precautions should be taken before shipping.

Let the strings down all the way to remove any tension from the instrument. Remove the strap peg from the butt of the instrument. Pack crushed newspaper around the head and neck area of the case to prevent the guitar from moving around during rough handling.

Guitars with hardshell cases can usually be shipped safely without boxing, but if you have a soft case, talk one of the music stores in your area into giving you one of the large cardboard shipping cartons they receive instruments and cases in and pack case and all into the carton with crushed newspaper, shredded paper, or what-have-you, around all surfaces of the case. If you have a couple of pieces of scrap ¼" plywood large enough, add this to the inside of the carton over the top and back of the case. Use filament type strapping tape and strap things up good and tight.

Be *sure* to insure the instrument, so if there should be any damage, it will be covered.

In flying, use only a hardshell case and if you are traveling with the guitar, try to take it on board with you. Barring this, try to get them to allow you to deliver and pick up the guitar at the plane personally. Most airline damage occurs in the handling between the plane and the terminal. Pack as for regular shipping, string tension down, crushed newspaper, etc., insure fully, and check the guitar at the baggage counter for damage *before* leaving the airport.

If this sounds kind of nit picking, just remember, I'm speaking from experience, having done quite a bit of work for the insurance companies. To quote an old cliché that I think particularly applicable here, "An ounce of prevention is worth a pound of cure." Old Ben had the right idea.

Suppliers for Parts and Materials

The following names are a list of suppliers where parts and various materials may be purchased. This is not a complete list, but is a list of the ones that I have had dealings with. Some of these will sell wholesale to established shops and some are strictly one price to everybody. Before selling wholesale to shops, they will probably want your sales tax number, and you should write them on your letterhead stationery. If you want to buy on an open account basis, they will want to check out your credit rating also. Otherwise any dealings will be on a C.O.D. basis.

C. F. Martin & Co., Inc.
Box 329
Nazareth, Pa. 18064

Most repair parts for Martin guitars are available from the factory. The availability and price can be obtained from sending the style and serial number of the instrument with an itemized list of the parts requested. Some frequently used parts are available for stock purposes to Martin dealers and to repair shops. The Darco string division of C. F. Martin & Co. manufactures the full line of Martin, Marquis, Vega, and Darco strings. As of 1995, C. F. Martin & Co. carries a full line of guitar-making supplies, exotic woods, and complete guitar-making kits. Catalog.

Vitali Import Company
5944 Atlantic Blvd.
Maywood, Calif. 90270

Just about anything in the guitar repair and making needs from "how to" books to woods of all kinds, hardware, tools, strings, inlays, purfling, and many other items used by the repairman and luthier. Catalog costs $2.00 and will be refunded on the first order. Will sell wholesale to established shops.

C. Bruno and Son, Inc.
1215 Walnut Street, Compton, Calif. 90220;

3443 E. Commerce Street, San Antonio, Texas 78294;
and
55 Marcus Drive, Melville, N.Y. 11746

Hard parts and accessories of all kinds including strings of various brands, machine heads, fret wire, electric pickups, etc., and also several lines of guitars and banjos, etc. Must be an established shop for wholesale purchases, which are necessary in most cases.

Rare Woods, Inc.
3160 Bandini Blvd.
Los Angeles, Calif. 90023

Rare domestic and imported woods of all kinds. You have to visit his shop and select what you want. *He positively does not ship.*

Original Musical Instrument Co., Inc.
1404 Gaylord Street
Long Beach, Calif. 90813

Dobro parts and supplies.

Erika Banjos
14731 Lull Street
Unit #3
Van Nuys, Calif. 91405

Banjo parts and supplies as well as completed instruments. Excellent source for pearl and abalone shell already ground for inlay purposes.

Stewart MacDonald Guitar Shop Supply
21 N. Shafer Street, Box 900
Athens, Ohio 45701

As of 1995, Stewart MacDonald carries a full line of repair parts and materials. They have everything needed for a guitar shop dealing with guitars, banjos, mandolins—you name it. Must be an established shop to receive wholesale parts. Catalog.

Craftsman Wood Service Company
2727 South Mary Street
Chicago, Ill. 60608

Rough and finished planed wood of all kinds, veneers of fancy domestic and imported woods, finishes, "how to" books, tools, and other woodworking supplies. One price only with discount for quantity. Catalog.

Star Chemical Company
8255 Forney Road, Dallas, Texas 75218
and
9830 Derby Lane, Westchester, Ill. 60153

Just about anything and everything needed in the finishing line. Sells almost entirely to established shops and manufacturers. Catalog.

"Hard-To-Find"-Tools
Brookstone Company
Dept. C. 12 Brookstone Bldg.
Peterborough, N.H. 03458

Plenty of useful items for the repairman. Vernier calipers, files of all kinds, jeweler's saws and blades, other small saws of all kinds, drill bits of all sizes, cutters for piano wire, and many other hard-to-find items. Catalog.

Luthiers Mercantile International, Inc.
P.O. Box 774
Healdsburg, CA 95448

This company issues a 230-page catalog/handbook containing informative articles, tables, fine woods, tools, finishing materials, books, plans, and a complete list of Lutherie supplies.

Abalone. Colored pearl. Comes in many shades from plain white through the whole spectrum of reds and greens to a purple-black. Used for decorative work and position markers.

Acoustic guitar. Unamplified guitar.

Action. Height of the strings from the fingerboard of the guitar.

Adjustable bridge. Usually found on F-hole guitars. Has a provision to adjust the string height up or down. Also found on some standard models. Some also have provision for forward or rearward movement. See bridge.

Air brush. Miniature spray gun used for touch-up finishing, etc.

Alignment pins. Pins of various types used to prevent the movement of a piece while gluing and clamping.

Back. The opposite of the top or front of the body, usually made of two book-matched pieces of wood with marquetry separating them.

Belly. Central or main vibrating area of the top.

Bending iron. Heated brass or copper tube used for bending wood to shape.

Binding. Material used on edges of guitar body for protective purposes as well as decoration and to seal the end grain of the wood. Wood or plastic.

Blushing. Moisture or vapor bubbles trapped under the surface of a finish caused by spraying while the humidity is too high.

Bone. Can be used as a substitute for ivory in making nuts and bridge saddles.

Book-matching. Splitting a single piece of wood and folding it out in two pieces like the pages of a book and edge-gluing them to form a symmetrical grain pattern from side to side.

Bout. The two widest parts of the guitar from the front or back. The upper bout is at the neck end of the body and the lower bout at the butt end of the body.

Bow. Description used when the neck is warped out of shape, either forward or backwards.

Bracing. See struts.

Bridge. The piece set on the face of a guitar with the strings running across it under tension to transfer the vibration of the strings to the top of the guitar. On the acoustic guitar, this piece is usually wood with an ivory inset for contact with the strings. See bridge saddle.

Bridge pins. Small tapered pins fitted to holes drilled in a bridge used to hold the strings in place.

Bridge plate. Thin piece of wood glued to the underside of the top under the bridge area to add extra strength to the belly area of the top.

Bridge saddle. That part of the bridge, usually ivory or bone, but in some cases may be wood, plastic, ceramic, or metal, as on some electric guitars, that the strings contact. This piece is harder in most cases than the bridge proper to prevent wear at the contact point with the strings.

Brilliance. Clearness of a string or note. Brilliance is lost as the string ages.

Burrs. Small high-speed cutters used with the Moto-Tool in fret work, inlay work, etc.

Bushings. Small metal pieces pressed into the wood where the machine head shafts come through the wood to prevent wearing out the hole as would happen with plain wood.

Butt. Lower end of the body of an instrument.

Butt block. Large block inside of the guitar where the two sides come together at the butt or bottom end of the body.

Butt peg. See strap peg.

Capo. Also known as a clamp, cheater, etc. Device used to clamp on a neck over the strings to raise the key or pitch of all the strings at one time.

Celluloid. Earliest known plastic. Used for bindings and purflings on instruments. Also used for pickguards and in some cases for position markers in the fingerboards.

Clamping caul. Various types of blocks used to assist in clamping a particular part such as a fingerboard, etc.

Clamping pads. Soft material such as leather, cardboard,

etc., used to protect the finish from clamps and blocks while using clamps.

Classic guitar. A wide, flat-fingerboard, flat-top, round-hole instrument strung with gut or nylon strings and played with the fingers. See text.

Coefficient of expansion. Expansion rate of one wood or material in comparison with another.

Compensated bridge. Bridge with saddle set to where each string is set to the proper length to note out accurately. See text.

Compromise tuning. Slightly sharping or flatting a given string in relationship with another to achieve a balance in tuning the strings of an instrument.

Course. A string or combination of strings played as one. The guitar is usually a six-course instrument with the exception of the tenor guitar, which is a four-course instrument. The twelve-string guitar is a six-course instrument, with each pair of strings forming a course.

Cracks. Any separation of a glued seam or between the grain of a piece of wood.

Cross-patch. Small piece of wood usually square or diamond in shape used to reinforce under a repaired crack. Grain of the patch runs across the grain of the piece being repaired, hence the name cross-patch.

Dehydrator. System of silica gel equipment used to remove moisture from air lines, etc.

Dehumidifier. Equipment used to remove moisture from the surrounding air.

Dessicant. Material used such as silica gel to remove moisture from the air.

Dovetail. Double-tapered joint used to join the neck to the body on the European style construction. The female part of the join is cut into the neck block and the male part is cut on the butt end of the neck.

Dreadnought. Large, almost straight-sided (shallow waist) guitar designed in 1917 by Martin and widely copied today by other companies.

Dressing. Flattening or cleaning up a surface such as a fingerboard, frets, etc.

Electric guitar. Any guitar, whether acoustic or solid body, that uses an electronic system to amplify the sound by means of an electric pickup.

Face. See top.

Fan strutting. Type of belly strutting used for nylon or gut strings with the braces under the belly in the shape of a "fan." See text.

F-hole guitar. Guitar with arch carved into top and back and having sound holes on either side of the face in the shape of an "f." Some are laminated under pressure to form the arch. See text.

Filling. Closing up the pores in wood with a special filler compound.

Fingerboard. The hardwood board laid on the surface of the neck and containing the frets.

Finger rest. See pickguard and tap plate.

Finish. The material used to seal off the bare wood and improve the looks of an instrument. Usually lacquer, French polish, shellac, and various plastics and varnishes.

Fish eyes. Round pits occurring in a finish coat that had been polished during a refinish job with a silicone polish at one time or the other. See silicone.

Flamenco guitar. Guitar used mostly by the Spanish gypsies to accompany dancers. Usually has friction pegs instead of machine heads and softer wood in the body along with a harsher sound than the classic guitar. Used with gut or nylon strings. See text.

Flat-top guitar. Spanish guitar.

Fourteen-fret neck. Neck that joins the body with the fourteenth fret directly over the neck to body joint. Usually steel strings.

Frets. Metal pieces laid across the fingerboard. By pressing the string behind the fret with the finger, one changes the pitch of a string by changing the string's working length.

Fret board. See fingerboard.

Fret file. Special file with teeth in the concave edges used to round the tops of frets flattened by too much dressing down.

Fret nut. Fret set into the fingerboard where edge of nut would normally be to determine the height of the strings over the first fret. Regular nut piece slightly behind it separates the strings only. See nut.

Fret slots. Small slots cut across the fingerboard to receive the frets.

Fretted instruments. Any instrument such as the guitar, banjo, mandolin, dulcimer, etc., using frets to change the string pitch.

Friction pegs. Non-geared, one-to-one ratio pegs inserted through the head of an instrument to tune the strings. May be made of wood, metal, or ivory. They keep the string up to pitch by friction between the peg and head. See machine heads.

Garbaged. Damaged badly or beyond repair.

Gauge. A measurement of size such as the diameter of strings, etc.

Glue. A material used between two pieces of wood, metal, etc., to cause a bond between the pieces, or, in other words, to cause them to stick together. There are many types of glue. See glue chapter.

Grafting. Inserting new wood to take the place of missing wood as in repairing a hole caused by impact damage.

Guitar. A musical instrument usually with from four to twelve strings with a long neck and played with the fingers or picks. See text, classic, flamenco, electric, and steel-string guitar.

Hardshell. Type of instrument case made of moulded plywood, fiberglass, etc., and padded to prevent damage to the instrument enclosed.

Harmonics. High pitched overtones obtained by touching the strings at certain points while plucking instead of fretting the string.

Head. Also known as peg head. The upper part of the neck to which the tuning mechanisms are attached.

Heel. The lower part of the neck where it curves down against the guitar body.

Heel cap. Decorative and protective piece, usually plastic, celluloid, ebony, or rosewood, covering the grain on the bottom of the heel.

Hot knife. Knives of any kind heated with a heater or boiling water and used to separate a glue joint.

Humidifier. Anything used to add moisture to the air.

Hygrometer. Humidity indicator which shows the percentage of moisture in the air.

Inlays. Usually pearl, abalone pearl, or plastic laid into the wood surface of an instrument for position markers and/or decorative purposes.

Intonation. The ability of an instrument to note out properly and accurately.

Impact damage. Damage caused by a blow to the instrument causing holes, broken necks, heads, etc.

Ivoroid. Imitation ivory, usually celluloid.

Ivory. The best material to use for nuts and bridge saddles. Comes mostly from elephant tusks but may also be from walrus tusks. See bone.

Jigs. Various fixtures or setups used in combination with various tools and clamps to facilitate repairs.

Ladder strutting. Lute strutting. Struts running across the face of the instrument at a 90° angle to the center line of the top. Can be compared to the steps of a ladder in relation to the sides of the ladder.

Laminated construction. Instrument constructed of plywood.

Linings. Notched pieces running around the sides of an instrument to give a larger area to glue the top and back to. In some cases, the linings may not be notched but bent with a bending iron to conform to the shape of the sides.

Lute strutting. See ladder strutting.

Machine heads. The mechanically geared pieces on the head of an instrument used to tune the strings to pitch. They may be all on a plate or individual machines for each string. They are mechanically geared to reduce the ratio to facilitate fine tuning instead of the one-to-one ratio of friction pegs. See friction pegs.

Marquetry. Decorative strip separating the two pieces of the back of an instrument. Usually made up of many small pieces of wood glued up in a single strip for ease of installation.

Moto-Tool. High-speed miniature grinder and hobbyist's tool made by the Dremel Company. When used with a special base, can be used as a miniature router for inlay work, etc. See text.

Neck. Sometimes referred to as the handle of the instrument. That part of an instrument extending out from the body containing the fingerboard or fret board, and on the upper end, the nut, head, and tuning mechanisms.

Neck block. Large block inside the guitar body where the sides join at the neck end of the body. On the Spanish style of construction, this block is integral with the neck. In the European construction, a dovetail joint is cut into this block, and the neck is set into this dovetail.

Nut. The slotted piece, usually ivory, wood, or plastic, located at the head end of the fingerboard that separates the strings and determines the height at which they clear the first fret. See fret nut.

Oval fingerboard. Same as regular fingerboard except that it has a convex or slight oval to the surface instead of being flat. Found on almost all steel-string instruments.

Overtone. A faint tone above the principal tone.

Pearl. Lining of the large ocean clam shell used for position markers and decorative work. See abalone.

Pearloid. Imitation pearl, usually celluloid.

Peg head. See head.

Peghead veneer. Thin layer of wood or plastic covering the face of the head. Some markers do not use it, and others simply paint the face of the head a solid color to imitate a veneer.

Pickguard. Plastic guard used on the face of steel-string instruments to keep from scratching up the finish with the plectrum or pick. Also known as finger rest or tap plate.

Plane and fret. Method of straightening a non-adjustable neck.

Plectrum. Also called pick or flat pick. Thin piece of plastic, nylon, or tortoise shell used to strike the strings.

Plywood. Wood joined together with glue from thin layers to form a thicker piece. There are three or more pieces with the center section grain running across the grain of the outer pieces. See laminated construction.

Position markers. Pearl or plastic pieces inlaid into the fingerboard used as an aid to playing.

Purfling. Thin layers of various colored materials used inside the binding on instrument tops and sometimes on the backs and sides. Some models are quite fancy, using abalone, pearl, etc.

Quarter-sawn. Describing tree trunk cut into four quarters and sections are cut from this so that the grain is running up and down at a 90° angle to the surface of the piece.

Refinish. To remove the old finish and apply a new one. See finish.

Resonance. Vibrations given out by an instrument when thumped or played.

Retarder. Slow-drying thinner for lacquer.

Rosette. Fancy or plain material used around the instrument sound hole for decorative purposes as well as to add some strength to the area. Some makers simply use a decal or paint to simulate an inlaid rosette.

Rotation. Tendency for a bridge to rotate, pulling the top up behind the bridge and caving it in in front of the bridge.

Rottenstone. Superfine polishing powder usually mixed with water for hand polishing. May be used with lemon oil for a very high-sheen satin-type finish.

Rubbing compound. Material ready mixed and used to polish out lacquer finish.

Sandpaper file. Auto body shop tool used for dressing bowed fingerboards, frets, etc.

Scale. Vibrating string length of a particular instrument.

Screwed-on neck. Has neck fastened to body with screws instead of glue and is removable.

Sealer. Undercoating used under finishing coats to seal off the filler, stain, etc., from the finish coats.

Shading. Darkening of a certain area and blending out to a lighter finish for hiding a damaged area or decorative "sunburst." See sunburst.

Sides. The curved wooden sections of the body of an instrument separating and connecting the top to the back.

Side reinforcements. Cloth or wooden pieces running across the grain of the sides to prevent spreading of cracks, should any occur.

Silicone. Very slick ingredient of some polishes. Raises havoc with refinishing work.

Silicone leveling fluid. Product used to make lacquer flow out smooth where silicone polish has been used. Prevents "fish eyes."

Slab-sawn. Wood sawn across the whole section of the tree. Grain will change at opposite sides of the board. See text.

Solvent. Anything used to dissolve or thin a particular element, e.g. water, lacquer thinner, naphtha, alcohol, etc.

Sounding board. See top.

Sound hole. Any hole or holes in the face of an instrument allowing air movement inside the body to escape to the outside.

Steel-string guitar. Any guitar designed for steel strings.

Steel-reinforced neck. Neck with T-bar, U-channel, or any other rigid piece laid into the neck under the fingerboard to help the neck resist the pull of the strings.

Strap peg. Wooden, plastic, or metal peg at the butt end of the guitar to which to attach a shoulder strap. May be screwed to the body or in a tapered hole. Metal peg may be attached to the heel of the guitar with a screw so strap may be attached there instead of the head.

Strings. Also called threads, wires, and a few unmentionable things. Gut, nylon, or various types of metal pieces plucked to vibrate the top.

String action. See action.

Stripper. Chemical compound used to remove old finish.

Strobotuner. An electronic strobe unit manufactured by the Conn Organ Company for measuring pitch of musical notes.

Struts. Reinforcing bars of wood used to brace the top and back of an instrument. See "X," fan, and ladder strutting.

Strut jack. Small jack used to raise loose or split strut back into position from the inside of the guitar. See text.

Spanish guitar. Any flat-top guitar with a round sound hole is commonly called a "Spanish guitar."

Spraying. Technique used to apply various finishing products with a spray gun. See air brush.

Sunburst. Special finish technique where light area of an instrument is surrounded by a darker one for special effect. Sometimes done with finish and also with stain.

Table. See top.

Tack coat. Also called mist coat. Very thin preliminary coat of finish allowed to dry until "tacky" or sticky before application of a heavier coat. Commonly used with varnish or enamels to prevent sags or runs.

Tailpiece. Used on F-hole guitars, mandolins, banjos, and certain standard flat-top guitars. Metal piece fastened to the butt end of an instrument with the strings attached to it rather than to the bridge.

Tang. Beaded part of fret that fits into fingerboard slot to hold the fret in place. Looks like the bottom leg of a T.

Tap plate. Very thin plastic guard used to protect the area of the top of a classic or flamenco guitar where the fingers come into contact while playing. See pickguard.

T-bar. Neck reinforcement shaped like a T.

Tension rod. An adjustable rod laid into an instrument neck which, when put under tension, causes the neck to straighten or flatten out. There are several types of tension rods. See the text.

Top. Often called the face, table, or sounding board. The front of the instrument to which the bridge is attached. The primary source of sound, vibrating with the vibration of the strings. Probably the one most important part of the guitar.

Touch up. Spot finishing of a damaged area. See shading.

Tuning. Raising or lowering the pitch of the strings until they resonate on a predetermined frequency.

Twelve-fret neck. Neck joins the body with the twelfth fret directly over the neck to body joint. Used on almost all classic and flamenco guitars and some steel-strings, particularly the twelve-string models, because it is stronger than the fourteen-fret neck.

Waist. The narrowest part of the guitar body viewing it from the front or back.

Wetordry sandpaper. Sandpaper designed to be used with or without water.

Wetting agent. Detergent. Breaks down surface tension of water allowing it to penetrate or flow out better.

Woods. See chapter on materials and hardware for discussion on woods used in guitar repairs.

Woolwax. Rubbing lubricant for use with fine steel wool and water to achieve a satin or antique-type finish.

Work piece. Part being worked on.

X-strutting. Type of strutting designed originally by the Martin factory and has the main belly struts in the shape of an "X." See text.

Baines, Anthony (ed.). *Musical Instruments Through the Ages*. Baltimore, Penguin Books, Inc., 1961.

Bellow, Alexander. *The Illustrated History of the Guitar*. Long Island, Belwin/Mills Publishing Corporation, 1970.

Brown, H. E. *Classic Guitar Maker's Guide*. Tulsa, Oklahoma, International Guitar and Import Company, 1967.

Fine Hardwoods Association. *Fine Hardwoods Selectorama*. Chicago, Fine Hardwoods Association, n.d.

Guitar & Accessory Manufacturers Association of America. *Fretted Instrument Service Manual*. Long Island, Guitar & Accessory Manufacturers Association of America, n.d.

Sharpe, A. P. *Make Your Own Spanish Guitar*. London, Clifford Essex Music Co. Ltd., 1957.

———. *The Story of the Spanish Guitar*. London, Clifford Essex Music Co. Ltd., 1954.

Sloane, Irving. *Classic Guitar Construction*. New York, E. P. Dutton & Co., Inc., 1966.

———. *Guitar Repair: A Manual of Repair for Guitars and Fretted Instruments*. New York, E. P. Dutton & Co., Inc., 1973.

Most of the books listed here are available from Vitali Import Company and/or H. L. Wild. Check with them on availability and price.

The *Fretted Instrument Service Manual* may be obtained from the C. F. Martin Organisation.

The *Fine Hardwoods Selectorama* may be obtained from Craftsman Wood Service Company. THIS BOOK IS A MUST. It tells you about practically all the available woods from all over the world and shows pictures of most.

In reference to the guitar making books, *Make Your Own Spanish Guitar* by A. P. Sharpe is probably the easiest to understand from the rank amateur's standpoint. It details the European (dovetailed neck) construction. The others are good also and are concerned primarily with the Spanish (integral neck-neck block) construction.

If you used the listed books for nothing but reference, they would still give you a better understanding of the guitar and its history.

There are other books on the market pertaining to guitar making and repair. This is not, to say the least, a complete list. These are ones that I own and have read. I keep adding to my library as I get the opportunity.